Inflation Accounting

Inflation Accounting

W. T. BAXTER

Emeritus Professor of Accounting
The London School of Economics

Philip Allan

First published 1984 by

PHILIP ALLAN PUBLISHERS LIMITED
MARKET PLACE
DEDDINGTON
OXFORD OX5 4SE

British Library Cataloguing in Publication Data

Baxter, W. T.
Inflation accounting
1. Accounting and price fluctuations
I. Title
657'.48 HF5657

ISBN 0-86003-524-7
ISBN 0-86003-623-5 Pbk

Typeset by *Sunrise Setting,* Torquay
Printed in Great Britain by
Billing and Sons Ltd., Worcester

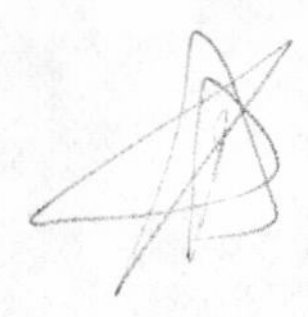

Contents

Preface

This book has grown out of an earlier one, *Accounting Values and Inflation*, published in 1975. Since then, principles of inflation accounting may not have changed, but accountants have engaged in much debate on them, have made important experiments, and have followed some false trails.

It now seems possible to omit or condense parts of the first book, while other parts have called for clarification or change of emphasis. In particular, this book analyses the good and bad features of the inflation Standards issued in Britain and the USA; it draws on the many recent publications by other authors; it simplifies the treatment of depreciation; and it includes new examples and diagrams.

One can marshal the problems of inflation accounting as two sets of questions and answers. First, is reform necessary? Accounting grew up as a day-by-day record of business dealings. Its figures are a series of snapshots, each a glimpse of some event as it happens. They may be faithful history. But usually they are left as historical records; traditional accounting seldom revises them if conditions change at later times. Thus it normally goes on measuring assets and inputs at their original cost, no matter how far their current values move. Particularly during inflation, the values are apt to move a long way.

One can imagine a science-fiction society in which money's purchasing power and the relative worth of assets never vary. In such a sleepy setting, historical accounts would be admirable. In the world as we know it, they invite criticism. When the price level is rising briskly, they are beset by several ailments: their asset values become anachronisms; they ignore important forms of appreciation and loss; and an invisible error creeps into income measurement, so that income is overstated in profit and loss accounts—and then in tax assessments.

The book sets out the case against historical accounts, and the benefits of reform. It describes the various proposals for improvement—asset revaluation, measurement of loss on holding money, adjustment of input costs with price indices, and so on.

The second set of questions concerns principles. These must govern choice of reform technique. Often, indeed, one cannot decide how to draft inflation accounts without first making up one's mind on how certain difficult problems should be treated in times of general price stability. For instance, one must decide whether income is a matter of economic or physical growth; how depreciation should be measured; whether intangibles should be accorded the status of assets; and whether 'realisation' is a prerequisite of income recognition (i.e. upon the point at which the chicken is deemed to leave the egg). Unhappily, accounting literature is weak in its treatment of these fundamentals; so a writer on inflation accounting must try to plug the gap, and (however modest his nature) is forced willy-nilly to attempt an ambitious task. Several chapters of this book therefore explore first principles.

Probably the most important of the problems of principle is whether economic or physical growth should be looked on as income. Physical growth now seems to be winning. To my mind, this is a pity: accountants should have stuck longer to their original proposal of reform based on economic growth, found with general index adjustments—the 'constant purchasing power' (CPP) approach. This is fairly simple and easy to understand, and gives a far more logical measure of income than its physical rival ('current cost accounting' or CCA). It would have made an excellent starting point for reform.

The faults in the physical concept show most clearly in three sets of circumstances: where the replacement differs from the existing asset; where the firm's input prices are falling; and where the asset is bought and sold in the same market (commodities and securities). Chapter 8 discusses these faults at some length, and argues that they should be regarded, not as unfortunate exceptions to a sound rule, but as proof that the rule is unsound.

CPP, the economic measure, takes these circumstances in its stride. It also is much the better at assessing loss on holding money during inflation—surely a prime task of inflation accounts. But, alas, it is weak at another of the big tasks, asset valuation. Here CCA scores higher marks, particularly if (as Chapter 12 suggests) the figures accord with the selective notion of 'deprival value'.

So reform will be faulty unless it can employ both CPP and CCA. The ideal is a hybrid. This alone can make full use of the good, and reject the bad, in the two rival methods. Later pages describe the arithmetic. If the hybrid seems too elaborate for immediate adoption, it should at least be taken as guide for choice of interim short-cuts.

Though the book pleads for change, it accepts that no reform model can be free from criticism. Here as elsewhere, inflation is a powerful agent of evil, and our efforts will not offset it entirely. Still, a partial cure is better than none; we shall have cause to congratulate ourselves if we at least get out of the fire and back into the frying pan.

If the inflation rate falls, enthusiasm for reform will no doubt fall too. But we must hope that accountants will not forget their recent experiments. Only a bold man would say that we shall never again see inflation (or deflation). And, whatever the current rate, students will always have a powerful reason for exploring inflation accounts in some depth: few topics can give a clearer understanding of general principles.

The research committee of the Institute of Chartered Accountants in England and Wales has sponsored my book, and I am grateful for its aid. Needless to say, the committee is in no way responsible for my views.

Many friends have helped me at various stages of the book's growth. They include Professors Harold Barger and James Bonbright of Columbia University; and colleagues and secretaries at the London School of Economics, notably Michael Bromwich, Martin Churchill, Susan Dev, Harold Edey, John Flower, Edward French, Pamela Hodges, Jean Knowles, David Pendrill, and Peter Watson. My thanks to them all.

W. T. Baxter

1

General and Specific Price Change

This book uses the term 'price change' in two senses. The first is *general* change, i.e. change so widespread that one can say the purchasing power of money has altered, as during inflation. The other is change in the price of an individual good or service (with or without general change); this may be called *specific* or special change. Both are of importance for accounting, but it is general change that has sparked off the current debate on the need for reform, and this chapter begins with it.

The instability of money

Physical units and value units

We all started measuring things while we were still children; and, without knowing it, we acquired firm views on the units of measurement. We measured our heights with an inch-tape, our weights on a scale marked with pounds, and the price of eggs with money. If the number of inches rose, we believed ourselves to be growing tall; if the number of pounds rose, we were praised for eating manfully; if the number of pennies rose, eggs were dearer. Very naturally, we took the measuring units for granted. We did not wonder whether the inch–tape might somehow have shrunk, or part of the weights might have rubbed off; and neither did our small minds conceive of pennies losing their worth. 'Things are getting dear', we heard our elders say—not 'money is getting cheap'. Our fairy tales warned us of the moral risks of too much treasure; they gave no hint that precious metal, if created to the lavish standards of Aladdin's djinn, would cease to be precious.[1] And so we learned a lesson that is uncommonly hard to unlearn.

Perhaps because of those early impressions, most of us stand in awe of money. We may see that price is an exchange ratio between a quantity of money and a quantity of goods, but we attach muddled notions of absolute value to the money. Yet a change in price merely reflects a change in the market's attitude to the two things concerned *relative to one another*; and there is scant reason to suppose that the market's esteem for money is constant and for goods variable.

'Things-in-general' as a stable measure of value

However, we may be justified in regarding a large sample of 'things-in-general' as almost having a stable value, e.g. in terms of a given consumer's satisfactions. In this book, we shall have to think about 'keeping capital intact'. Money capital is not too hard to measure; accountants deem a man's money capital—of, say, £1000—to be intact so long as he still has assets whose book-values (by various conventional rules mainly based on original cost) add up to £1000. Nevertheless he may well want to apply a more useful test (particularly if prices are restless) to find whether he is still as well off in terms of purchasing power. For lack of a better test, we must assume that his real capital is intact so long as it enables him to buy the same bundle of 'things-in-general'.

This concept is admittedly not perfect. To measure 'things-in-general', we must rely on an index of many prices; and no price index that the statisticians can devise is free from flaws. Despite the flaws, however, a general index is often the best tool available.

Our troubles in this area are not merely matters of statistical technique (choice of goods and weights for the bundle of goods, etc.—see Chapter 2). We also face more fundamental difficulties. In the last analysis, 'capital' and 'wealth' must imply ability to yield satisfaction to human beings. But the concepts behind 'satisfaction' are elusive; and it evades numerical measure. So, when we try to increase our skill at measuring wealth, we must not pitch our hopes too high. Our task becomes even harder when we try to compare wealth at different points in time.

Price changes in history

If we hold money in undue respect, the reason is certainly not that money has behaved well in the past, but rather that our memories are short.

The relative attractions of money and 'things-in-general' can change for many reasons. Thus the volume of precious metal may rise (as when silver and gold poured into Europe after the discoveries of the late fifteenth century). But the most notable price rises have been due to tampering by government. The temptation to degrade money is nearly as old as money itself. Under the strains of the Peloponnesian War, Athens took to inflation, by both debasement and devaluation (i.e. reducing the fineness and the amount of metal in coins). The Romans in their turn took up the game, and 'gave the world the inestimable curse of practical knowledge of all possible forms of inflation apart from the issue of paper money'.[2] And English history adds plenty of examples, e.g. Henry VIII was as cavalier with his coins as with his wives.

Yet metal offered less scope for dilution than paper money. Fresh records were achieved when notes (and, later, bank credit) came into common use. In particular, the First and Second World Wars drove many countries to inflate in varying degrees: Germany's fantastic issues in the early 1920s caused a social tragedy of the first order (and inspired early experiments in inflation accounting).

After the Second World War, it was reasonable (remembering what happened after the First) to expect slump and deflation. In the event, prices tended to go up. For nearly thirty years the inflation rate was low in most lands (e.g. it averaged little over 2 per cent per year in the USA). After 1974, there was a sharp rise, mainly because the international oil cartel (OPEC) then began its series of savage price increases; inflation rates of 10 per cent or more became not unusual. In Britain, the rate averaged about 4 per cent till 1970; thereafter it rose fast, threatening to pass 30 per cent in the spring of 1975.

Fall in prices

However, the lesson of history is not so much that money loses value as that its value changes. The increases in price have indeed outweighed the falls, but this should not make us forget how often falls took place, and how steep they were. Figure 1.1 shows price movements in England during some seven centuries. A study of

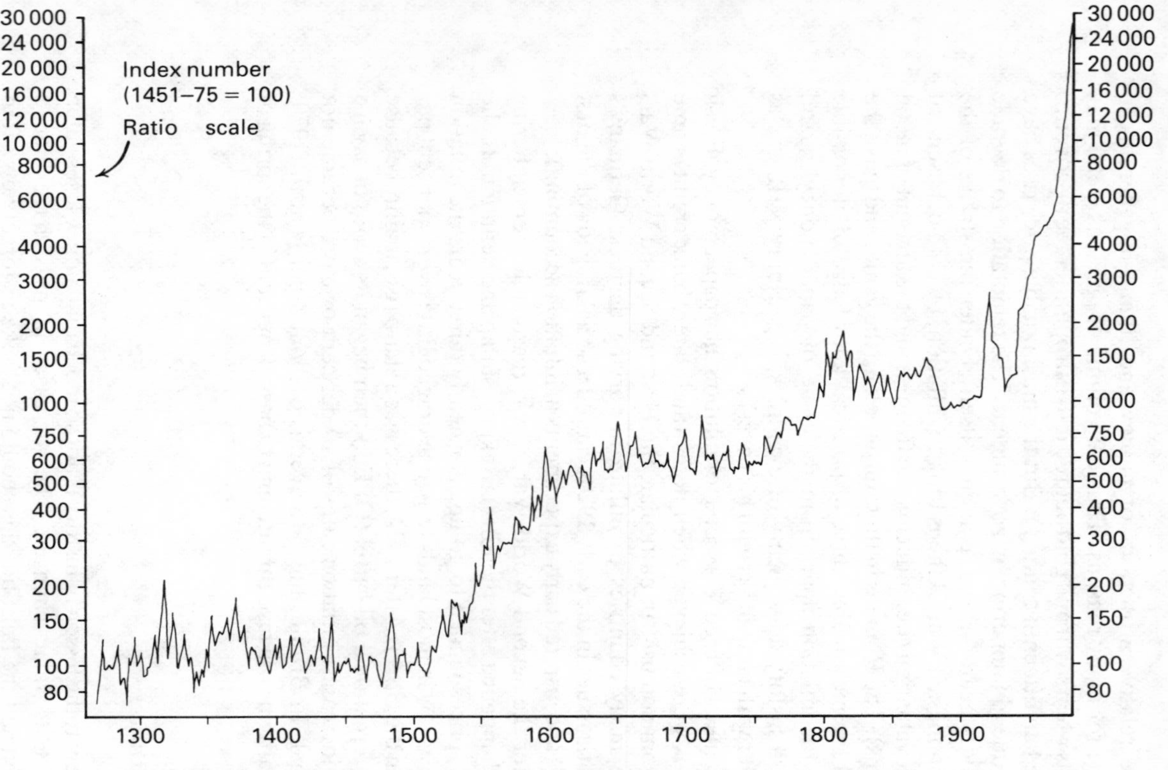

Figure 1.1 Price of a composite unit of consumables in Southern England, 1264–1982

Source: E. H. Phelps Brown and Sheila V. Hopkins, 'Seven centuries of the prices of consumables, compared with builders' wage rates', *Economica*, November (1956), p. 229, with later additions.

these movements suggests that prices fell in 328 years, were steady in 13, and rose in 367; further, if during this period 'we took a bet each year that the price level would be higher ten years from the date in question, we would be wrong more times than we would be right'[3] in all past centuries except the sixteenth and eighteenth. There was a markedly downward trend in the latter part of the nineteenth century; British prices fell by nearly one–third in the fifteen years after 1880, and US prices were nearly halved between 1864 and 1894. This half-century was the very time when accounting was evolving fast to meet the needs of companies and tax officials—which may perhaps help to explain why accounting principles ignore the dangers of rising prices.

Reasons for more inflation

It is tempting to argue that governments may at last be mastering powerful new ways of regulating economic affairs; that they are imbued with distaste for ever-mounting prices; and that accordingly they will soon be able to stop inflation—with enough skill to avoid overshooting the mark and landing us in a slump. This would be a high achievement. Is it likely?

There are strong reasons for thinking that inflation will persist. In many lands, governments now spend more than they raise in tax; as a consequence, they borrow from the banks and thereby swell bank deposits. Another influence is trade union power, which tends to push up costs. And a humane society cannot be single-minded in its struggle against inflation. Unfortunately success here may spell failure elsewhere; a tight monetary policy may contribute to slump and the major curse of unemployment. We must, despite our imperfect understanding of the economic issues, try to strike a balance between evils.[4]

So our chances of achieving price stability do not seem high. This being the case, we should face up squarely to instability. One of the ways of doing so is to admit that accounts based on the assumption of constant money values may be faulty and capable of improvement.

Specific change

Specific change calls for only a short introduction. We are all familiar enough with it. As children we learned that fruit becomes cheap when it is in season, and then gets dearer again as the months pass. Later we saw how the price of a raw material or stock exchange security can undulate in dramatic style, and how the price of a newly-invented gadget is apt to be high at first, and then sink. And so on.

Even when general prices are fairly stable, the specific prices of a firm's assets may fluctuate—sometimes in ways that bring great benefit or harm; thus it is perhaps surprising that accountants have stuck firmly to figures based on historical cost, i.e. a system that turns a blind eye to current values. When general change is superimposed on specific changes, the latter grow even more important, and the arguments for recognising them seem very strong.

Interplay of specific and general change

If the conditions for a laboratory experiment could be imposed on a human community, the experimenters could perhaps manipulate market forces in such a way that the price of every good and service would rise by precisely the same percentage. But in real life a general price rise of, say, 10 per cent must be some kind of 'average' rise: forces other than the money supply (e.g. gluts and shortages) will cause the prices of individual goods and services to move to varying extents above and below the 10 per cent average. General and specific changes differ and intertwine.

A rise in the price of a certain good from £1000 to £1300 is a 30 per cent specific change—regardless of what is happening to general prices. However, whether or not the owner of this asset feels much pleasure over his £300 of appreciation will in great degree depend on how general prices have behaved during the period. Naturally he will prefer his specific rise to outstrip the general rise.

Money gain versus real gain

Thus he should use two different sums to test his progress:

	£
1. Current price	1300
Original price	1000
Money gain	300

and (if general prices have risen by say 20 per cent):

	£
2. Current price	1300
Original price restated in current money, £1000 × (120/100)	1200
Real gain	100

The usual crude calculation, 1, shows *money* change; the more testing, 2, shows *real* change—the surplus or shortfall between the specific value and what this would have been if it had behaved like prices in general. In the example, the owner has beaten the general index to make a real gain of £100.

Summary

Our irrational faith in money

Mankind has been astonishingly reluctant to recognise that money is not stable. We have been slow to profit from experience, and quick to forget; men of high intelligence have often been no wiser than the fools. Except when some painful lesson is fresh in our minds, we have been apt to plan our affairs on the assumption that money has a fixed value—and to resent any contrary suggestion.

Accounting has shared the common attitude. For the most part, it has recorded values at historical cost, and ignored all subsequent changes in price.

Some accountants have been upset to a surprising extent by proposals for reforming this system. Such resentment may spring in part from loyalty to professional doctrines that for long were seldom criticised, and in part from dislike of scrapping hard-won mental equipment; perhaps it also reflects the general—and utterly misplaced—faith in the money unit.

Most accountants still seem to view their craft as something that is sound in fundamentals, but which has of late been exposed to shortsighted attack because of fleeting economic upsets. The aim of this chapter has been to suggest that, as both logic and experience stress the fickleness of money values, measurements based on historical cost are suspect right from the start.

Notes and References

1 A notable exception is 'The Snake with the Golden Teeth': 'The only other man I ever knew who had as much gold in his mouth was a pilot in the Yukon river in Canada, which goes past Klondyke, where there is a lot of gold. So gold is very cheap there. You can get a lot of gold for any ordinary sort of thing, like a loaf of bread or a book, so that means that everything else except gold is very dear.' Haldane, J.B.S. (1971) *My Friend Mr. Leakey,* Penguin Books, p. 128.

2 Burns, A.R. (1927) *Money and Monetary Policy in Early Times*, Kegan Paul, pp. 464–5.

3 Lipsey, R.G. (1960) 'Does money always depreciate?' *Lloyds Bank Review*, October, p. 7. The rise in the eighteenth century may have been due to the development of banks (and so, as credit transfers in a banker's records would be almost impossible without debits and credits, in a sense of accounting).

4 'Which horn of the dilemma should public policy embrace: unemployment or inflation? If the choice has to be made, I do not think it can be made on grounds of principle. On the one hand it can be claimed that for Uncle Sam to debase the dollar is the height of immorality, especially since he is net debtor for a large amount. On the other hand it can equally well be urged that nothing is more immoral than the deliberate adoption of a policy that must create unemployment, cause businesses to fail, and lead to the loss of billions of dollars' worth of output. Hence, as with so many other choices in this unhappy world, the rate of substitution is critical.' Barger, H. (1964) *The Management of Money*, Rand McNally, p. 302. The book quotes suggestions that about 5 per cent unemployment would be needed in the USA to maintain price stability, while a 4–5 per cent price rise per annum would keep unemployment down to 3 per cent.

2

Measuring Price Change

It is easy to talk about such and such a size of change in general or specific prices. But the actual measurement is often beset by many troubles, of both principle and technique.

General price change is measured with a general price index. The statisticians try to provide us with suitable indices, but with incomplete success (see below).

Specific change can be best measured by direct study of the particular asset. Thus an adequate current value for a stock exchange security may be found from its quotation in the stock exchange list; and a building can be valued by an appraiser. But, as a shortcut to approximate values, a specific index may be used for each class of asset (e.g. an index that shows the average movement in the prices of factory buildings). Such an index tries to reflect the price movements of a class of assets, with varying degrees of success.

General indices

A general index tries to measure how many money units (e.g. pounds or dollars) must be paid for a given quantity of goods and services at different times. Thus a general index of consumption prices tries to measure the changing retail prices of the goods and services in common use, and so may be said to show how the 'cost of living' is behaving. The statisticians who compile such an index must deal with—or skate over—many awkward problems. What sort of goods and services are to serve as the standard? Today's housewife fills her basket with goods that differ from those chosen by her grandmother. The goods may have changed in quality. The modern housewife's loaf is branded, wrapped, and sliced. Her peas may be podded, packed, and frozen—and possibly tasteless. Her shoes may fit, look, and wear better (or worse) than her grandmother's. Technical changes may indeed have gone much farther than these examples suggest, and have brought entirely new commodities and services into use: thus electricity has ousted candles.

Moreover, tastes vary with circumstances and people. The statistician cannot in fact find a 'representative consumer'; there is no such thing as a 'typical' housewife. Mrs A and Mrs B may have very different tastes and needs. Even if their incomes are equal, an elderly widow does not buy things in the same proportions as the adolescent, and a rise in the price of bread hurts the mother of six more than the bachelor-girl. Disparities of income heighten the contrasts: the rich stockbroker spends freely in directions that the poor student only dreams about.

So an index often fails to match one's own experience. It records a two-point drop in the cost of living (due to a glut of vegetables), just when I become worried by the rise in bus-fares and you by the higher charges at Jamaican hotels.

For these and other reasons, it is not hard to find plenty of faults in a general index series. The skill of statisticians can lessen them, but not overcome them.

However, despite the defects of the general index, it is the best tool that we possess for tracing money's value over time. Normally it does give a useful impression. To reject it in accounting is in effect to assume money's value to be stable; and this may lead to far worse error than does the index. When a series is based on prices of a remote year, we may be doubtful whether the best figure for the present year is 390 or 410; we can be quite sure that it is not still 100.

Most suitable type of general index

How general should be the chosen general index of accounting reform (e.g. should it include capital goods)?

Here one is dealing with a problem of *translation*—of giving as good an impression as possible of what money figures of some past date meant at that time. The most vivid and significant measuring rod for most people must surely be one related to their own everyday experience, i.e. to their consumption. This argues for the cost-of-living index. Further, an important (perhaps the most important) use of income figures is to give owners some picture of their material welfare, e.g. as a guide to their level of consumption; this too points to the cost-of-living index as a means of comparing 'well offness' at various dates.

However, it can also be argued that accounts are mainly intended as guides to the kind of man who owns a business or shares. Such a man is—directly or indirectly—a buyer of business assets, and so is not indifferent to the prices of capital goods. There are thus grounds for use of an index that covers such prices as well as the cost of living (e.g. the gross national product deflator). For simplicity, however, this book assumes the cost-of-living index to be adequate for both kinds of prices.

Specific indices

Because they are much less ambitious in aim and simpler in structure, specific indices may be less open to criticism than general indices. But they too are imperfect, e.g. an index of machinery prices may be far from typical of a given firm's machines, or at least of some of its machines.

There are, of course, many specific indices: governments, journals, and research institutes compile and publish them liberally, for wholesale prices in general and for each type of commodity, for capital goods and sub-divisions of capital goods, for securities, and so on. If this wealth of numbers does not provide an index to meet your particular needs, you can often (given modest skill in statistics) construct a private one without much trouble.

A general index is compiled from many specific prices, and so there may be some tendency for a movement in a general index to be matched by roughly similar movements in the underlying specific prices. However, this association is often far from close. In a diagram of curves for a composite index and its constituents, the latters' prices often fan out capriciously 'like a swarm of bees'. Thus the price of man-made fibres has in recent years risen much less steeply than the composite index of manufactures; whereas the price of coal has risen far more steeply.

It follows that, where assets are to be revalued at current level (as in a balance sheet), general index adjustment of historical cost may give results that are far from realistic; here it is better to reappraise each asset, or to use a narrow-range specific index. But for several other purposes, as we shall see, the general index can play a most useful role in inflation accounting.

3

Concepts of Wealth and Income

A proposal for accounting reform should presumably be judged by both intellectual and pragmatic tests. Is it right in principle? Will it work? This chapter will attempt to suggest the tests of principle—that is, to describe an intellectual framework within which the proposals of later pages can be set and judged.

One of the accountant's main tasks is to keep track of wealth: he has to measure both wealth at a given time (e.g. in the balance sheet), and changes in wealth between given times (e.g. in the income statement). The first problem is thus how to do the measuring—what to include, and how to value; and the second is how to compare figures of different dates.

Alternative concepts for measuring wealth

There are many ways of tackling the first problem (and probably we use all of them sometime or other, at least in our hazier thoughts). One group of concepts envisages wealth as the expectation of a stream of future benefits. Another looks to the existing assets; and, within this group, different concepts view the assets at various current or historical values.

Forward-looking concepts

An obvious example from the first group—the 'forward-looking' or *ex-ante* concepts—can be illustrated as follows. If the owner of a firm is asked at what price he would sell it, he may reason to himself: 'By keeping the firm as a going concern, I shall probably be able to take home various sums of money each year. I guess these will be about £*x* during the next twelve months, £*y* in the year after, then £*z*, and so on. So my price must be at least the total present value of £*x*, £*y*, £*z*, etc.' Let us say that the discounted value of these expected cash flows works out at £20 000.

Here, then, is one way of measuring the owner's wealth in the firm—and a profoundly important one, since it will guide him in deciding (among other things) whether or not to accept the buyer's offer. Such a concept is near kin to the discounted cash flow approach of internal capital budgets. It is highly personal and subjective. It looks at the expected future cash flows from the firm as a whole, and pays scant attention to the separate assets. These are relevant only so far as they will contribute directly to the flow (e.g. where they include cash in excess of working needs), or they can make the flow seem more secure and predictable (e.g. a shop in a prosperous street reassures investors more than a mine-shaft in a desert). Therefore they tend to be of only minor importance when a firm is flourishing. When a firm is doing badly, however, the best plan may be to sell off the assets piecemeal, and then their separate values as scrap, etc. become relevant since these will constitute the future cash flow.

The owner in the above example, like the rest of us, probably does not normally carry in his mind any precise figure (such as the £20 000) of his wealth. Unless he budgets in great detail, he will have only a vague impression; even if he does budget, he will admit that some of the estimates are likely to prove wildly wrong. Moreover his value figure will vary in time with changes in his expectations, due for instance to new information and whether his mood is cheerful or not. Other people (such as potential buyers) may also form opinions about the future cash flows from the firm, and their valuations are likely to differ a good deal from the owner's £20 000.

Thus we face a paradox. Forward-looking concepts are clear and attractive in principle, and do in fact guide us in our fundamental decisions; yet they can yield only shadowy figures that depend on personal opinion. For routine accounting, clearly they must give place to a concept of lowlier intellectual status, whose figures are, however, more precise, objective, and verifiable.

Under such an 'unanticipatory' concept, the firm's wealth does not depend on what is expected to flow in hereafter but on what is here already. It can best be measured by listing the assets and liabilities one by one, valuing each on some objective basis, and finding their net total. But, alas, this is not as simple as it sounds, for there are many ways of measuring an asset's value. Two sets of concepts call for particular attention.

The accounting (historical-cost) concept

Accounting has evolved a concept whose features are well defined (though admittedly the edges are fuzzy and there are lots of exceptions). It aims to show the firm's actual achievement to date in winning solid wealth, rather than prospects of future gain. So it records new assets at cost, and then—if applied rigorously—ignores all upward movements in value till these are vouched for by clear-cut realisation; thus some fixed assets (such as land) may be kept indefinitely at their original cost, despite manifest increase in their current value. Accordingly accounting is said to depend on a historical-cost concept—though the deference to history is probably a by-product of the realisation test (so that 'realisation concept' might be better).

Note that the concept is asymmetrical. It does not write up, but it does write down. It is built on caution. Thus it values most current assets at 'the lower of cost or market'; and fixed assets with limited lives are usually written down—regardless of any rise in market value—to allow for depreciation (found as some fraction of historical cost).

The realisation test has played, and still plays, a major role in accounting. Nevertheless its standing should not be exaggerated. It is not applied strictly to all assets. Thus some firms seem to flout caution by valuing stocks at net realisable value (sale price less costs still to be borne, e.g. delivery charges); such firms include farms, producers of precious metals, and exotic plantations. (One suggested generalisation is that the test is used where realisation is difficult and the sale price is doubtful, and not used where realisation is easy and the price is sure.[1] But the difficulties of finding cost may be the determining factor; how could a farmer fabricate a cost for lambs born in his own fields?) Again, firms engaged in long-term contracts (such as building skyscrapers) may in effect write up an unfinished asset, so that each year of construction shows a profit by a 'percentage of completion' test; they defend their deviation by the need to spread profit in smooth trends.

Increasingly, the test is being half disregarded in a way that is helpful for inflation accounting. Assets are revalued, and the increase is classed not as income but revaluation surplus (a 'capital reserve'). Even the EEC's staid Fourth Directive permits this device, and Britain's Companies Act 1981 follows suit.

Doubts on realisation date Even where the test is loyally applied, there may be doubt about its interpretation. One set of criticisms concerns the nature and date of 'realisation'. To some writers, the word implies merely physical usage (e.g. a factory's raw materials or depreciating plant may be said to be realised when they are consumed as input); far more often it implies an external transaction, such as a sale, that gives objective evidence of value growth. Even where an external test is used, the choice of date can seldom be justified by anything more profound than a convention. Where the contract is for the sale of goods, etc., their realisation date is normally deemed to be that at which the goods are sent off.[2] Where the contract is not for such sales (but is, e.g., for work by a building contractor or solicitor), the selected date may be that at which a claim for payment arises—a difficult matter, probably governed by the terms of the contract or by statute law, etc. But to be on the safe side, accountants sometimes treat realisation as occurring only at the later date of the cash receipt (e.g. where credit sales are beset by bad debts and lengthy delays of payment). Such caution may seem to put the figures beyond peril, but even cash receipts can afterwards be offset by, say, refunds for poor quality. Moreover, there are other circumstances that can make the realisation date hard to define: for instance, when cash at a foreign branch appreciates because of favourable exchange movements, is the gain realised instantly or only on remittance?

Doubts on whether an asset exists There may be doubt about whether a historical cost should be 'carried forward' or 'expensed', i.e. whether or not an asset has come into being. Expenditures on research and advertising are examples.[3]

This problem is not peculiar to the historical-cost concept, but is inherent in most asset-by-asset concepts.

Doubts on the size of historical cost Where bits of historical cost can be charged to different periods or physical units, etc., the question 'How much is the historical cost?' often permits of more than one answer. Unfortunately the accounting concept lacks any built-in logic for deciding which is right. So the accountant must willy-nilly rely on conventions, which may or may not happen to yield figures that make economic sense. He faces this choice between conventions when for instance, he must decide on:

1 *The scope of historical cost.* There may be doubt about the range of expenditures that should be included in an asset's historical cost. Thus a manufacturer must decide whether to charge overhead—and, if so, how much—to his finished stocks and work in progress.
2 *Depreciation.* The various methods of splitting up a depreciating asset's cost over the years of its life yield very different answers.
3 *Sequence.* The size of some costs may hinge on order of physical movement, e.g. of materials issued from store—the first-in-first-out (Fifo) *versus* the last-in-first-out (Lifo) type of difficulty.

The use of current values would remove or at least lessen these problems. In particular, problem 3 impinges a good deal on reform proposals, and its existence is very damning to the accounting concept. One can hardly argue that economic magnitudes depend on such piffling trivialities as physical sequence (real or assumed). A concept that stumbles here must tend to be discredited *in toto*.

The current-value concept

Another approach (important for inflation accounts) measures each asset at its 'current value'. This phrase can mean several different things, which a later chapter will look at more carefully. One is current *sale price* (or more accurately the asset's net realisable value). Another is current *buying price* (replacement cost). Yet another is the type of cost employed by perceptive managers in their decision budgets (e.g. in measuring the sacrifice that would result from using up existing stores on a job); as we shall see later, this is found by considering the whole set of relevant values and then selecting the one that seems most informative in the given situation. For reasons that will appear later, I call this figure 'deprival value'.

If an asset is revalued, the accounts must perforce recognise gain or loss *before* realisation. Caution suggests that such figures should be given some special name such as 'unrealised appreciation' or 'unrealised holding gain', and kept apart from traditional profit until realisation occurs.

Should the term 'current value' be stretched to cover a historical cost that is updated with the general index ? The resulting figure is still backward-looking, and therefore differs in principle from current market values; so it should probably be classed as a variant of the historical group.

Alternative concepts for measuring income

If wealth is compared at two different points of time, the growth is income.

This definition is not widely used. Accountants normally prefer one that compares revenues with costs—the approach of the profit and loss account. But the balance sheet approach seems to fit the facts and clarifies the problems of price change: this book will therefore make much use of it.

There are, however, a number of provisos to the bald definition above. Two of the more obvious are that allowance must be made (when the accounts are those of a firm) for wealth paid in by or out to the owners during the period (e.g. dividends) and that, as like must be compared with like, the same value concept must be applied at both points of time.

Needless to say, 'growth' and 'income' are sometimes negative. For convenience, this book will normally assume that such words include negative forms (and similarly that 'assets' covers 'negative assets', i.e. liabilities). It will also assume 'income' to be a general word that covers 'profit'; the latter is useful only in that it suggests an origin in trade, etc.

The simple diagram in Figure 3.1 may help to introduce later steps in the argument. Time is shown on the horizontal OX axis, and value on the vertical OY axis. Total wealth at 1 January is AB, and at 31 December it is CD; the growth ED is the income.

Value concepts lead to corresponding income concepts

The choice of value concept governs the sizes of AB and CD—and therefore of ED. Thus income, like wealth itself, is the creature of

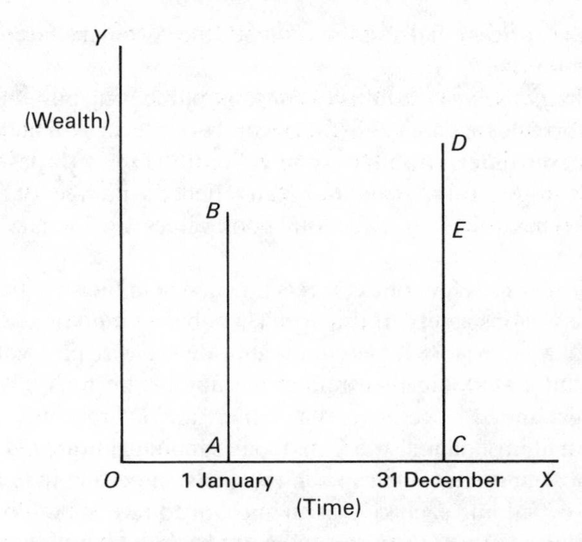

Figure 3.1 Simple comparison of wealth over time

value concepts; it must be defined by reference to the chosen concept.

If, then, there are *x* value concepts, there are *x* corresponding income concepts—possibly leading to *x* different income figures. A firm can legitimately have several different 'profits' for a year. To avoid imprecision, one should on some occasions say that profit is such and such a figure by such and such a concept.

Comparison units at different dates

A further difficulty now arises. *CD*'s growth may or may not be due in some part to price change. If price change has taken place, one must—whatever the chosen concept—give thought to the kind of units in the vertical measures *AB* and *CD*; there is now a danger of the opening and closing wealth being no longer measured in like units.

Three possible types of unit for measuring both *AB* and *CD* (i.e. for calibrating *OY*) suggest themselves:

1 *Money units*. Here one takes the money unit as the yardstick throughout, ignoring changes in both its purchasing power and

specific prices. This is of course the ordinary accounting procedure.

2 *Real wealth units* (i.e. units of constant purchasing power). Here one corrects for changes in the general price level with the help of a general index. In effect, one calibrates *OY* with baskets of goods-in-general; *AB* and *CD* then reflect the number of baskets that seem equivalent to the total book values at 1 January and 31 December.

3 *Physical units*. Here one corrects for change in the specific prices of the various assets. If the firm has only one kind of asset (e.g. tons of a given stock), one could calibrate *OY* with physical units; *AB* and *CD* would then reflect the number of tons, etc., at 1 January and 31 December. Where there are several kinds of stock (i.e. in almost all real-life firms), one cannot calibrate *OY* with a physical unit. But one can achieve the same effect with money units by valuing each kind at an unchanged rate in both opening and closing stock; thus an item might be valued in both *AB* and *CD* at its rate on date *A*, or (as under Lifo rules) on some remote base date.

Comparison between *AB* and *CD* would be absurd if the former were measured in, say, francs and the latter in lire. It likewise smacks of absurdity if the value of the money unit in the given country changes during the year: then too the opening and closing units can be deemed unlike. This is why orthodox accounting methods, based on money units, are now under fire; when prices change markedly, real wealth (or perhaps physical) units may be preferable.

Example of comparison units

Suppose a firm starts at 1 January with a capital of £100 in cash, and uses this to buy 100 tons of stock at £1 per ton. It turns over its stock several times during the year, and uses all the resulting revenue to buy fresh stock; the last such replacement takes place at 31 December. Prices are rising; the general index goes from 100 to 110, but the price of stock per ton goes from £1 to £1.32. At 31 December, the only asset is still 100 tons of stock (i.e. all the sales receipts have been needed to maintain a constant physical volume), valued at £132.

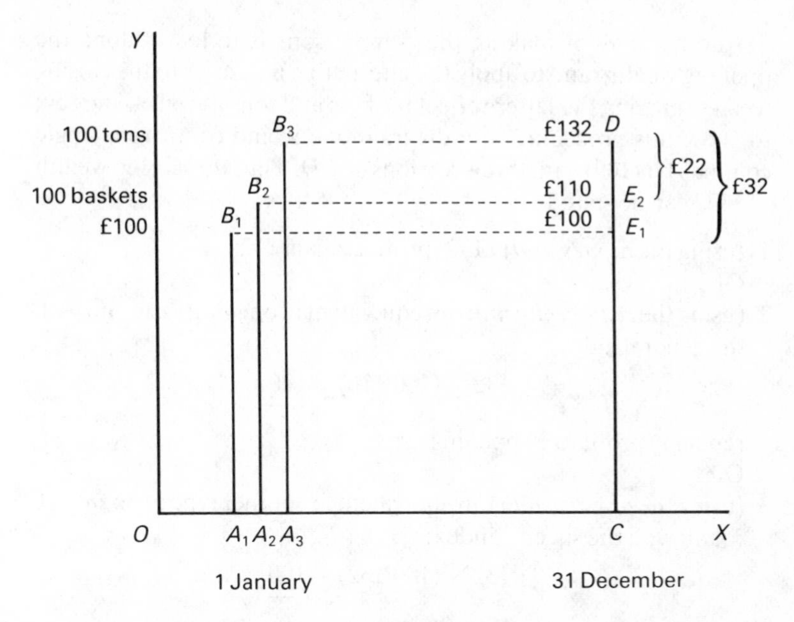

Figure 3.2 Comparison of wealth using alternative units

Has the firm's wealth grown? One way of tackling the comparison is to accept the £132 figure for closing wealth, and to restate the opening wealth in the three alternative units. In Figure 3.2 opening wealth is shown by three different columns:

A_1B_1—100 money units.

Comparison of A_1B_1 with CD puts growth at E_1D. £100 has become £132; *money profit* is £32 (as in ordinary accounting).

A_2B_2—100 real-wealth units (baskets of goods-in-general).

At the end, 100 baskets cost £110; so opening wealth is restated at the equivalent of 110 end £s, A_2B_2. This notional £110 grows to £132; *real profit* (= $CD - A_2B_2 = E_2D$) is £22.

A_3B_3—100 physical units.

At the end, 100 tons cost £132, so opening wealth is restated at the equivalent of 132 end £s, A_3B_3. By the physical maintenance test, there happens in this example to be no growth—a capital of £132 has merely been maintained; $A_3B_3 = CD$, and profit is zero.

Another way of making the comparisons is to leave alone the opening wealth, and to apply the alternative measures to the closing wealth, making the latter reflect baskets and tons as well as money; to show this procedure in a diagram one would compare a single column *AB* (100) with three versions of *CD*. Thus the closing wealth of £132 can be stated as:

1 (using the *money unit*) £132; profit is again £32.
Or
2 (using the *real-wealth unit*) an equivalent in opening £s, found with the general index:

$$132 \times (100/110) = \underline{\underline{120}}$$

reducing profit to 20 opening £s.
Or
3 (using the *physical unit*) an equivalent in another type of opening £ found with the specific index:

$$132 \times (100/132) = \underline{\underline{100}}$$

and profit is again zero.

However, we are likely to prefer the earlier calculations, because these state the current profits in recent rather than remote pounds.

Sub-concepts of income

It was pointed out on p. 19 that there are as many 'incomes' as there are value concepts, and succeeding pages added the further complexity of the alternative units of comparison. The accountant may thus seem to face a confusing welter of income figures.

However, it is not too hard at least to marshal these income figures in a comprehensible pattern. The first step is to make the fundamental choice of value method—whether to measure *AB* and *CD* by, for instance, the historical-cost or current-value concepts. Once the concept has been chosen, the next step is to decide on the comparison method (i.e. the capital maintenance idea): the three possibilities may be regarded as giving rise to three sub-divisions within the chosen concept. Thus the accountant who uses Fifo and ignores price change has in effect opted first for the historical-cost concept and then for its money-capital sub-concept.

Comparison unit:	*Money*	*Real-wealth*	*Physical*
Concept: historical cost			
Current: buying price			
selling price			
deprival value			
Etc., etc.			

Figure 3.3

In other words, if there are x feasible value concepts, and three ways of comparison for each, there are altogether $3x$ feasible sub-concepts of income. It follows that there are $3x$ possible ways of setting out the income statement, and that up to $3x$ different income figures are likely to emerge. They could be arranged in a table as shown by Figure 3.3. Ordinary accounting profit fits into the box at the left-hand side of the top row.

The 'truth' of an income figure

Some readers may find it hard to swallow the notion that there are many rival 'incomes'. They may feel that only one can be 'true' and the rest must in some sense be impostors. Or they may liken the figures to those obtained during an experiment in a laboratory, where different readings presumably cluster round the result that would be given by extremely accurate measurement.

Such views are mistaken. There are some respectable arguments in favour of almost every one of the rivals (arguments of principle or ease of calculation); conversely, there are sensible objections to each one. Probably indeed it is a mistake to suppose that there is a 'true' income. What can be said is that some of the rivals are preferable to others because they are more useful. And 'useful' means not only honest, but also informative. Thus the different figures should be thought of, not so much as nearer to or further from truth, but rather as more or less able to give information that helps the reader. This ability may vary with the type of problem being studied; each version of profit may light up some aspect of a firm's progress better than other versions, or suit one kind of firm better than other kinds.[4]

For some legal purposes, admittedly it is convenient to enjoin the use of a particular concept. The ordinary accounting concept has obvious merits: it is familiar and (inflation apart) cautious, and most of its figures are based on objective data; its widespread use has therefore been sensible where the decisions are about cash payments (e.g. tax and dividends), since it reduces the scope for bickering and the danger of paying out cash before the revenue has been realised. But judicial blessings on this score do not make it more 'true' than any other version. Nor should they stop us from trying to improve it; for judges must in time give weight to reform that becomes accepted business practice.

If this view of income is right, the main test of proposals for reforming accounts during price change is whether the revised figures give a more useful picture of the firm and its progress than do orthodox figures. If the reformer can show this, he has made his point.

The uses of income figures

The last paragraph in the section above raises further questions: who are the users of the accounts, and when and why do they want information?

Clearly there are many types of users, both inside a firm (e.g. directors and managers) and outside (e.g. actual and potential shareholders). And they will seek information on many problems, notably:

1 *Consumption*. The individual investor wants information about each of his investments, in order to form some idea about whether he is growing richer or poorer—in particular, so that he can over the years regulate his consumption to whatever kind of pattern he deems most suitable. This is the view behind Professor Hicks's famous definition of income: 'The purpose of income calculations in practical affairs is to give people an indication of the amount which they can consume without impoverishing themselves.

Following out this idea, it would seem that we ought to define a man's income as the maximum value which he can consume during a week, and still expect to be as well off at the end of the week as he was at the beginning.'[5] This consumption-power criterion is perhaps a corollary of the common-sense view that the main reason why we work is to earn our living—that the end of production is consumption.

2 *Investment*. Present owners presumably want guidance on whether to keep or sell their shares, and so would welcome information that helps with comparisons between a particular company and other outlets for investment. Potential investors also want help with such comparisons. True, past performance is an unsure guide to future prospects; but the size and trend of the income figures, interpreted in the light of economic and other circumstances, can be useful aids.

3 *Efficiency*. Both 'outsiders' and 'insiders' want to know about the efficiency of management; they may be helped if, for instance, they are enabled to work out the rate of return on capital employed. Insiders may have a further need for detailed study of the efficiency of new methods, etc.; an income calculation should give guidance here, especially by providing costs that are meaningful.

4 *Legal arrangements dependent on profit*. Often more than one person has a legal interest in profit—i.e. partners, different classes of shareholders, the tax-gatherer, and employees paid by commission on profit. Again, trustees may be required to pay income to one person during his life, and then capital to another. Some forms of government control are linked with profit. Thus public utilities may be enjoined to keep their profits under a stated ceiling; and one way of controlling prices is to limit profit margins.

And there may be other users. Profits are sometimes cited during wage negotiations with trade unions; they may be relevant too in debates on social problems, a government's economic and fiscal policies, etc.

The different users will seek somewhat different types of information. Investors are concerned with all types, but particularly types 1 and 2; and, as investors are an important (arguably the most important) group of users, surely the published income figure should be one that caters as well as possible for them. But this view does not always dispose of all difficulty. The interests of different groups of investors may conflict: thus over-caution probably tends to be bad for ordinary shareholders, whereas preference shareholders and long-term creditors may think that they benefit from it (if it holds down the ordinary dividend and so increases retained wealth).

If insiders want other sorts of accounts for use 3, there is nothing to stop them drafting extra accounts for their special purpose. Use 4 has played a big part in the historical development of accounting concepts. But it has perhaps been accorded more weight than its deserts warrant. Legal income should presumably be the figure that is in some sense most acceptable to people in general, i.e. it should follow tamely from uses 1 and 2. But, as the size of the legal income may well govern the size of cash payments for dividends, commission, tax, etc. the men who determine such income must be influenced by a wish to curtail disputes, delays, and excessive cash drains; their resulting rules may differ from those most helpful for the other uses.

It is one thing to want helpful information and another to get it. Like other human devices, income figures are imperfect.[6] Indeed, some critics say they are so bad that accountants should cease to publish them,[7] and should provide users instead with condensed cash accounts—thereby enabling each user somehow or other to form his own conception of the firm's progress.[8] Even if we reject this defeatist view, we must freely concede that any given figure, reformed or unreformed, is likely to have limitations in plenty, and will not tell readers all they want to know.

Proprietorship versus entity, or who is boss?

No-one seems likely to question the notion that, from a shareholder's personal standpoint, income figures should be guides to consumption. But managers are apt to take a different view of their firm's income. They may feel their paramount concern to be the firm's welfare (and maybe its aggrandisement); and therefore that if an income concept leads to levels of dividend and tax that starve the firm, the concept must be wrong.

This clash of interest (which echoes the 'proprietorship' *versus* 'entity' debates in accounting theory) colours much of our later discussion. Where capital maintenance is at issue, managers will stress their firm's physical capital; shareholders, more concerned with their personal welfare, will stress real capital.

For the managers, it can be argued that the notion of shareholder supremacy has become naive. In the giant corporation, management is top dog; managers in fact hire the shareholders, not *vice versa*. Moreover, the firm's sickness or collapse would harm not only managers but the workforce and society at large.

Against this is the legal view of the shareholder as owner and ultimate controller; and, given a situation grave enough to provoke group action, the shareholders can in fact prevail. As the person who accepts the residual position and provides the retained earnings, the shareholder surely deserves respect. Another argument is that wealth depends on human satisfaction; and so economic concepts are likely to be more rational and simple if based on the individual rather than the corporation ('a damned abstraction . . . with neither a soul to be saved nor a stern to be kicked'). This may mean no more than that it is convenient to measure income as if the firm were only a one-man enterprise (managed by its owner). But the philosophers assure us that 'as if' arguments can be respectable as well as useful.

The shareholders' viewpoint seems the more human and democratic. My own inclination is to say that it should win.

Capital gain

The order and wording of the balance sheet can show abnormal gains in very different lights. Accountants have been adept at arranging the figures in alternative ways that may or may not suggest income. Suppose a firm's capital is £1000, its profit from ordinary trade is £400, and it has realised a gain of £100 from sale of a fixed asset. Somewhat extreme alternative forms of the balance sheet might be:

(1)			(2)	
		£		£
Capital		1000	Capital	
Profit on:			Share capital	1000
trading	400		Reserve from	
sale of fixed asset	100	500	sale of fixed asset	100
		1500		1100
			Profit	400
				1500

Forms 1 and 2 give quite different impressions of whether the £100 has the quality of income.

Where gains fall squarely within the historical-cost concept, attempts (e.g. by tax experts) to treat some as income and others as non-income must tend to sound thin in logic; the attempted distinction will often hinge on 'usualness', and then must be arbitrary. However, where gains fall into different concepts, some distinction can be justified. Thus reformed accounts might reasonably (in the interest of caution) separate realised from unrealised gains—even though the size of the figures on each side of the line may admittedly depend on rule-of-thumb, as when material costs rely on sequence (see p. 17), and machinery costs are 'realised' via depreciation charges of questionable size.

Various other solutions to this problem have been suggested, notably by lawyers. Thus growth in 'fixed' assets has been distinguished from growth in 'circulating' assets; and the analogy of the tree and its fruit has been seized on eagerly.[9] Such solutions are too superficial to be of much service.

It does not get us out of the wood to call some gains 'capital'. The word seldom means more than 'unusual' or 'unforeseen'; and though there may be some advantage in pointing to unusual or unexpected items (e.g. because windfalls do not affect our expectations, and thus our behaviour), these items may none the less seem in other respects to be income. There are, however, two exceptions:

1 Suppose a testamentary trust starts with a capital £100 000 and invests this in irredeemable fixed-interest securities to earn £6000 a year, the market rate of interest then being 6 per cent. Later the rate drops to 5 per cent, i.e. the value of the securities rises to £120 000. In one sense, there is here a gain of £20 000. But if the trustees now sold £20 000 of the securities and paid out the proceeds, future revenue would drop to only £5000 a year; the recipients of income would be delighted this year but very dismayed next year. So, where gain is due to change in the market rate of interest, at least part[10] of it may usefully be excluded from some definitions of income.
2 Where there is gain in money terms but not real terms, it may sensibly be treated as a restatement in current pounds of an unchanged real capital rather than an increase. But such treatment implies acceptance of the real-wealth sub-concept.

The discussion of capital gains, etc. in this section might have been broached in a rather different way—by questioning the earlier statement (p. 18) that all growth should be called *income*. Should not some forms of growth be excluded? Again, if an accountant decides that asset values should be written up to higher levels, does he thereby commit himself to a new income concept and a higher income figure?

The best answers to such questions probably hinge on the notion of multiple incomes. By the narrow test of a single concept (e.g. that employed by ordinary accounts), many forms of growth no doubt can be excluded. Once we admit the existence of the other concepts, we must concede that every gain has a place in some part of the framework (on p. 23), and so can be called income.

The case for using multiple figures of income

Perhaps therefore accounting should aim at giving several income figures rather than one—at setting out different pictures of the firm side by side.[11] This would put users of reports on their guard, and might also remind them of the nature of accounting measurements.

Multiple figures would unfortunately make reports still more complex and unintelligible to laymen. However, a skilfull draughtsman should be able to compress several alternatives into a fairly simple table. For instance, Professor E. O. Edwards and Professor P. W. Bell, in a book that has had a major influence on inflation accounting,[12] show two very different approaches in twin-column format. This must now be described.

'Operating' profit versus 'holding gain'

The normal income statement throws little light on management's skill at buying cheap and selling dear, i.e. at making holding gains while the assets await realisation. The statement might try to repair this deficiency by unravelling profit into two parts.

1 Profit that would arise even if all relevant specific prices were stable. It is thus the firm's reward for the narrow task of manufacturing, retailing, etc. as distinct from holding. It is called

operating profit. It is found by charging inputs that have 'lain in stock' (notably goods and depreciation) not at historical but current cost—just as if the inputs had been bought on realisation day.

2 Specific appreciation on these inputs, i.e. the difference between their current and historical costs. This part is *holding gain*.

So an ordinary income account might show both parts, which would add up to ordinary accounting profit.

This analysis is helpful to theory and to inflation accounting. Would it be useful to ordinary accounting in the absence of inflation (e.g. by showing the skills of the buying and operating departments)?[13] Practical men are unenthusiastic about it. Some of their reasons are sound (e.g. holding entails hidden costs such as storage, insurance, and interest). Other reasons are less sound—for instance, the view that production technicalities are more important than price fluctuations, so that a manufacturer should be judged by his skill on the workshop floor, not in the market. But price movements are a fundamental part of economic life, and a manager's prowess in this area deserves surely to be shown as clearly as his prowess elsewhere.

Example Suppose that a shopkeeper buys three units of goods in year 1, at the wholesale price of £10 apiece. They remain in stock till June of year 3, when two units are sold at the current retail price of £21. There are no other transactions. Accounting profit for year 3 is thus £22:

Income account, year 3

		£
Sales	2 units at 21	42
Cost of goods sold	2 units at 10	20
	Profit	22

Specific prices (i.e. the wholesale buying prices per unit) during the three years are:

		£
Year 1	Purchase date	10
Year 3	1 January	12
	30 June (sale date)	16
	31 December	17

(General prices are here ignored, but could readily be superimposed on the calculation.)

With the aid of the specific prices, the above income account can be redrafted as in Table 3.1, which tries to illustrate the Edwards and Bell model.

Its income account starts with stage (a), the calculation of operating profit. This is found by charging the sold goods at current instead of historical cost, i.e. by ignoring the holding gain (appreciation) now realised. The two units appreciated from £10 to £16 while in stock, so the realised holding gain is £2 × (16 − 10) = £12.

Stage (b) rounds off the account in two alternative ways. Its columns both start with the £10 operating profit brought down from (a). Then they add holding gain, but in different doses.

Column (1) is only a fuller version of the ordinary account. It brings back the £12 realised holding gain; so it reaches the historical profit of £22—but by what may be a more informative route. Variations on its two-step analysis have greatly influenced some forms of inflation accounting.

Column (2) uses current values. But it is more emancipated than most CV models, in that it rejects the realisation test as an over-timid convention, and merges unrealised and realised gains as equals. Further, it deals exclusively with year 3, by taking in holding gain for that year only; thus, unlike most income statements, it does not credit the current year with good buying in earlier years. Because current values here exceed historical ones, its profits for the three years (£29) exceed the accounting profits (£22) of column (1). Its balance sheet shows stock at current value.

Price-change reforms and wealth concepts

Ill-results of ignoring price change

Accounts that ignore price change give poor information in several ways:

1 Because they blend £s of unlike value, they blur real trends—for instance in a comparative table of results for several years.
2 They fail to show how inflation eats into the value of cash and other 'monetary items'.

Table 3.1 Accounts Showing Two Versions of Profit

Income Account

(a) Current trading section

	£
Sales	42
Cost of goods sold (as at 30 June, year 3): 2× 16	32
Operating profit	10

(b) Alternative treatments of profit

	(1) *Only realised gains shown*	£	(2) *Both realised and unrealised gains shown*	£
(i) Operating profit, b/d		10		10
(ii) Holding gain				
	Appreciation in years 1–3, realised in 3:		All appreciation during year 3 only, on assets:	
	2 × (16 − 10)	12	sold: 2 × (16 − 12)	8
			still held: 1 × (17 − 12)	5
		—		13

Total

	Accounting (= realised) profit:	'Current profit':
For year	22	23
Brought forward	—	6
	22	29

Balance Sheets, year 3

	1 Jan. £	31 Dec. £	1 Jan. £	31 Dec. £
Cash	—	42	—	42
Stock	30	10	36	17
	30	52	36	59
Capital	30	30	30	30
Profit: realised		22		22
unrealised			6	7
				29
	30	52	36	59

Note: Reconciliation of profit figures:

		£
Accounting profit		22
less Gains of years 1–2, realised in 3	(4)	
add Year 3 gain, still unrealised	5	1
'Current profit'		23

3 They may, by what seem important tests, misstate cost; and in consequence
4 may likewise misstate realised profit.
5 They show assets at out-of-date values; and in consequence
6 they ignore unrealised gain and loss.

These faults can be important for all the uses and users mentioned on pp. 24–5. The following chapters study each fault at some length.

Reform means movement over the conceptual framework

There are many different proposals for curing the faults. Most of them involve some degree of switching within the conceptual framework already described. Thus the reform of cost and profit figures must mean a switch at least from the money sub-concept to a real-value or physical sub-concept; and reform of asset values forces a switch from the historical to a current-value concept.

Because the orthodox accounting concept, despite its defects, confers certain safeguards (p. 24), plainly we should not abandon it without awareness of what we are about. We should appreciate the size of the conceptual change in a given reform proposal, the better to assess its risks as well as its benefits. And probably a change from the historical to the current concept is not justified during the stress of inflation if it would not seem defensible in more serene times. Therefore a reformer strengthens his case by showing how his proposals fit into the full framework. He is less than honest if, bent on reform of concept, he slips this in as part of a seemingly modest programme for dealing with inflation.

Meanings of 'inflation accounting'

A warning is perhaps needed at this point. The above discussion of general and specific indices shows that accounting reform can use alternative tools, leading to different values. And in fact the possibilities are even more varied; 'inflation accounting' is not a single model—the one and only substitute for historical accounts—but can take many shapes.

The rival models can be sorted by *value concept*, and then again by *degree of completeness*. To keep our minds clear, we must therefore classify any given proposal by two different tests (and also must know the many names—and initials—that are commonly used):
First we must ask which value concept is to be paramount:

1 *General index* (GI). Here ordinary historical cost (HC) figures are restated in terms of artificial units of constant purchasing power (CPP). *Real* wealth is stressed.
2 *Specific values*. Here HC is restated with the aid of individual reappraisals or specific indices (SI). The result can be called current value (CV) or current cost accounting (CCA). *Physical* wealth (e.g. number of tons of a given stock) is stressed.

Or reform may draw strength from both concepts—'hybrid models'.

Secondly we must ask how completely the proposed model reshapes HC accounts. Its scope can be restricted (e.g. it may only revalue a few items in the balance sheet, or raise some costs in the income statement). Or its scope can stretch much further; at the extreme, reform extends to every item including the equity ('full stabilisation'). Thus a reform programme should seldom be thought of as a seamless robe, to be accepted or rejected as a whole. On the contrary, its various parts should be considered one by one; and a firm may reasonably decide to adopt some parts and to reject or postpone others.

Notes and References

1 This idea is suggested in Wright, F.K. (1970), 'A theory of financial accounting', *Journal of Business Finance*, Autumn.
2 'Shipment is taken as the occasion for the credit to revenue. . . . In many cases, title doubtless actually passes at this point; but this is certainly not always the case'. Paton, W.A. (1922) *Accounting Theory,* p. 450, Ronald Press.
3 Morison, A.M.C., (1974) 'W/o or C/f', *The Accountants' Magazine*, September, p. 357, discusses this point well.
4 'If, indeed, one believed that annual profit was in some sense an objective phenomenon, one might well take the view that careful search was bound to disclose the appropriate formula, in the same way that a scientist by looking deeply into the nature of the real world is able sometimes to produce a formula describing, within very close

approximations, a natural phenomenon, such as the propagation of light. But this is not the case. The terms 'profit' and 'income' are in fact used in our language to indicate a whole range of ideas. It is true that all these ideas have something in common. They all imply in some sense the receipt of a benefit during a given period of time. But there the common element ends. In fact, the systematic use of any one of the many concepts of income arises only because thereby a convenient social purpose is fulfilled; and for different social purposes it is convenient to use different concepts. Edey, H.C. (1962) 'Income and the valuation of stock-in-trade', *The British Tax Review*, May–June p. 164.

5 Hicks, J.R. (1939) *Value and Capital*, Oxford University Press, p. 174. But 'well-offness' is there subdivided. It may mean *ex-ante* maintenance of either ('Hicks 1') capital value, or ('Hicks 2') future consumption—different things if the interest yield changes.

6 Professor Hicks ends his discussion of income with: 'We have come to see how very complex it is, how unattractive it looks when subjected to detailed analysis. We may now allow a doubt to escape us whether it does, in the last resort, stand up to analysis at all, whether we have not been chasing a will-o'-the-wisp' (*op. cit.*, p. 176).

7 'We are led to the conclusion that periodic income is not an effective tool of financial planning or control. This conclusion seems to accord ill with the fact that income measurement has long been a central theme of accounting and the main preoccupation of the accounting profession. Yet this fact need not impress us. The practice of medicine once consisted largely of blood-letting . . . just as in the first half of this century we saw the income statement displace the balance-sheet in importance, so we may now be de-emphasizing the income statement in favour of a statement of fund flows or cash flows. Each of us sees the future differently, no doubt. But my own guess is that, so far as the history of accounting is concerned, the next twenty-five years may subsequently be seen to have been the twilight of income measurement.' Solomons, D. (1961) 'Economic and accounting concepts of income', *Accounting Review*, July, pp. 118–19.

8 See, for example, Lee, T.A. (1981) 'Cash flow accounting and reporting' in T.A. Lee (ed.) *Developments in Financial Reporting*, Philip Allan.

9 'For a long time the relationship of income to capital was likened to the relation of the fruit to the tree. Just as there was no difficulty in separating the crop from the tree, so there need be no difficulty in distinguishing income from the capital which produced it. It was in line with this thinking that, for the first thirty-six years after Peel had re-introduced the income tax in Britain in 1842, no relief was given by the British tax code for the using up of fixed assets in the course of carrying on a business. The introduction of income tax depreciation allowances in Britain in 1878,

and their growth in importance there and here since then, constitute a movement away from the idea that you can evaluate the fruit without giving thought to the value of the tree— that realised profits can be measured in disregard of what have sometimes been called "mere value changes" in the assets.' Solomons, *op. cit*.

10 Professor Frank Paish (1977) explains the theoretical distinction between the 'income' and the 'non-income' parts in 'Capital and income', in W.T. Baxter and S. Davidson (eds), *Studies in Accounting*. Institute of Chartered Accountants of England and Wales.

11 Stamp, E. (1981) 'Multi-column reporting', in T.A. Lee, *op. cit*.

12 Edwards, E.O. and Bell, P.W. (1960) *The Theory and Measurement of Business Income*, p. 218, University of California Press. This important book approaches the problem of price change by pleading persuasively for specific revaluation; the general index is introduced as a concluding refinement. The authors have up-dated their argument in their *Accounting for Economic Events*, Scholars Book Co., 1979.

13 For a discussion of the pros and cons of this analysis see Drake, D.F. and Dopuch, N. (1965) 'On the case for dichotomising income', *Journal of Accounting Research*. Autumn, and Prakash, P. and Sunder, S. (1979) 'The case against separation of current operating profit and holding gain', *Accounting Review*, January.

4

Price Change Makes Accounting Figures Unlike

The critics of orthodox accounting point to several faults that appear when prices change. Historical figures of different dates then tend to be expressed in unlike units, i.e. in units of different purchasing power. Australians and Americans both call their money unit the dollar. But 'in spite of the deceptive similarity of sound' the two units are unlike, e.g. they will each buy different quantities of goods. To stop confusion, we may write Aus$ and US$. We readily agree that it would be wrong to add together the two kinds of dollar.

Similarly the £ of 1950 was unlike the £ of 1980 by the test of what each could buy. To avoid confusion, we should use symbols such as $£_{1950}$ and $£_{1980}$; indeed, within a year's account we may find it helpful to distinguish the $£_{June}$ from the $£_{Dec.}$ Unfortunately accountants have not been averse to adding and subtracting these different units.

Combinations of unlike units foster various types of misinformation. Two of the more obvious are:

1 Figures of different dates, even if each was correct at its own date, are not comparable. To arrange them side by side is to invite false impressions.
2 If a year's accounts contain figures found by adding or subtracting unlike units (e.g. a profit found by subtracting an old cost from a current revenue), then these figures are in a significant sense incorrect even at the date of the accounts.

Trends

The first of these faults (non-comparability of figures of different dates) is important to anyone who tries to discern trends in a time series of accounting figures. For instance, company reports often include tables showing the main figures (e.g. sales, profits, and fixed assets) over the last ten years or so. This is excellent. But, as such a period has, since 1939, invariably been one of inflation, the figures are almost sure to display an upward trend—whatever the physical turnover, the efficiency of management, and so on. The same holds for almost all other kinds of long-term accounting series.

To give better information to users, such figures ought to be made comparable. This can be done with an index; the arithmetic is simple and familiar enough. The main problem is what kind of index to choose.

Physical trends and the specific index

Trends of physical activity can sometimes be detected by adjusting the money figures with a specific index. For example, suppose the manager of a shop wishes to find out the trend in the physical volume of sales over the years. He may (subject to provisos about the unchanged nature of the physical units and mix) sometimes obtain an adequate impression by deflating the money sales with an index for the type of goods, so getting the 'stabilised' figures (shown below in italics):

Year	*1*	*2*	*3*
Sales	£4000	£7000	£10 000
Specific index for these goods	100	200	300
Sales adjusted by index	*£4000*	*£3500*	*£3333*

The adjusted figures here suggest that the physical volume of sales has fallen—though the money figures suggest a steep rise. Similarly trends in physical volume of stocks held, or of any type of fixed asset, can on occasion be best studied with the help of a specific index for the particular asset.

Where one accounting figure covers several types of asset (for instance, stock usually comprises more than one commodity), the sub-total for each type should be separately adjusted with its own index. Or an adequate answer may be obtained by making up an index that is weighted to allow for the approximate volumes of each type.

The general index and trends

Where physical quantities do not matter, the general index may be more helpful than specific indices. Thus it usually affords the best means of comparing cash flows of different dates. Suppose a man's consumption outlays are:

Year	*1*	*2*	*3*
General index (average for year)	100	£120	£140
Outlays	£1000	£1320	£1680

The real trend in his style of living can be seen more clearly if he measures his outlays with a common footrule, by converting each year's £s into equivalent numbers of the £s of some convenient base date, say year 1:

Year	*1*	*2*	*3*
Outlays—average £s of year 1	*£1000*	*£1100*	*£1200*

This series shows the trend plainly enough; the values are now comparable. His standard of living has been rising, though not so much as the raw figures suggest.

Choice of base date

In both this example and the earlier one on stocks, the revised figures for years 2 and 3 are statistical abstractions based on the average prices of year 1 (perhaps the actual prices of June of that year), and therefore divorced from those of year 3, when the man makes the study. He may feel that the figures will be a trifle less abstract if they are instead linked with the £s now current—that is, if they are adjusted with an index of year 3 instead of year 1. The year 3 average of 140 may serve; but the index at 31 December, year 3, may be still better. Suppose it has by then risen to 150. The cash flows become:

Year	*1*	*2*	*3*
Outlays—£s of 31 December, year 3	*£1500*	*£1650*	*£1800*

For that matter, the man could take as his base a £ of year 2, or of any other suitable date in history; or he could take the average £ of several successive years. His own convenience and understanding are the main tests.

Where fresh figures must be added each year to a long series, there is an obvious clerical economy in basing the adjustments on the £ of an early year. In this way, one avoids the annual readjustment of all the past figures to the new end-£. But such readjustment, though it entails more work, gives a contemporary and so more meaningful picture, and thus is often worth the trouble.

'Mixed' figures within an account

In the historical-cost ledger, an account may hold a series of unlike figures. A good example is the account for retained earnings. Each year sees the addition of a new figure; a mature firm's account holds a long range of additions, each expressed in a money unit peculiar to the given year. The successive figures can best be interpreted in terms of general purchasing power—the base-date equivalents of what the owners gave up when they ploughed back each year's bit of profit.

Example of mixed figures within an account

Suppose the owner has ploughed back profits of 1000 (year 1), 1100 (year 2), and 1200 (year 3). For a clear picture, this mixed series can be re-stated in (say) $£_3$s, the conversion factors being found from the general index series. If this has been 100, 130, 160, the result is:

	(1) *Historical figure*	(2) *Factor*	(3) *Stabilised equivalent* $£_3$
Year 1	1000	160/100	*1600*
Year 2	1100	160/130	*1354*
Year 3	1200	160/160	*1200*
	3300		*4154*

In real terms, the sums retained each year have been sinking.

The ledger account of column (1) adds up to £3300. But this total comes from the addition of 'jumbled £s', and so has little meaning. The adjusted total of £4154 is better. It is the current equivalent, in terms of the purchasing power of year 3 £s, of all the past savings. For instance, if the owner wants to see whether his investments in the firm have maintained their value, the £4154 plus the year 3 equivalent of his original capital can sensibly be compared with a revalued total of the net assets.

Comparison of cost: revenue structure

To be most helpful, the comparison of income statements, etc., for different years should point clearly to any interesting developments. General price change tends to make such comparison hard. Once again, the user's task may be lightened by adjustment with the general index.

Examples of cost: revenue variation over time

Suppose that a firm's profits are £400 a year in a stable period before inflation starts (its costs being £1000 and its sales £1400). Then inflation sets in: next year, the general index rises smoothly from 100 (1 January) to 120 (31 December), and is at 110 'on average' during the year (say at 30 June).

All sorts of things could now happen to this firm's costs and revenues. Table 4.1 shows three of the many possibilities. The pre-inflation income account is given in column (1) on the left. To the right, under A, B and C, are some possible variants for the first year of inflation, namely:

A. *Ordinary figures vary exactly with the general price level* Here sales go up in strict proportion to the general rise in prices—by one-tenth on the average, so the £1400 of revenue now becomes £1540 in the ordinary accounts, as in column (2). Similarly costs move in step with the inflation from £1000 to £1100. (It does not matter much whether we envisage a steady flow of small transactions over the whole year at prices increasing from, say, week to week, or a single outlay and revenue at 30 June.) Thus profit rises from £400 to £440.

To help comparison with the pre-inflation accounts of (1), an extra

Table 4.1 Comparison of Income Accounts during Inflation

	Before inflation	During first year of inflation								
		A			B			C		
		Ordinary figures vary exactly with price level			*Ordinary figures are fixed*			*Mixed case—say, sales vary, costs are fixed*		
	(1)	(2) *Ordinary accounts*		(3) *Stabilised accounts*	(4) *Ordinary accounts*		(5) *Stabilised accounts*	(6) *Ordinary accounts*		(7) *Stabilised accounts*
	£	$£_0$		£	$£_0$		£	$£_0$		
Costs	1000	1100	× 10/11 =	*1000*	1000	× 10/11 =	*909*	1000	× 10/11 =	*909*
Sales	1400	1540	× 10/11 =	*1400*	1400	× 10/11 =	*1273*	1540	× 10/11 =	*1400*
Profit	400	440	× 10/11 =	*400*	400	× 10/11 =	*364*	540	× 10/11 =	*491*

column (3) restates our ordinary figures in opening £s. The stabilised figures, obtained by multiplying the ordinary figures by the factor 100/110, show that sales are unchanged in real terms (and perhaps in physical volume), as are inputs; a profit of £440 earned on average at mid-year is worth only as much as 400 of the £s circulating before the inflation began. This firm has neither been helped nor harmed by the inflation, as its owners can buy the same quantity of goods and services as hitherto. Such consistent movements are not likely to occur in practice. A rise in general prices may, for instance, be reinforced by a growth in the number of units sold; or the specific prices of this particular firm may go up faster than the general index. Money profit will here rise by more than 10 per cent, and the firm's real income will rise too, though by a lesser percentage than the money figures suggest.

B. *Ordinary figures are fixed* Some firm's figures are not responsive to price changes. Thus the rents earned by a property company may be subject to government control or long leases; interest from government stocks, etc., also remains constant. Input prices may likewise be regulated by controls or long-term contracts.

Under B in Table 4.1, the ordinary figures for revenue and cost do not alter as prices rise—see column (4). But the £s are now less desirable than in earlier days. The stabilised column (5) shows that each item has sunk, and the unchanged profit of £400 in the ordinary accounts is worth only 364 pre-inflation £s.

In private life (as distinct from business), type B firms have their parallel in the *rentier*—the man who depends on a fixed income such as interest on government stocks. He is in clover if the price level falls (as in the early thirties); but in an inflation his real capital and income dwindle—despite static money figures—and so his lot may become tragic.

C. *Mixed case* In practice, probably most items change more or less in step with the inflation, but a few are eccentric. A vast range of possibilities exists. Example C deals with rising revenue (like example A) but fixed expense (like example B). The ordinary accounts (column (6)) now show a much increased profit, and the stabilised accounts (column (7)) confirm that this increase is both real and substantial. But they also show that it comes, not from the apparent rise in sales (steady in real terms), but from the decline in the real burden of expense—the unchanged payment of £1000 in the ordinary accounts now represents a sacrifice equal to only 909 starting £s.

However, mixed change is not kind to every type of enterprise. The landlord of houses subject to rent restriction has a fixed gross income, but his maintenance costs show a delicate awareness of upward pressures. He may, therefore, not earn enough even to keep his houses in repair; an appreciable number of homes in the UK each year sink into slumdom.

Comparisons between firms

Unlike units may also mar comparisons between firms. Suppose the current (19x9) balance sheets of companies X and Y both include land, valued at its historical cost of £10 000. X bought its land in 19x1, and Y in 19x7. More revealing figures can be found if a specific index for this kind of land is to hand. Suppose its figures are 100 (19x1), 200 (19x7), and 240 (19x9). A realistic comparison can be made thus:

	X	Y
Cost	£x1 10 000	£x7 10 000
Factor	$\frac{240}{100}$	$\frac{240}{200}$
Current value	£x9 24 000	£x9 12 000

The seeming similarity of the balance sheets hides the fact that X's land is probably twice as valuable as Y's.

5

Revaluation and Stabilisation

As earlier chapters have hinted, the essence of most proposals for the reform of accounts during inflation is the restatement of accounting figures of different dates in terms of the prices at a common base date. One example is the revaluation of assets at current prices.

When accounts talk about 'revaluation', they normally mean a limited degree of modernisation—probably confined to the corner of the balance sheet that encloses the fixed assets. However, it is possible to restate every figure in both income account and balance sheet with the help of price-index factors, and so to create a consistent whole in terms of the price level of some chosen base date. We shall call this full treatment 'stabilisation', by way of compliment to the late H.W. Sweeney, of Columbia University, who first explained the matter in English and used the word in this sense.[1] Other words, such as 'revaluation', can then serve as names for some of the incomplete programmes.

Stabilised accounts

As Chapter 4 explained, the real trends in a series of accounting figures can be made clearer by adjusting the raw figures with index factors. But stabilisation has also a far more valuable function: it can cut out most of the flaws and inconsistencies that mar a given year's accounts after price change, and make such accounts almost as useful as they would have been in the absence of change.

Probably no-one can really appreciate the impact of price change on accounts unless he can stabilise them. We may decide in the end that stabilised accounts are too elaborate for this or that kind of report; but they are essential for an understanding of our subject, and so a serious student must drill himself in their use.

Analogy with foreign currency translation

Stabilisation will remind accountants of a more familiar subject—their treatment of figures for foreign subsidiaries. When exchange rates are varying, the conversion of foreign money figures into home equivalents involves problems very like those of dealing with home price change. Suppose a businessman in Utopia (the 'head office') runs a branch in Britain. At the end of each year, the head-office accountant probably converts the British results from £s sterling into Utopian dollars (in order to draw up consolidated accounts for the group). Let us say that the business year ends on 31 December; that the only branch asset is land; that branch profit is £400 p.a. (net rents received smoothly over the year, i.e. on average at 30 June); and that the branch balance sheets run:

	1 January	*31 December*
	£	£
Fixed assets (land), at cost:		
At start of year	10 000	10 000
Bought with the year's profits, on average at 30 June		400
		10 400
Capital	10 000	10 000
Profit—net rents, earned on average at 30 June		400
		10 400

The head-office accountant can translate these sterling figures into Utopian $s easily enough if the exchange rate is £100 = $100 throughout the year; then the closing sterling values are also the Utopian values.

But suppose instead that British prices start to rise on 1 January (when the general index in Britain stands at 100) and go up steadily—to 110 at mid-year and 120 at the end; that profits rise in harmony, and thus (being earned on average at mid-year) are £400 × 110/100 = £440; that these profits are promptly invested in more land; and that the exchange rate exactly mirrors the depreciation of the £, so that:

At 1 January, £100 sterling exchanges for $100;
at 30 June, £100 sterling exchanges for 100/110 of $100; and
at 31 December, £100 sterling exchanges for 100/120 of $100.

One possible procedure—which links well with the accounting conventions for valuing assets—has been to convert the branch's opening assets and capital at their original exchange rate; additional fixed assets at the rate when bought; profit at the average rate for the year; and current assets at closing rate.[2] So the closing balance sheets are now:

	31 December		
	Sterling (1)	*Factor* (2)	*$* (3)
Fixed assets, at cost:			
Original	10 000	100/100	*10 000*
Bought with the year's profits, on average at 30 June	440	100/110	*400*
	10 440		*10 400*
Capital	10 000	100/100	*10 000*
Profit	440	100/110	*400*
	10 440		*10 400*

The converted results of column (3) show that the British income, up from 400 of the old £s to 440 of the new ones of mid-year, remains unchanged in the units that mean more to the Utopian owner (e.g. as a guide to further investment in Britain). They also measure the different assets in consistent terms, i.e. the total of $10 400 is no longer 'mixed' (see p. 41).

With stabilised accounts, in effect we pretend that the ordinary accounts are those of a foreign branch, and we convert them into the units of a conceptual head office in a far-off, happy land with stable money. Index factors (based on the price level of any convenient time) take the place of exchange rates. In simple examples, the mechanics are much the same as for the Utopian firm.

Example revaluation versus stabilisation. The $ figures in the above account are the same thing as British figures stabilised with 1

January as the base date, i.e. in *opening* £s. But stabilisation in the money units of the close of the period—i.e. in *end*-£s—is often preferable (see p. 40). If these closing units are used, the figures must be raised to match the rise in the closing index to 120. Table 5.1 shows what happens then; it also contrasts stabilisation with the half-hearted reform of revaluation. It has three columns: (1) is for the ordinary figures, and (2) and (3) for their revalued and stabilised counterparts. Column (2) assumes that all the land has appreciated in step with general prices, i.e. that the specific index for such land has behaved just like the general index.

1 The *ordinary* form is the one in everyday use. Its figures are historical, and therefore out of harmony with current values; as they date back to times with different price levels, they are mutually inconsistent.
2 The *revalued* form is being adopted by a growing minority of firms. In many countries, Accounting Standards tend to require it for bigger companies. It gives up-to-date values to some or all the assets; but it leaves alone the equity (capital, retained earnings, etc.), and therefore needs a balancing figure—the 'gain on revaluation of assets' or 'current cost reserve'.
3 The *stabilised* form is seldom met with, even in textbooks. It completes the process of revaluation by extending it from the assets to the other balances, here capital and profit. These are raised by factors that match the time between their 'arrival' and the end of the year—capital by 20/100 and profit by 10/110. Because the same factors are in this example applied to both asset and the corresponding equity item (i.e. no real gain intrudes), a balancing figure is not needed.

   How can we best explain the new equity figures shown in column (3)? The owner should argue that 12 000 of the depreciated end-£s mean the same to him as 10 000 undepreciated beginning-£s: both buy the same basketful of goods. Similarly 480 of the low-value end-£s are the same to him as 440 mid-year-£s.

Most balance sheet figures are the sum of many entries at different dates with different price levels. Thus more than one factor is in practice needed to revalue or stabilise each of these 'mixed' accounts. For instance, if undistributed profits have grown from year to year, the total must be analysed so that each increase can be separately multiplied by the factor appropriate to its date.

Table 5.1 Simple Balance Sheet, in Alternative Forms Showing Revaluation, and Stabilisation in End-£s

	(1) *Ordinary figures* £	(2) *Revaluation* *Factor*	£	(3) *Stabilised figures* *Factor*	end-£
Fixed assets					
Original, bought at index 100	10 000	120/100	12 000	120/100	*12 000*
Bought with the year's profits at index 110	440	120/110	480	120/110	*480*
	10 440		12 480		*12 480*
Capital, issued at index 100	10 000		10 000	120/100	*12 000*
Profit, earned at index 110	440		440	120/110	*480*
Gain on revaluation of assets			2 040		
	10 440		12 480		*12 480*

Nature of gain on revaluation

Revalued accounts (column (2) in Table 5.1) need a balancing figure of £2040. This 'gain on revaluation' cannot but give an impression of growth. Such an impression is here misleading, since it reflects merely the cheapening of money. Accountants distinguish such an unrealised gain on fixed assets from ordinary trade profits, and justify the distinction on the dual grounds that the asset is fixed and is unrealised. If, however, one adopts the real capital sub-concept, gain due to inflation becomes non-existent (whether or not it is realised). And this is exactly what the stabilised accounts show; so here stabilisation and caution are allies.

It is important to make up one's mind firmly on the principle at stake in this example. In less clear examples, as later chapters will show, the illusory gain from inflation can seep undetected into realised trade profit; and orthodox accounting usually leaves it there.

Some problems of stabilisation

Stabilisation becomes less easy when the values in the accounts change at differing rates.

General versus specific indices

Our simple example assumes that the general and the specific indices rise equally. So it evades the problem of choosing between them when they differ.

The specific index (like direct revaluation) gives more information about the size of assets. Thus it seems the better tool for updating asset values.

But the equity balances—capital, profits, etc.—are not linked with particular assets. They reflect a series of investments by the owner (cash paid in or dividends forgone) at various dates. The problem is how to interpret such historical sums in the most meaningful way. The general index is probably the best device for enabling us to look at yesterday's cash flows through today's spectacles: if we want to see how the owner's wealth has fared in a period, there are strong grounds for using units that measure it in terms of his general purchasing power. And even if we are tempted to use a specific index, we should have a hard time deciding which one is appropriate where the other half of the balance sheet covers a range of assets with diverging indices.

We shall next adapt the example so as to introduce problems that arise when the specific and general indices diverge. Here the values of the assets and the equity will diverge too, unless the equity is increased by the real gain. We can conveniently distinguish two kinds of movement.

1 Real-value change in non-money assets (more clumsily called 'non-monetary items') like land, whose money value changes.
2 Real-value change in money assets ('monetary items'), such as cash and debtors.

Real change in the values of non-money assets

Suppose in the example that, while the general index moves from 100 to 120, the specific index moves from 100 to 130. Then the original land appreciates during the year from £10 000 to £13 000, instead of £12 000 as in Table 5.1. For simplicity, let us suppose too that the only asset is this original bit of land (i.e. that trade profit is zero, and so no land is bought at mid-year).

If the accounts show the £13 000, the surplus on revaluation is £3000; but £2000 of this is mere paper gain due to inflation, and only £1000 is real gain. Stabilised accounts ignore the £2000, but will, if suitably drafted, show the £1000 as in Table 5.2, column (3).

Is it wise for the balance sheet to recognise real but unrealised appreciation? A useful mental approach to problems of inflation accounting often is to start by thinking about comparable change in a time of general stability. If the value of an asset goes up by £1000 while the general index stays at 100, should the asset be revalued? Recognition of the £1000 gives a more informative picture of the firm's wealth and progress, and accordingly seems desirable. This being the case, it is desirable also when specific change is superimposed on general change.

Table 5.2 Simple Balance Sheet, in Alternative Forms, with Real Appreciation on Assets

		(1) *Ordinary*	(2) *Revalued*		(3) *Stabilised*	
		£	*Factor*	£	*Factor*	*end-£*
Fixed assets	Cost	10 000	130/100	13 000	130/100	*13 000*
Owner's balances						
Capital	Historical	10 000		10 000	120/100	*12 000*
Appreciation (unrealised) on revaluation of assets						
Nominal			10 000 × (30/100)	3 000		
Real					10 000 × (130 − 120)/100	*1 000*
				13 000		*13 000*

Stabilisation and real change in the value of money assets

Let us go back to Table 5.1. Suppose that the £440 of rents received at mid-year are held as cash (instead of being invested at once in more land). The closing balance sheet—see Table 5.3—now contains £440 of cash.

Unlike its counterpart in Table 5.1, the stabilised column in Table 5.3 does not change the £440. The column uses end-£s; there are 440 end-£s in the till; change would be wrong. Whereas the money value of land can move, that of money cannot.

The £440 cash figure disagrees with the £480 profit figure—though the profit arose from earning the cash. There is no error here. True, cash and profit were both £440 in accounts at 30 June. But then, between July and December, inflation cut the value of the cash. The fall is $440 \times (110 - 120)/110 = -40$. A loss of this amount is shown in the equity. This information is important; an alert manager might have avoided the loss by buying land at 30 June.

The analogy with foreign exchange is again apt. If a foreign branch earns cash in June, the June exchange rate is used to translate the profit. If it still holds the cash at year end, the end-rate is used for this cash. If the rate has worsened, there will be a gap between the two translated figures. The gap (euphemistically named 'translation adjustment') measures the loss from neglect to remit promptly.

Gain and loss on money seems to fit under the heading of 'real change', just like the £1000 appreciation on land in Table 5.2. One could say that money has a very specific index of its own; no matter how far the general index moves, this specific index stays doggedly at 100, and every fluctuation in the general index alters the gap between the two indices, and so signals real gain or loss on money. Whether or not such gain or loss is *realised* is a nice point, which will be discussed in Chapter 6.

Gain and loss on money can have immense importance for individuals, firms, and society. Yet ordinary accounts make not the least attempt to measure it. Here is one of the strongest arguments for stabilisation.

Stabilisation in £ of dates other than the end of year

When accounts are stabilised, the end-£ normally seems to be the

Table 5.3 Balance Sheet Showing Loss on Holding Money

		(1) *Ordinary* £	(2) *Factor*	*Stabilised end-£*
Fixed assets	Cost	10 000	120/100	*12 000*
Cash		440		*440*
		10 440		*12 440*
Capital	Historical	10 000	120/100	*12 000*
Trade profit	Historical	440	120/110	*480*
Loss on holding money				*– 40*
		10 440		*12 440*

most convenient unit to choose. But the raw figures can as easily be stabilised in £s of any other date (e.g. some of our examples have used opening-£s, and a table comparing the results of many years might possibly use the £ of a remote date). Moreover, one of the virtues of stabilisation is that any set of stabilised figures can be converted directly to another base with the help of a single factor. We can, for instance, turn the figures of column (3) on the balance sheet on p. 48 into those of column (3) in Table 5.1 by multiplying by 120/100 throughout, and the reverse change can be made with the factor 100/120.

The stabilised income statement

The income account also can be stabilised—that is, the costs and revenues of, say, each month can be restated in the £s of some base date (perhaps mid-year or end-year). The results are specially helpful where a statement is 'mixed', in the sense that costs are incurred at dates other than those of the corresponding revenues (e.g. where materials are bought in the summer for peak sales at Christmas); the twisted results of such time-lags in ordinary statements will fill several later chapters.

The stabilised figures are, however, in one respect hard to digest. There are clearly strong grounds for stabilising the income statement at the same base date as the balance sheet. For the latter, the end-£ usually seems the obvious unit. But an income statement that is stabilised in end-£s must disagree with the ordinary figures of earlier months, and thus strike a manager as unfamiliar and odd. During inflation, they may seem too big. (A partial remedy—when cost studies, etc., are being made—is to stabilise the relevant figures at some 'average' date, e.g. mid-year.) As an illustration, suppose one of a firm's ventures costs £1000 and brings in £1540; that both the outlay and the sale take place at mid-year, when the index stands at 110; and that the accounts are stabilised at the year-end, when the index is at 120. The ordinary and stabilised versions of the income statement will run:

	Ordinary £	*Factor*	*Stabilised Closing-£*
Cost	1000	120/110	*1091*
Sale	1540	120/110	*1680*
Profit	540		*589*

The enlargement of the stabilised figures is at first disconcerting.

Notes and References

1 Sweeney, H.W. His pioneering *Stabilized Accounting* (Harper, 1936, republished by Holt, Rhinehart and Winston, 1964) was based on German experience during the inflation of the twenties, and is still excellent on the mechanics of stabilisation.

2 This is the 'temporal' method of translation. The alternative is the 'current' method, which translates assets at end-rate.

6

Gain and Loss on Money

The proposal that accounts should show change in the value of money, as in the example in Chapter 5, is more alien to ordinary practice than any other part of inflation accounting. So let us tackle it at once.

Money assets and non-money assets

Stabilised accounts show change in money's value automatically, because they give different treatment to:

1 *Non-money assets* (such as land, buildings, etc.), whose values are free to float as the price level changes; and
2 *Money assets* (such as cash and debtors), whose values are firmly fixed to the money unit. (It is unfortunate that *fixed* is the obvious adjective to use both in such phrases as 'fixed assets' and 'fixed money rights', which are at opposite ends of the inflation spectrum.)

The ordinary balance sheet splits its contents into current and non-current groups; the definitional distinction is none too clear, but usually hinges on the firm's ability and willingness to liquidate the asset within, say, twelve months. The process of stabilising lays great stress on a different line of cleavage—that between 1 and 2 above. For stabilisation purposes, all 'money assets', whether current or not, belong to the same family. The corresponding claims on the firm (e.g. creditors) also belong to it. If a balance sheet is stabilised in the end-£, all the members of this family are left at their face values. If it is stabilised in the £ of some other date, all members are multiplied by the same factor. Indeed, they might all be reduced to one net figure of money owned or owed (which would show the firm's structure in an interesting light) and then be stabilised *en bloc*.

Presumably firms do not obtain their asset structures by chance. The structure normally results from some sort of plan—an attempt to hold the assets best suited to economic and technical conditions. However, the plan may be marred by carelessness, shortsight, or bad luck. Stabilised accounts make one wonder whether most managers realise how much they stand to make or lose by regulating the volume of monetary items.

Types of money assets and non-money assets

Many of the current assets (cash, debts due to the firm, etc.) are money assets, or near enough to be treated as such. Investments held as current assets may or may not be money assets: the value of some (e.g. short-term government stocks) is closely linked to money, whereas the value of equities is free to fluctuate. Stocks, though current assets, are not tied to money; their values can change between acquisition dates and the end of the business year.

The heading 'investments in subsidiary companies' may cover dissimilar items. Loans to such companies are money assets, whereas holdings in the equities are non-money assets.

Fixed assets are almost invariably non-money assets. Deductions from their value (e.g. depreciation provisions) also must normally obey the same rules.

On the other side of the balance sheet, the equity of the ordinary shareholders (i.e. the balances for capital, retained profits, etc.) form a non-money group. But preference shares carry rights that are defined mainly in rigid money terms, and thus are subject to much the same forces as money assets; so too are debentures and loans. Current liabilities to creditors also fall into the money group, as do provisions for the payment of fixed sums of money.

Sometimes the item will have affinities with both groups, and then its classification must be arbitrary. Examples are participating preference shares and convertible loan stock.

Gearing

Inflation makes a money liability less burdensome, and so gives a 'gain on owing money' to those who are in debt. An important example is the company with high gearing ('leverage' in USA), i.e. one that is financed in substantial part by loans, preference shares, etc., rather than by equity capital. Inflation transfers part of that company's wealth from the holders of the money claims to the holders of the equity; the latter obtain a gain on owing. Stabilisation reveals this gain.

Gearing also affects annual cost. The borrowing costs of a company with gearing—interest and preference dividends[1]—stay constant during inflation (i.e. fall in real terms), and so the ordinary shareholders then reap an agreeable harvest.

Balance sheet example

By way of example, again consider (as in Chapter 5) firms whose pre-inflation capital is £10 000; general prices again rise by 20 per cent, as do the values of fixed assets, etc. But we now vary the patterns of assets and liabilities, and illustrate (in Table 6.1) three of the possibilities.

A. *Real values are constant*. Here the net money assets are assumed to be *nil* (throughout the year).
B. *Money values are constant*. Here the wealth is assumed to consist entirely of money assets (throughout the year). So £10 000 is the net sum of cash, debtors, etc., less money liabilities.
C. *Mixed structure*. A normal firm owns some money assets and some non-money assets. An interesting mixture is provided by high gearing, shown here.

To avoid complications, no trade profit appears; i.e. such profit is assumed to be zero, or to be paid out in dividends as fast as it is earned.

Table 6.1 sets out the differences between firms A, B and C in three possible forms of balance sheet: (1) ordinary, (2) revalued, and (3) stabilised. The stabilised accounts are likely to use the £ of either the start or the end of the year as base. Both possibilities are shown here.

Some rather dramatic contrasts emerge.

A. *Constant real values*. Because it has no money, the assets of this

Table 6.1 Balance Sheets Showing Effects of Owning Money

	(1) *Ordinary*		(2) *Revalued*		(3) *Stabilised* *In opening £*		*In closing £*	
A. *Constant real values* (money zero)		£	*Factor*	£	*Factor*		*Factor*	£
Land, property, etc.	Cost	10 000	120/100	12 000	100/100	*10 000*	120/100	*12 000*
Capital	Historical	10 000	Historical	10 000	100/100	*10 000*	120/100	*12 000*
Surplus on revaluation of fixed assets assets			Balance	2 000				
				12 000				
B. *Constant money values*								
Cash, etc.	Actual	10 000	Actual	10 000	100/120	*8 333*	Actual	*10 000*
Capital	Historical	10 000	Historical	10 000	100/100	*10 000*	120/100	*12 000*
Loss from holding money					20/120 (−10 000)	*−1 667*	20/100 (−10 000)	*−2 000*
						8 333		*10 000*
C. *Mixed pattern* (with high gearing)								
Fixed assets, etc.	Cost	30 000	120/100	36 000	100/100	*30 000*	120/100	*36 000*
Less Debentures	Actual	20 000	Actual	20 000	100/120	*16 667*	Actual	*20 000*
Net assets		10 000		16 000		*13 333*		*16 000*
Capital	Historical	10 000	Historical	10 000	100/100	*10 000*	120/100	*12 000*
Surplus on revaluation of fixed assets				6 000				
Gain from owing money					(20/120) ×20 000	*3 333*	(20/100) ×20 000	*4 000*
				16 000		*13 333*		*16 000*

firm can be shown in the stabilised accounts at a figure that still represents their full original value—stated as either 10 000 opening £s or 12 000 closing £s; there is no real gain or loss. The revalued accounts of column (2) show a £2000 'surplus on revaluation'. This suggests rightly that the managers have been clever to buy land and property; but a more apt title would be 'nominal gain from avoiding money assets'.

B. *Constant money values*. Because the managers stick to a policy of holding money assets while money is losing value, the firm is clearly worse off at the end of the year. But the ordinary and the revalued accounts still put the assets and capital at £10 000, i.e. show no loss. We can expand the ownership side of the stabilised balance sheets to show what has happened. The full consequences of holding money then hit the eye: 1667 opening £s, or 2000 closing £s, have evaporated.

C. *Mixed pattern*. Here our example is a firm whose financial policy is superlative: it holds no money assets, and it is deeply in debt. Its debt is £20 000 borrowed on debenture, which, with the capital of £10 000, allows it to start the year with £30 000 invested in non-money assets.

At the end of the year, the assets have retained their real value. Debentures, however, have become a far lighter burden. Ordinary accounts give not the slightest hint of this important change; the net totals in column (1) are exactly the same for firm C as for firms A and B, which have fared so differently. Revalued accounts do tell us that C is the winner, but overstate the gain and ascribe it to the fixed assets. Stabilised accounts correctly put the gain at 3333 original £s or 4000 current £s, and explain that it comes from borrowing: this part of the debentures has in real terms been cancelled. The gain should presumably not yet be deemed to be 'realised'; but it is an indication that the firm could now pay off its debentures more easily than at the start of the year (e.g. by selling fewer of its properties), and that in real terms the interest charge has shrunk. Firm C in fact gains much the same benefits as it would (in a time of stable prices) from a reconstruction scheme under which the debenture-holders are forced to scale down their claims to principal and interest by one-sixth.

It may be worthwhile to put the above in rather different words. Asked to explain firm C's story, someone not steeped in stabilisation is apt to answer sagely: 'Firm C did well because its assets rose in value.' True—but hardly helpful; we should take it for granted that the price of non-money assets tends to rise with inflation. What then matters is real gain, whether on monetary or non-monetary items. And real gain on owing is what distinguishes firm C.

Fixed interest and gearing

Table 4.1 (p. 43) illustrated real changes in cost and revenue structures. Fixed-interest receipts and payments are important examples of such changes.

A highly geared company has a profit and loss account like example C on page 43; if the money cost of interest stays constant during inflation, real cost falls and the company gains. So too does the man who pays interest on (say) a mortgage over his home. The snug position of borrowers is the obverse of the *rentier's* discomfiture. Someone must get what the *rentier* loses; an interest payer is one of the gainers. He might be called a negative *rentier*.

Gearing's rewards and risks

By real-life standards, firm C's gearing is somewhat exaggerated. Nevertheless, many companies have big overdrafts and long-term loans, and manage to get ample credit from suppliers. Much has been written about the harm done by inflation to business, and (as will appear in later chapters) inflation does indeed inflict a harsh extra tax on many firms. We must, however, in fairness recognise that some firms obtain substantial benefit from the lightening of their money liabilities.

If borrowing brings such easy gains, why are not all men of foresight deep in debt, and why are not all firms as highly geared as their credit status permits? One answer is of course that firms subject to marked ups-and-downs of trade may in the bad years be acutely embarrassed by high interest costs. Another is that though high gearing is very pleasant if prices happen to rise, it can be disastrous if the cat jumps the other way. Then the real burden of paying the interest each year, and the capital at maturity, becomes very onerous; and a firm that has already borrowed heavily may in an emergency be unable to borrow more.

Note that each annual gain on owing must decrease existing real liabilities—and thus the potential future gains. In firm C, for instance, each gain reduces the real size of the debentures, and so the scope for further gain on them. To maintain the annual gains, a firm would have to borrow more each year. But lenders then become wary; and interest rates tend to rise with inflation.

Importance of failure to show results of holding money

How important is it that ordinary accounts give no inkling of the loss or gain from holding money?

Most managers and investors are appreciative when accounts show the size and source of various trading gains; we should all denounce accounts that failed to report large cash losses due, say, to theft; and we go to great pains to devise costing systems that pinpoint small wastes in a factory. So there is a presumption in favour of showing any sizeable profits or losses—including those on money.

The argument will in any case seem somewhat needless to anyone who remembers what has happened in major inflations. When prices go up steeply by the hour, people soon grasp the notion of loss from holding money. In 1923, German workmen would on payday race from job to shops in order to change their wages into goods before prices rose again.[2] In such extreme circumstances, figures for this loss or gain might well be the most significant part of accounts. They could still be helpful in less extreme circumstances.

The next few pages will amplify the results of such movements in value—to the individual and the state as well as to firms.

Personal investment

Balance sheet B in Table 6.1 illustrates the position of the *rentier*—the traditional modest investor in 'safe' securities. His trust has been betrayed. Indeed many investors who put their savings into fixed-interest securities (early in the inflation) have done worse than balance sheet B suggests. The value of their securities has fallen even in money terms, especially where redemption date is remote. The full story would be shown by stabilised accounts that allowed for the specific index, i.e. quotation of the particular security.

The losers

An extreme example is provided by irredeemable securities with a low rate of interest, such as Britain's $2\frac{1}{2}$ per cent consols. Consider the investor who took up £100 of the 1947 issue at par, and held on to it. By the 1980s, not only had the £ depreciated to one-eleventh of the 1947 value, but the market quotation fell to about 23. The balance sheet showed:

		Ordinary accounts £	*Factor*	*Stabilised in 1947-£*
Investment				
Cost		100		
Current market value	23		100/1100	2
Capital		100		*100*
Loss on holding government loan				*–98*
				2

So stabilisation shows that this holder, like many others, has lost some 98 per cent of the wealth that he entrusted to the government. The wide use of stabilised accounts might well have led to strong, and probably beneficial, political pressures against inflation.

The gainers

But not every private investor has a balance sheet of type B. The more shrewd or lucky have achieved types A or C.

Inflation is a powerful educator. Many investors have switched from fixed-interest securities to equities (and from no-profit life insurance to with-profit). Equities have tended to keep in step with inflation; where they do, the investor has a stabilised balance sheet of type A. But, alas, there are many exceptions to this happy situation: individual companies may buck the trend, and the whole market can slump as in 1974.[3]

The man who runs deeply enough into debt has a stabilised balance sheet of type C in Table 6.1, and also an income statement like column C in Table 4.1. Provided the rate of interest lags behind inflation, his real yearly costs fall; and he can finally repay his loans easily from his rising salary, etc. As we have observed earlier, it pays to have a mortgage.

The state

If the government published its accounts in commercial form, we should see that it is the outstanding example of type C (Table 6.1).

The state's balance sheet

The state's balance sheet would show immense money liabilities—the national debt. This is incurred to meet deficits on current account, and to pay for non-money assets such as hospitals and houses. At the time when the payments take place, the state checks our grumbles by raising some of the money as loan rather than tax. Afterwards, the service of the loans becomes burdensome. By lowering the value of money, we in effect repudiate part of the loan; we avoid more obvious taxes by imposing an invisible capital tax on ourselves as holders of loan and other money assets. Such furtive manoeuvres are hardly conducive to sound fiscal policy.

Stabilised accounts would show the state's vast gains from owing money, and might lessen our self-deception; and stabilised interest figures could show how we evade the burden of interest on old loans. Collectively we are negative *rentiers*. We are here behaving rather like our ancestors when they used the press-gang to man the navy, instead of sharing the burden fairly.

The nationalised industries

Inflation cuts also the real costs of nationalised industries, since these are mainly financed by fixed-interest securities. Presumably part of the gain is passed to consumers; part may go to the state (the holder of the unrecorded equity capital) as reduction of real subsidies.

These transfers are very big, and should be shown.

Some related accounting matters

Results of holding money should be segregated

Enough has been said to stress the vast importance, in times of changing prices, of a firm's skill in controlling its net money assets. Accounts showing a 'loss of holding money' or a 'gain on owing money' would provide one test of this skill.

A careless person may be tempted to lump these gains and losses with the other accounting distortions (treated in later chapters) that inflation causes. Yet they are so different in logic that we must—if we are to see clearly what is afoot—keep the two things severely apart in our analysis. This book will therefore always try to unravel the 'gain on money' from the other effects of inflation, even though they tend to be confused in practice.

Correcting entries for money gain and loss in ordinary accounts

Money gain and loss fit neatly among stabilised figures, but hardly seem at home in ordinary accounts (because the latter do not revalue their equity items). With a little ingenuity, however, such gain and loss could be inserted, by making transfers between equity items. Thus loss could be shown by reducing profit and increasing a 'reserve' that in effect revalues equity.

Consider again the successful firm C (page 60). Its ordinary accounts could helpfully analyse the nominal gain of 6000 thus:

	£
Fixed assets, current value	36 000
Less Debentures	20 000
	16 000
Capital	
Historical	10 000
Inflation allowance	2 000
	12 000
Unrealised real gain, on owing money	4 000
	16 000

Is gain on money a realised profit?

One may agree that gain and loss on money should be shown, and yet hesitate over their classification. Is gain an addition to current profit, or is it more akin to unrealised appreciation on fixed assets?

We shall be helped with this problem if we follow the reasoning suggested on page 52, and consider the treatment of comparable gain and loss in times of stable general prices. A deduction of discount by debtors at such times is not unlike inflation loss on debtors and cash; discounts received are not unlike inflation gain on current creditors. Unrealised appreciation on land seems comparable to inflation's lightening of long-term liabilities; another parallel is the fall in liability where loan-holders, as part of a reconstruction scheme for an ailing firm, agree to cuts in the redemption payment and annual interest.

The ordinary rules (for times of stable prices) tell us that the discounts on current items, being measurable and either realised or sure to be realised, should go into the income statement. On the other hand, the remote and unguaranteed appreciation of land is ignored by historical cost accounts; and, if more emancipated accounts write up the asset, they very rarely use the growth to swell current profit.[4]

It seems reasonable to stretch this reasoning to inflation (particularly where the realisation test is deemed important). Gain and loss on short-term (i.e. current monetary) items may then be shown in the income statement. But gain on long-term liabilities should not be put there until the loan is repaid; if I have a mortgage repayable twenty years hence, inflation will lighten the ultimate burden, but this hoped-for gain hardly justifies my spending more now. (However, these views do not commend themselves widely. Thus the British form of 'gearing adjustment' has been far from clear-cut on principles.)

Inflation makes realisation harder than ever to define in cautious terms. The distinction between current and non-current is always arbitrary. Gain that is realised in the conventional sense can still be lost during inflation if it is left as a money asset. One might perhaps say that it is not certainly realised until cash is paid out as dividend, so that the owners have the chance to put it back into the safety of non-monetary assets.

Some writers argue that, when interest rates have risen during inflation, an ideal system should use part of the expected final gains to offset the extra yearly interest costs. Probably it should. But, as no-one knows what the interest rate would have been in the absence of inflation—and therefore the size of the extra cost—such offset seems impracticable. (And one can think of many other costs that are cautiously 'expensed' despite hopes that they may some day yield capital gain.)

Calculation mechanics

Strictly, current gain and loss on money should be found by applying general index factors to day-to-day or monthly balances. If, however, the balances do not vary much during the year, the gain and loss can be found approximately from the amounts in the opening balance sheet. Where the balances do vary somewhat, a short-cut calculation that assumes the changes to take place at a single date (such as mid-year) may well come close enough. (Page 77 has an example.)

Interest rates and inflation

Traditionally the interest yield on gilt-edged securities has been below the earnings yield on equities (e.g. in 1938 the two British rates were about 3.4 per cent and 6.2 per cent); because of the greater commercial risk attaching to equities, the investor would not buy them unless they seemed to offer an extra return. But inflation changed the market's preferences. Prices in the gilt-edged market fell—which is of course just another way of saying that interest yields rose. Thus the gap between the two types of yield dwindled. In the UK, the gilt-edged interest yield rose above the earnings yield on equities in 1960. Many investors are now content with a low immediate yield on equities if there are reasonable prospects that dividends and capital value will rise with inflation.

High fixed versus low but rising yields

Some investment pundits from time to time tell us that the fixed-interest yield has become big enough to make money securities attractive despite the inflation risk. Whether or not this is true depends on one's expectations regarding rates of inflation and one's own income tax.

Suppose for simplicity that a debenture yields 10½ per cent, and an equity 3 per cent; and that a given investor expects the inflation to run at 5 per cent per annum (equity dividends keeping pace). Then he must, to maintain the real value of money securities that are worth £100 at the start of any year, invest a further £5 by the end of the year to make good the loss on holding money; whereas his equity dividends and prices look after themselves. Accordingly he should budget somewhat as in Table 6.1, substituting his own marginal rate of tax for the specimen rates shown—say *nil*, 33⅓ per cent, and 66⅔ per cent. Fixed-money investment is, on the given assumptions, worthwhile only to investors blessed with low tax rates (such as charities); to be as attractive as equities to tax-payers with higher rates, the fixed-money security needs a gross yield of 10½ per cent where tax is 33⅓ per cent, and of no less than 18 per cent where the tax is 66⅔ per cent. (But *redeemable* securities, if bought well below the sum repayable on redemption, may be more attractive to those with high tax rates.)

Trusts—the need for new rules on capital and revenue

Where different persons are entitled to a trust's income and capital, inflation makes it hard for the trustees to keep a fair balance between them. Presumably the aim should be to maintain (at least) both income and capital in real terms. Investment in equities perhaps offers the best chance of doing so. But there must be some rate of interest high enough to make fixed-interest securities seem attractive to trustees. Under existing rules, such investment will yield a high immediate income; but this will dwindle in real terms over the years, and is obtained at the cost of a dwindling real capital.

If the trustees had power to retain some of the annual interest and transfer it to capital (as loss on holding money assets during inflation—see column (1) in Table 6.2), real capital could be preserved; money income would at first be penalised, but would grow over the years as the retentions were invested and bore interest (i.e. real income would be constant).

Table 6.2 Comparison of Hypothetical Real Income (after Tax) from Money Investments and Equities

Type of investment	(1) *Fixed money*			(2) *Equities*		
Tax rate—(say)	*Nil*	*$33\frac{1}{3}\%$*	*$66\frac{2}{3}\%$*	*Nil*	*$33\frac{1}{3}\%$*	*$66\frac{2}{3}\%$*
Gross money income	$10\frac{1}{2}$	$10\frac{1}{2}$	$10\frac{1}{2}$	3	3	3
Less Tax	—	$3\frac{1}{2}$	7	—	1	2
Money income after tax	$10\frac{1}{2}$	7	$3\frac{1}{2}$	3	2	1
Loss on holding money during inflation	5	5	5	—	—	—
Net sum for spending	$5\frac{1}{2}$	2	$-1\frac{1}{2}$	3	2	1

On the other hand, growth stocks may sometimes seem the best investment in all respects, save that dividend yield is below the average for sound equities. Here the trustees should have power to transfer the annual shortfall from capital to revenue.

Discounting during inflation

It is important during inflation to distinguish between nominal and real rates of interest.

To find the real rate, one must do something akin to stabilising. Suppose £100 grows into £125 in a year. The nominal growth rate is 25 per cent. But, if the inflation rate is 12 per cent, the real growth rate is only $(125 \div 1.12) - 100$ or about 11.6 per cent.

DCF budgets When he is using discounted cash flow budgets to test long-term projects (e.g. to find whether investment in a new machine is worthwhile), a budgeter must clear his mind on two questions. Should his estimated figures rise each year with inflation? Should he use real or nominal rates for discounting?

He can answer the first question in three ways. He can either:

1 Ignore inflation, i.e. use data that assume constant ('frozen') prices. This is probably the usual method. In its defence, a budgeter can plead that sophisticated estimates become silly in face of wild uncertainties; and rising figures, when stabilised, become much the same as frozen figures. Or
2 Estimate the actual prices and flows for each year—distinguishing between prices that will rise (e.g. materials) and those that are fixed (e.g. rent). Or
3 Employ both 1 and 2 by using rising prices for the first few years, and constant prices for the vague thereafter.

The budgeter can answer the second question in two ways. He must throughout use either (a) actual (rising) flows and the nominal rate, or (b) deflated (frozen) flows and the real rate. The two methods end with the same answer.

Example Suppose a £100 investment is expected to yield £140 after a year; the firm tests projects with a 25 per cent nominal interest rate; the inflation rate is 12 per cent and so the real rate is again 11.6 per cent.

Method 1
End receipts, discounted with the nominal rate:

140 ÷ 1.25 £112

Method 2
Step (a) Deflate:

140 ÷ 1.12 = 125

Step (b) Discount with real rate:

125 ÷ 1.116 £112

After discounting, the £100 project yields £112, and so is worthwhile.

The danger is that one muddles the two methods. This is not unlikely where the budgeter uses frozen flows, but then discounts with the high current (i.e. nominal) rates that must be in the forefront of his mind.

Indexation

Not unnaturally, lenders have sought for devices that will guarantee real income and capital. Thus one occasionally hears of money contracts with a 'gold clause' linking the debt with the price of gold. But a simpler plan is to link contracts with the general index.

A few countries have gone a long way in this direction. Brazil is the prime example. Since 1964, it has included government and private loans in a comprehensive system of indexation that also covers rents, minimum wages, tax rates, tax allowances, and inflation accounts for all firms. The British Government was long hostile to indexation, and began to issue indexed loans only in 1975. At first it hedged them with restrictions (lump-sum investment was permitted only to the old, and in small doses). The rules have been grudgingly relaxed; anyone can now invest in loans whose interest and redemption payments are indexed.[5]

Appendix: Further illustration of money gains in stabilised accounts

It may be useful to illustrate stabilisation a little further, by showing the arrival of extra money assets during the year. Assume that firm C (otherwise as described on p. 60) retains £540 of profit earned by a single set of transactions (including payment of a year's interest) at mid-year (index 110), or a series of transactions with the same average date; the ordinary and stabilised income figures are thus the ones explained in Table 5.1 (p. 50). If the net receipts of £540 are promptly reinvested in non-money assets (which appreciate with the general index), the figures for these assets and for their source (profit) remain equal, and stabilisation is still a simple matter (much as it was in the example in Table 5.1). But let us now suppose that the new assets are kept as cash. The latter does not appreciate, and so stabilised cash and profits cannot remain equal. Columns (1) and (2) of Table 6.3 compare the ordinary and stabilised figures. Column (2) shows that the £4000 gain on the debentures is slightly offset by a £49 loss from holding the £540 of cash from mid-year.

It may be salutary to show also what happens to a highly geared firm in a year when prices *drop*. In a second version of firm C's story, we suppose that the index falls from 100 to 80, being at 90 when profits are earned. As trade is likely to languish in such a recession, realism suggests that the profits should here be lower, say £260. Once again, the new assets are kept as cash. The ordinary and stabilised accounts appear in columns (3) and (4) of Table 6.1. The main interest of the column (4) balance sheet is that it shows clearly the disaster entailed by borrowing during deflation—a loss of £4000.

When stabilised accounts are being drafted, special calculations of some of the figures may be helpful. Thus Table 6.3 can be backed up with detailed calculation of the loss on money.

Calculation of gain or loss on money items

The gain or loss during a period, in £s of the close of the period, is:

$$\text{Amount of money assets (net)} \times \frac{\text{Change in index during period}}{\text{Index at start of period}}$$

Where the stabilisation date is some date other than the close of the period, the answer must be multiplied by:

$$\frac{\text{Index at stabilisation date}}{\text{Index at close of period}}$$

Table 6.3 Balance Sheets with New Assets in the Form of Money

	Index rises to 120					*Index falls to 80*		
	(1) *Ordinary accounts* £	*Factor*		(2) *Stabilised accounts closing-£*	(3) *Ordinary accounts* £	*Factor*		(4) *Stabilised accounts closing-£*
Income Account								
Gross profit—say	1 540	120/110		*1 680*	1 260	80/90		*1 120*
Interest on loan—say	1 000	120/110		*1 091*	1 000	80/90		*889*
Trade profit	540	120/110		*589*	260	80/90		*231*
Balance Sheet								
Fixed assets	30 000	120/100		*36 000*	30 000	80/100		*24 000*
Cash	540	Actual		*540*	260	Actual		*260*
	30 540			*36 540*	30 260			*24 260*
Less Debentures	20 000	Actual		*20 000*	20 000	Actual		*20 000*
Net assets	10 540			*16 540*	10 260			*4 260*
Capital	10 000	120/100		*12 000*	10 000	80/100		*8 000*
Trade profit	540	120/110		*589*	260	80/90		*231*
Gain on money:			£				£	
Unrealised			*4000*				(Loss) –*4000*	
Realised			*–49*				*29*	
				3 951				*–3 971*
	10 540			*16 540*	10 260			*4 260*

For complete accuracy, each period would have to be short—say 24 hours. In practice, one might well approximate by working in months, etc., and (in the absence of violent cash changes within a month) by using the opening balance (of net money assets) for each month. One could then, if the year runs from January, either:

1 find the gain on the 1 January balance, from 1 January to 31 December; then find the gain on extra cash, etc., received by 1 February, from 1 February to 31 December; and so on. Or
2 (more clumsily) find the gain on the 1 January balance, from 1 to 31 January; then find the gain on the 1 February balance, from 1 to 28 February, and, by adding the gain brought forward (adjusted with the February factor) find a cumulative total; and so on.

Table 6.4 applies both methods to the examples.

Notes and References

1 Strictly, a preference dividend is of course not a legal 'cost'. But it is one in the economic sense (since it is the price paid for the use of resources); for our present purpose, loan interest and preference dividends are indistinguishable.

2 One tale of this time is specially poignant. An old couple, whose pension had become valueless, lived by selling off their furniture. Finally they sold their house, for an enormous number of marks. They went to collect this cash a week later. Prices had so risen during the week that the price was just enough to pay their tram-fares back again.

Hungary in 1946 achieved inflation at the annual rate of 1.3×10^{55} per cent. A housewife could join a bread queue when the price was 10 000 pengo per kilo; within half-an-hour, when she reached the counter, the price was up to 50 000. Falush, P. (1976) 'The Hungarian hyper-inflation of 1945–46', *The Westminster Bank Quarterly Review*, August, p. 49.

3 The short-run results can be disturbing. See Bodie, Z. (1976) 'Common stocks as a hedge against inflation', and Nelson, C.R. (1976) 'Inflation and rates of return on common stocks', *Journal of Finance*, May. The reasons are discussed in Moore, B. (1980) 'Equity values and inflation', *Lloyds Bank Review*, July.

4 This reasoning assumes that the accounts mirror the owners' views, i.e. back the 'equity' and not the 'entity' approach. The latter holds that wealth switch from loan to equity is irrelevant to the whole firm. See Kennedy, C. (1978) *Cambridge Economic Policy Review*, no. 4, March.

Table 6.4 Calculation of Gain and Loss on Money

	Index rises from 100 to 120			*Index falls from 100 to 80*		
	Actual £	*Factor*	*Gain in closing-£*	*Actual* £	*Factor*	*Gain in closing-£*
Method a						
Debentures, 1 January	−20 000	−20/100	+4000	−20 000	20/100	−4000
Money received, 1 July	540	−10/110	− 49	260	10/90	+ 29
			3951			−3971
Method b						
1 January–30 June period						
Debentures, 1 January	−20 000	−10/100	+2000	−20 000	10/100	−2000
1 July–31 December period						
Adjustment of £2000 above		10/110	+ 182		−10/90	+ 222
Money received	540			260		
Balance, 1 July	−19 460	−10/110	+1769	−19 740	10/90	−2193
Total gain or loss			+3951			−3971

On the broad problems of realisation, see Horngren, C.T. (1965) 'How should we interpret the realization concept?', *Accounting Review*, April.

5 Rutterford, J. (1983) 'Index-linked gilts', *National Westminster Bank Quarterly Review*, November.

7

The Time-lag Error in Accounting Profit: (A) General Price Change

Chapter 6 accused the accountant of failing to report certain real gains. This chapter accuses him of reporting gains that do not exist.

'Mixed' money figures in the income statement

Subtracting cost of one date from revenue of another date

To understand this accusation, one must think again about 'mixed' sets of figures (Chapter 4). In a time of general price change, a ledger account may contain entries that each deal with £s of different worth. For instance, in a year when prices are rising the transactions of January are expressed in more valuable £s than are those of the following December. Thus unlike units are added and subtracted; the totals and balances become 'mixed' and perhaps meaningless; it is almost as if we subtracted 2 horses from 9 oranges.

The ledger account that is most vulnerable to this error is the profit and loss account. Typically, a firm must obtain and use inputs ahead of sales; and so the cost £s in that account are older than its revenue £s, and the balance (profit) is distorted. This book calls the distortion the 'time-lag error'.

Unfortunately, the error cannot be analysed simply. Theory is here charged with controversy, and its application varies with the type of information needed and asset owned. Not surprisingly, this compexity has created much confusion in discussions on reform: almost anything said about the time-lag can be either sensible or silly according to the context envisaged by the speaker. To avoid muddle, he should specify what context he has in mind.

Possible contexts

He should, in the first place, be clear on the familiar point of whether the price change is general or specific. But a second point then obtrudes. Cost figures can be needed for different purposes. They may be used for income measurement, i.e. in the income statement. Or they may be used as guides to whether a particular job, etc., is worthwhile, i.e. as measures of sacrifice in budgets employed by managers when making decisions (and in any postmortem cost accounts to check these budgets). And perhaps the two figures should not always be the same. So the first step in analysing any pronouncement on the time-lag is to decide into which of the four boxes shown in Figure 7.1 it falls.

	Income statement	Decision budget
General change	(1)	(2)
Specific change	(3)	(4)

Figure 7.1

We start with (1)—i.e. this chapter deals solely with the income statement in a period when general prices change but the relevant specific indices move exactly in step with the general index and so can be ignored. Later chapters will broaden the argument.

Costs and revenues—simultaneous and separated

Costs and revenues can often be looked on as a series of linked pairs—inputs and corresponding sales. When there is no delay between input, sale, and the withdrawal of the resulting profit, the income statement is free from the time-lag error even in a year of big price change. When there is delay, distortion follows.

Simultaneous costs and revenues Suppose, for instance, that a man starts and ends a venture in January (general index 100) and another in July (general index 110), and that his income account for the year can be set out as shown in Table 7.1.

Table 7.1 Income Account With No Time-lag Between Input and Sale

Date	*Index*		*Cost*		*Sale*	*Profit*
			£		£	£
1 January	100	Venture 1	1000	→	1400	400
1 July	110	Venture 2	1100	→	1540	440
			2100?		2940?	840?

Each horizontal line here deals with the same kind of £s; taken separately, the January and July profits are sensible guides to, for instance, the sums available for drawings just after each venture. But the totals of each vertical column are mixed, and thus are of doubtful meaning—as is the total profit of £840.

Time-lag between input and sale However, production is often a lengthy matter, with inputs preceding outputs and sales. Here a time-lag occurs between a cost and the corresponding output's realisation; the debits and credits in the income account no longer form neat horizontal pairs, but are 'slanting', and so are recorded in £s of different dates and value. If the two ventures in the example each need a half-year turnover, the account in Table 7.1 changes into something like Table 7.2. This assumes that the general index goes

Table 7.2 Income Account With Six Months' Time-lag Between Cost and Sale

Date	*Index*		*Cost*	*Sale*	*Profit*
			£	£	£
1 January	100	Venture 1	1000 ↘		
30 June	110	Venture 1		1540	540?
1 July	110	Venture 2	1100 ↘		
31 December	120	Venture 2		1680	580?
			2100?	3220?	1120??

up during each venture by 10 points, and that the sale prices also rise with the index. Thanks to the time-lags, the profits on each venture—let alone their total—are now suspect.

Typically an income account contains some costs that synchronise with revenues, so forming horizontal pairs and doing little harm, and some slanting pairs. Then one may say that the cost column does not on average synchronise with the revenue column. When the average time-lag between the two columns is big, the figure for profit is stretched in an odd fashion.

The balance sheet approach to profit measurement

Capital maintenance as the base line for income measurement

Earlier chapters have tended to define income more as growth in wealth than as a gap between revenues and costs. They have, in other words, treated capital maintenance as the base line for calculating income; the measurer's task is to see whether or not the initial capital has been maintained exactly. The same approach will serve to clarify reasoning on the time-lag. Moreover, arithmetical illustrations to such problems are often more helpful if the figures are put in successive balance sheets rather than a profit and loss account. Assets are mostly familiar and easy to envisage; costs and revenues are less clear—being mere measures of asset changes. So, probably, we see more of the truth when we compare the net assets at two dates than when we try to visualise the streams of arrivals and departures.[1]

Balance sheet illustration, with historical values

To illustrate the balance-sheet approach, let us apply it to the first (January to June) venture in Table 7.2. The starting data and price changes are here much the same as those used in Table 4.1 (p. 43); we can treat this venture as an important extension to the range of sample firms (A, B, and C) shown there, and call it D.

We can trace firm D through all its stages by putting a series of balance sheets in successive columns. The approach of ordinary accounting needs columns for only three stages:

1 Date of *opening figures*—morning, 1 January (index 100).
2 Date when *stock bought*—afternoon, 1 January (index 100).
3 Date when *stock sold*—30 June (index 110).

Bearing in mind that profit ran at £400 per venture before the inflation began (see p. 43), we see that the owner of firm D has cause to feel delighted by the increase to £540. This promotes him to the level of C, the firm that is so successful because of its gearing; whereas he may well have thought that his business is in its nature more like firm A, whose profit merely keeps pace with inflation. He has often heard that a slow turnover is rather a bad thing; but, merely by having a slower turnover than firm A, he has far outpaced it in the race for profit.

Is there something spurious in this upward leap in the profit of firm D? The answer depends on our old problem of how to compare amounts of wealth at different dates. If we are content with pound notes as the unit, the increase is genuine: firm 4 began with 1000 bits of paper, and now has 1540 bits of paper; there is nothing wrong with our sum by the money sub-concept.

Table 7.3 Comparative Balance Sheets, Using Historical Values Only

Date	(1) *Opening figures* £	(2) *Stock bought* £	(3) *Stock sold* £
Cash	1000		1540
Stock		1000	
Initial capital:			
Historical figure	1000	1000	1000
Trade profit			540
			1540

Consequences of using historical values

However, doubts about the usefulness of this paper measure begin to arise if the owner treats his accounts as a meaningful guide to action.

We may reasonably suppose that his main problem is what to do next with his £1540—in particular, how much of it he needs to reinvest in the firm if his capital is not to be impaired, and how much is surplus. He now faces issues discussed in Chapter 3, i.e. the nature of capital and income, and the wisdom of choosing the measures that give the most useful information. Here a good measure of income may be especially helpful in shaping his views on, e.g. how much to withdraw for consumption, and whether he has used the assets efficiently.

The historical measures suggest that he must put back £1000 as capital, and that his income is now running at £540 per venture. This is misleading on two different scores. First, it suggests that the rate of return has gone up from 40 per cent to 54 per cent per venture. But on the assumption that the firm's methods, etc., are unchanged, the profit rates depend solely on the behaviour of money; for instance, if the index now levelled off at 110, the rate would tend to revert to 40 per cent. Fifty-four per cent is thus a poor guide to the rate of future earnings. Secondly, and much more important, the future yield by a capital of only £1000 is likely to seem inadequate to the owner, notably because it will fail to maintain his real standard of life. We are assuming, it must be remembered, that the index measures the prices of consumers' goods (as well as business assets); henceforth, the profits on £1000 will tend to buy fewer of those goods, and so the owner will feel poorer than he did before the inflation.

This can be seen easily if we look into the next stage in the firm's story. The balance sheet of 30 June tempts the owner to withdraw £540; and, even if he himself has qualms about the wisdom of so doing, his tax collector will have none. Let us suppose that he does take out £540 for consumption and tax, and so leaves his money capital once again at exactly £1000. Then 1 July finds him about to undertake the next venture. But when he comes to buy more inputs—for a similar or any new type of venture—he realises to his dismay that their prices have gone up by 10 per cent. His £1000 will now finance only about 10/11 of his former trade, measured in real terms. He cannot automatically buy the whole July input envisaged in Table 7.2. He faces a painful choice between:

1 Working henceforth at only 10/11 of his former scale of real investment—earning perhaps the same money profit as before the inflation, but unable to buy as much with it as hitherto, i.e. with a reduced real capital by the consumption test. Indeed, even his

money income will perhaps fall, since shortage of real capital may for example deprive him of quantity discounts, or force him to work with assets that are no longer in such good proportions to one another;[2] or

2 Paying in, or borrowing, an extra £100. Then the firm can go on at the same real level; but the owner must pay interest, and the net level falls. His consumption is reduced as in (1).

In short, the owner's increase in drawings from £400 to £540 means that he takes out real capital. Other things being unchanged, he must sooner or later see a consequent fall in his real income; to think otherwise is to regard the firm as a cornucopia. By the test of real consumption and investment, his accounts are untrustworthy guides.

Balance sheet illustration, with current values

The next step is to adapt the balance sheets to make them illustrate the 'real-capital maintenance' sub-concept. We must add a column to those in Table 7.3 to restate historical figures in current terms of the moment just before the sale. As the index has risen to 110 at this time, initial capital is now reset at £1100, and so also is the stock's cost.

By restating capital and stock in current £s, we reduce trade profit to £440. This is the same real amount as the pre-inflation £400. The owner can withdraw it, and still maintain capital at a level (£1100) that preserves his living standards.

The columnar analysis confirms our explanation of why and how distortion creeps into conventional balance sheets—wherein assets valued after the sale in new £s are placed alongside a capital still valued in old £s. If we attach weight to what money can buy, rather than to money *per se* (i.e. if we prefer the real-wealth sub-concept to the money sub-concept), then we should update initial capital as in column (3) in Table 7.4. The £100 nominal increase in initial capital may be called a capital reserve[3] or, better, an inflation allowance. Column (5) supports this interpretation by showing the figures of (4) in stabilised £s.

Table 7.4 Comparative Balance Sheet, Using Current Values

Date	(1)	(2)	(3)	(4)	(5)
	Opening figures	*Stock bought*	*Just before sale*	*After sale*	*After sale, stabilised at 110*
	£	£	£	£	£
Cash	1000			1540	*1540*
Stock (current value)		1000	1100		
Initial capital					
Historical figure	1000	1000	1000	1000	
Allowance for inflation			100	100	
Initial capital in current £s			1100	1100	*1100*
Trade profit				440	*440*
	1000	1000	1100	1540	*1540*

Cost, revenue, and the time-lag

Distortion of the profit and loss account

It is easy to repeat the time-lag argument in terms of cost and revenue, explaining how distortion arises when the price level changes between the dates of input and sale. It is also easy to explain the mechanics for correcting the profit and loss account. But the logic perhaps becomes less obvious than in the balance-sheet approach, and must in the end fall back on capital maintenance.

The profit and loss account corresponding to the conventional balance sheet of firm D, at the stage of column (3) in Table 7.3, is set out below. To show what is really happening, a stabilised version is also given. Remember that to obtain the stabilised counterparts, different factors must be applied to transactions of different dates. The stabilised accounts show that real wealth is flowing in merely at the old rate, as in firm A (p. 43). The ordinary accounts, when compared with those of pre-inflation years, suggest instead that

Table 7.5 Profit and Loss Account with Time-lag Error

		Index	(1) *Ordinary accounts* £	Factor	(2) *Stabilised accounts* £ *of 30 June*
1 January	Cost	100	1000	110/100	*1100*
30 June	Sale	110	1540	110/110	*1540*
	Profit		540		*440*

trade has been exceptionally good—that cost and profit are just like those of the fortunate firm C.

Thus ordinary accounts give a rosy picture during inflation. They are likely to make the owner more cheerful than the facts warrant. So they may not only induce him to raise his real consumption, but also (as investment now seems to yield such easy winnings) to expand his business. If many other owners are also misled by their accounts, their combined actions may have social effects of some magnitude.

'Correction' of the cost error in the ordinary profit and loss account

The time-lag error, as we have seen, arises when an account sets off cost of one price level against revenue of another. Table 7.5, for instance, subtracts January £s from June £s. It would be less apt to mislead if it subtracted like £s. The simplest way to make the £s uniform is to restate the costs at the June level, by inserting an 'inflation charge' among the ordinary figures to raise historical cost. (Note that we are here considering only something in the nature of first-aid to the ordinary profit and loss account. This restricted reform must be distinguished from full stabilisation, which not only aligns cost and revenue £s, but also ensures that all the figures in both the profit and loss account and the balance sheet are expressed in some common unit.)

The size of the error equals the appreciation on historical cost between cost date and sale date. A convenient way to express it is as follows. Let C stand for the historical cost shown in the ordinary accounts, *c* for the general index at cost date, and *s* for that index at sale date. Then the error is

$$C\left(\frac{s}{c} - 1\right)$$

To correct the figures in Table 7.5, raise the cost by £1000 [(110/100) − 1], i.e. £100.

The correction can easily be put into the ordinary profit and loss account, e.g. in this way:

Table 7.6 Profit and Loss Account with Time-lag Error Corrected

	£
Cost:	
Historical	1000
Inflation charge to raise historical cost to current price level	100
Total current cost	1100
Sale	1540
Corrected profit	440

The inflation charge is, of course, the other end of the double entry that leads to the credit of £1000 in Table 7.4, column 3.[4] Because 'inflation charges' (or 'cost of sales adjustments') are novel, it seems desirable that their presence in an account, and their size and method of calculation, should be made abundantly clear.

Nature and limitations of a 'corrected' income account

The 'corrected' ordinary account is, in this simple example, the same thing as an account stabilised at 30 June, as can be seen by comparing Table 7.6 with column (2) of Table 7.5.

So this form of correction appears here to do just what is needed to put right the cost and profit figures, within the ordinary framework and with far less labour than is demanded by the worksheets of full stabilisation. And, indeed, it is an easy and effective trick for improving ordinary accounts (even where they are less simple than here), and has the great merit of calling for the bare minimum of change in familiar methods and figures. It has some resemblance to the system introduced in 1964 by Brazil—which was workable enough to be adopted at once by almost every firm.

But correction cannot claim to be more than a rough-and-ready cure. It suffers from several faults. For instance, an income statement that is corrected at some date *during* the year (average sale date) does not fit in with the balance sheet of the *end* of the year (ordinary or stabilised), and may not be a good basis for a dividend decision at a still later date. So the correction should be regarded as valuable first-aid rather than a complete solution.

Table 7.7 recapitulates these points by comparing the rival forms of profit and loss account that are now at our disposal:

1 *Ordinary accounts*. These make no attempt to correct the raw figures.
2 *Ordinary accounts with time-lag correction*. These try to stick as closely as possible to the form and figures of ordinary accounts, and yet to improve profit with a short-cut correction—the insertion of an inflation charge.
3 *Stabilised accounts*. These adjust the crude costs and revenues with the help of a general index factor and so produce almost completely new sets of figures, all in homogeneous £s (of some chosen base date) and thus automatically free of the errors due to the time-lag and mixing.

The figures in Table 7.7 are set in accounts for the year to 31 December. The index is assumed to reach 120 at that date. Thus, the figures of column (3), being stabilised in end-£s, must differ from those of earlier months in columns (1) and (2). They must also show (if the profit has been retained in the form of cash) a loss on holding money from July to December.

Chief cost items subject to the time-lag

In practice, the error is likely to be material for three kinds of cost:

1 *Cost for capital gain calculations*. When fixed assets, investments, etc., are sold, their historical cost may have been carried forward for many years. If the gain is to be seen at its real size, the cost must be updated with an inflation charge.

Table 7.7 Comparison of Ordinary, Corrected, and Stabilised Income Accounts

	(1) *Ordinary* £		(2) *Corrected* £	*Factor*	(3) *Stabilised* *end-£*
Income statement					
Cost (index 100)	1000		1000	120/100	*1200*
Inflation charge		1000 × (10/100)	100		
			1100		
Sale (index 110)	1540		1540	120/110	*1680*
Trading profit	540		440	120/110	*480*
Balance sheet					
Cash	1540		1540		*1540*
Capital	1000		1000	120/100	*1200*
Inflation allowance			100		
Loss on holding money				1540×(–10/110)	*–140*
Trading profit	540		440	120/110	*480*
	1540		1540		*1540*

2 *Stocks*. There may be a time-lag of at least some months between the purchase of stocks and their sale, engendering 'inventory profit'. (Stocks are so important that the whole of Chapter 9 is devoted to them.)
3 *Depreciation*. The life of a depreciating asset is normally long enough for the index to change greatly. So a considerable error is apt to arise when the later slices of historical cost are written off. (Chapter 10 deals with depreciation.)

As the error raises taxable income during inflation, one may regard it as imposing an extra tax, never authorised by Parliament, on the owners of stocks and depreciating assets.

Other items subject to the time-lag

Any marked carrying-forward of historical figures can lead to the use of outdated values. Cost is the main but not the only victim. 'Revenue received in advance' is also carried forward in the ledger, and not put into the profit and loss account until the date at which the revenue is deemed to be earned. This may lead to a different form of time-lag error: when the historical revenue is credited in the profit and loss account, old revenue £s are offset against new cost £s, and so (if prices are rising) profit is understated. Thus magazine publishers (so far as they receive subscriptions in advance) and correspondence schools may habitually understate their profits.

Charges for tax, dividends, etc., may relate to dates many months away from average revenue date. For instance, the income statement may contain a closing adjustment for a final dividend to be paid some months after the end of the year. Here is another example of the subtraction of unlike £s. During inflation, such belated charges are in fact less expensive than the ordinary figures suggest. In cold logic, the charges should be reduced by 'inflation credits'.

Date of historical cost

The historical cost date (with index *c* in the formula on p. 88) is normally the date at which the firm invests in the input, and as at which the books record its acquisition. The date of *c* does not depend on whether the input is bought for cash or on credit: both forms of transaction at once change part of the firm's wealth from net money assets to non-money assets—which is what matters here. (But credit, loans, etc., give rise to an interesting point that will be discussed on p. 95.)

Consider for instance the accounts of a tenant who pays a rent of 1200 a year. If this whole sum is paid at the start of a year of inflation, the cost £s do not in value match the revenue £s of later months; to make them match, they must be corrected with an inflation charge (*c* being here the index at the start of year). If instead £100 is due monthly, probably each instalment will almost coincide in time with the month's revenue, and little or no cost correction is needed. This accords with common sense: inflation gives the former arrangement a higher real cost than the second.

Visible and concealed time-lag errors

Where inputs are bought in one business year for the benefit of another, they will show up as assets in intervening balance sheets, and the scope for time-lag error will be fairly obvious. But some inputs are bought for use within the same year, and then the annual accounts can give no hint of the error. To correct costs, therefore, one must look at both (a) inputs carried forward at a year-end, and (b) inputs acquired and consumed within the accounting year.

1 *Inputs carried forward at a year-end*. Typically, a balance sheet may show machinery, stocks, rent paid in advance, and so forth. Such assets point to the likelihood of time-lag error (though they give little indication of its size).
2 *Inputs acquired and consumed within the same accounting year*. This source of error is most likely to be important where firms have peaks of activity within each year, for seasonal or other reasons. For instance, a maker of skis may buy heavily in the spring in order to meet the winter rush; and the maker of fireworks may incur costs throughout the year to build up stocks for sale near Guy Fawkes' Night or Fourth of July. If, as is not unusual, the accounting year ends after the peak (when stocks are at their lowest), the stock figure in the year-end accounts can give no hint of the time-lags. Nevertheless, these lead to 'inventory profit' just

as surely as if the stocks were recorded in inventory sheets at the year-end.

This type of distortion must usually be small compared with that under (1).

Sluggish sale prices

In most of the earlier examples, sale price has been made to respond freely and promptly to inflation. These buoyant figures seem not unrealistic; they are also a good means of stressing the upsurge in general prices between buying and selling dates. But they may leave some impression that increased sale prices are what cause the overstatement of profit. Such is not the case. The error comes from mixing £s of different worth: sale price is irrelevant.

So the error still occurs if sale prices are kept low, e.g. by the firm's own policy (notably selling at cost-plus), or by government controls. Then the profits in ordinary accounts are smaller than those envisaged in our examples; and real profits (after correction with an inflation charge) are smaller still, or perhaps negative.

The time-lag and partnership rights[5]

Chapter 6 explained how the money-effect can transfer wealth between the various groups who finance a company (e.g. from loanholders to ordinary shareholders). In a partnership, a corresponding transfer can take place if the firm obtains fixed money loans (from outsiders or some of its own partners). But the time-lag can induce a second and subtler transfer, in the following way.

The time-lag error makes a hidden switch of capital to profit. This might not matter much if all the false profit could be retained and returned to capital, in the proportions needed to restore each partner's balance to its original real size. Such a cycle may exist where the partners share profits in the ratio of their capitals; but not where they share profits in another ratio. If partner X's fraction of the total capital exceeds his fraction of annual profit, the error diverts some of his real capital to his partner. If Y's fraction of profit exceeds his fraction of capital, then he gets some of his partner's real capital. We may guess that, where the capital fraction differs much from the profit-sharing fraction, X is likely to be the senior partner and Y the junior. If this is true, there must in recent years have been some levelling as between junior and senior partners—none the less real because neither side planned or detected it. Inflation here plays Robin Hood.

Example As usual, one should use a rather extreme example to stress the facts. Suppose X and Y become partners in a venture that needs £100 000 of capital. X provides £80 000, and Y only £20 000; but X works only part-time, and Y full-time. They agree that these contributions of capital and work will be fairly compensated if all profits are split fifty-fifty. At its end, the venture brings in £150 000, so its uncorrected profit is £50 000; but, as the index rises from 100 to 150 during the period, the time-lag error (50 per cent on the capital of £100 000) is also £50 000, and corrected profit is *nil*.

	Ordinary £		*Corrected* £
Cash, etc.	150 000		150 000
Partner's capitals			
X. Opening	80 000		80 000
Inflation allowance		50/100	40 000
Profit	25 000		—
	105 000		120 000
Y. Opening	20 000		20 000
Inflation allowance		50/100	10 000
Profit	25 000		—
	45 000		30 000
	150 000		150 000

Ordinary accounting here gives Y a handsome present, as one can see by comparing an ordinary balance sheet with the one that would have resulted if the time-lag error had been corrected.

If (as is true of most professional firms) the partnership holds a substantial amount of work-in-progress, the time-lag error may well be fairly high, and it may also be big where a capital gain arises. Any surplus when the partners' rights are restated at a retirement or admission is probably such a gain.

The time-lag and borrowed capital

Let us now go back to firm D (see p. 82). Thoughtful readers may have detected an unconvincing point in the treatment of its figures. Surely there is one circumstance, they may object, in which the owner of firm D *does* make a genuine profit of £540, not £440. What if he has borrowed the original £1000—does he not then end up £540 to the good after repaying his debt?

The answer is that he does. But now we have returned to the discussion of p. 67—the money-effect. His gain does not all come from trading; £100 of it comes because he was in debt.

Here the time-lag is superimposed on gearing. Stabilised accounts would throw up two different facts, both obscure in ordinary accounts: (a) the ordinary profit is swollen by £100 of synthetic gain, which must be omitted in real calculations, reducing trade profit to £440; but (b) the firm's owner has made a gain of £100 from the scaling down (in real terms) of his debt. The ordinary closing balance sheet and its stabilised counterpart run as in Table 7.8.

Table 7.8 Balance Sheets Affected by Both Time-lag and Money Gains

	(1) *Ordinary balance sheet* £	(2) *(1) stabilised at 110* £
Cash	1540	*1540*
Less Loan	1000	*1000*
	540	*540*
Trade profit (after interest, etc.)	540	*440*
Gain on owing		*100*
		540

Interplay of time-lag and money-effect in practice

Both the time-lag and the money-effect are sure to be present in most real firms. Even if there are no formal loans, the usual flow of credit purchases and sales will create money liabilities and assets, and so give rise to a money-effect.

Time-lag and money-effect may well be interlinked on purpose. An alert firm will try to manipulate its current position so as to make the best of the market from the viewpoints alike of trade and finance. Thus, if the firm foresees higher prices, it may tighten up its credit terms to customers, and so lessen the vulnerable period on its debts. It may also buy supplies farther ahead. If it gets longer credit for such extra purchases, its suppliers suffer; if it borrows from the bank, its bank suffers; if it invests idle cash, it avoids losses on holding money. For instance, firm D in our example may well buy the repeat dose of input before 30 June, the sale date; it then seems to benefit by buying while prices are still low, but in real terms the benefit comes from the gain on owing, etc. (As was stressed on p. 63, however, a policy of heavy borrowing does not always end in success. Prices may start tumbling just after the purchase, and then the real gain is transmuted into real loss—as in the example on p. 77; and when further loans are wanted in a time of dire need, they may prove unobtainable. In an uncertain world, borrowing is far from being the rather one-sided and unsporting manoeuvre that Table 7.8 suggests.)

When the purchase and sales are those of a busy firm, one must treat them not as discrete incidents but as streams of transactions. Plainly, the time-lag errors and money-effects will here multiply and intertwine in a way that is hard to follow. But no matter how complex their interrelations, a clear-headed observer will try to keep them apart in his thinking, and to form at least an approximate idea of their separate sizes.

Falling prices

Nowadays it comes naturally to describe the time-lag in terms of rising prices. But the argument holds equally well when prices are falling.

Example Table 7.7 can be adapted to deflation. Suppose again that profit has been £400 per venture while the index was stable. This year's venture begins at index 100, but the index falls to 90 at sale date and 80 at the year-end. For realism, the sale proceeds should be reduced, say by 10 per cent to £1260. Then the ordinary accounts run

Table 7.9 Ordinary, Corrected, and Stabilised Accounts with Falling Prices

	(1) *Ordinary* £	Factor	(2) *Income Corrected* £	*Factor*	(3) *Stabilised* *end-£*
Income statement					
Cost (index 100)	1000		1000	80/100	*800*
Less Deflation credit		1000 × (10/100)	100		
			900		
Sale (index 90)	1260		1260	80/90	*1120*
Trading profit	260		360		*320*
Balance sheet					
Cash	1260		1260		*1260*
Capital	1000		1000	80/100	*800*
Less Deflation adjustment			100		
			900		
Gain on holding money				1260 × (10/90)	*140*
Trading profit	260		360		*320*
	1260		1260		*1260*

as in column (1) of Table 7.9; ordinary profit (£400 in stable times) falls steeply to only £260.

Capital maintenance in deflation

If the owner treats the accounts of column (1) as a guide, he will now leave at least £1000 in the firm (i.e. he will increase his real stake in it) by restricting his withdrawals to a £260 ceiling. A fall of this size may bring much suffering to him and his family. The low profits will also make him wary about further investment in productive assets, so that his extra cash will tend to lie idle. As other owners will likewise at such a time be prompted by their accounts to spend less on consumption and investment, real demand by the whole community may fall, making the slump worse than it would have been in the absence of accounts.

Yet, judged by the test of a constant living standard, the owner does not now need to leave a capital of £1000 in the business; £900 in June, and only £800 in December, should thereafter (thanks to lower prices in the shops) yield a big enough flow of cash drawings to maintain his old standard. More helpful accounts for June would write down initial capital by £100 as in column (2), and thus raise surplus from £260 to £360, the correct profit by the real-wealth sub-concept. A profit of £360 is the exact equivalent, at June prices, of the £400 that was the profit for the same real activity when the index stood at 100.

Profit correction

The first-aid correction of the accounts is again simple. In column (1), the cost £s of January are too big relative to the sale £s of June. So total cost must be reduced to allow for the rise in the value of the £ during the turnover period. The error is £1000[(90/100) − 1] = −£100. In column (2), £100 is deducted from cost in the income statement, and also from capital in the balance sheet.

Where space permits, this deduction in the income statement might be explained as:

Less Reduction to allow for fall in general prices during the turnover period £100

But a short name is convenient: 'deflation credit' will perhaps serve. The corresponding deduction in the balance sheet should be made from a suitable figure in the owner's equity (e.g. reserves, but ideally from an inflation allowance created on the upswing of the price cycle); presumably company law would frown on any change in the capital figure itself, though in fact the original £1000 is now equivalent to a lesser number of current £s.

Correction and caution

At first blush, the raising of profit in column (2) may be disturbing. It seems at odds with the normally cautious tenets of accounting. So this side of reform may be much harder to swallow than its counterpart for inflation. One must concede, for instance, that it would tend (if tax were based on the reformed figure) to put up a firm's tax at an awkward moment. Again, many directors will yearn for a strong liquid position when bad times threaten, and will regard low profit figures as a welcome pretext for cutting dividends.

The analogy of the 'dividend equalisation reserve' may be helpful here. Some companies subject to profit fluctuations used to transfer profits in good years to such a reserve, and then retransfer enough to cover the dividends of poor years. The most prudent of directors should not object—if the productive assets have been kept in good heart and there is enough cash for all likely calls—to drafts on such a reserve in bad times. An inflation allowance may be thought of in the same light. But in fact the case for the higher profit figures rests on still stronger ground: they measure real growth better than uncorrected ones. Moreover, as was pointed out on p. 98, if low figures appear also in the annual reports of most other companies, they may aggravate depression and become self-defeating.

Stabilised accounts and deflation

The reasoning of column (2) in Table 7.9 is confirmed by stabilised figures. If these are based on the £ of June, stabilised profit is £360. In column (3), they are based instead on the £ of December (to conform with the usual custom of covering a whole year in accounts); the equivalent profit, because of the rise in money's worth, is then £320.

Capital is likewise restated at only £800.

If the sale proceeds are kept as money assets from July to December, they appreciate in purchasing power. Accordingly column (3) shows a £140 gain on holding money.

Appendix: Arithmetical troubles of correction and stabilisation

The simplicity of the examples in this chapter leads to tidy and precise results (e.g. the equality of the stabilised and corrected profits set out on pp. 87 and 88). But in real life, alas, the figures are seldom so amenable. The number of costs and revenues in a year will be great. These costs and revenues are apt to form unwieldy patterns (some spread evenly over the year, some bunched, and some carried forward from or to other years), and do not always centre on mid-year. The price level continues to change after the central date has passed. Further, inputs do not always link up surely with individual sales. Even if they do, many firms lack the detailed cost records that trace the flow of costs from input to sale. Thus, it is often hard, if not impossible, to correct profit or to stabilise exactly, and some rough-and-ready arithmetic may be inevitable.

Example Profit correction and stabilisation: In Table 7.10, the figures are less simple and regular than those of earlier examples. The second half-year's venture is much bigger than the first, so that the 'centre of gravity' is near to December. The index goes up at an accelerating pace, from 220 at the first input to 280 at the last sale and 285 at the year-end. Therefore, as correction of the time-lag error must be linked with the 'average sales date', the corrected accounts are *not* the same thing as accounts stabilised at mid-year, and also differ considerably from those stabilised at the year-end.

Because inflation has been so brisk during the year, both correction and stabilisation take a big bite out of accounting profit. The inflation charge is the difference between the totals of columns (4) and (1), £41. It cuts down the ordinary profit of £120, column (3), to a corrected profit of £79, column (5). Stabilised profit in the end-£ is £86, column (8).

Table 7.10 Less Simple Income Account—Ordinary, Corrected, and Stabilised Figures

Date	*General index*		(1)	(2)	(3)	(4)	(5)	(6)	(7)	(8)
			Ordinary accounts			*Accounts with cost correction*		*Stabilised accounts*		
			Cost	*Sale*	*Profit*	*Cost raised to current index*	*Corrected profit (2)–(4)*	*Cost*	*Sale*	*Profit*
			£	£	£	£	£	*£ stabilised at 31 December (index 285)*		
14 February	220	Input	110							
15 April	230	Sale		140	30	115	25	*142.5*	*173.5*	*31*
15 September	250	Input	300							
15 December	280	Sale		390	90	336	54	*342*	*397*	*55*
			410	530	120	451	79	*484.5*	*570.5*	*86*

References

1 This is at odds with the view, nowadays popular with many leading accountants, that the income statement is significant, whereas the balance sheet is merely a cold-store for unripe costs and revenues (see Yamey, B.S. (1962) 'Some topics in the history of financial accounting in England, 1500–1900' in W.T. Baxter and S. Davidson, (eds) *Studies in Accounting Theory*, 2nd edn, Sweet & Maxwell, Irwin, p. 38). In fact, the two accounts depend on one another, and thus to belittle the values in the balance sheet is also to belittle the values in the profit and loss account.

2 These points are developed by Professor F.W. Paish (1953) *Business Finance*, Pitman, p. 66.

3 'Capital reserve' may suggest an addition to capital in its narrow, legal sense. This is only part of the truth. Here 'initial capital' is the whole of the owner's investment at the start of this accounting period, and may consist of accumulated profit as well as legal capital (in a partnership, current accounts as well as capital accounts). Both of these become understated in ordinary accounts during inflation. Part of the inflation allowance is thus a corrective to accumulated profit, and can scarcely be dealt with as a capital reserve.

4 If the correction is made by a closing adjustment, the journal entry might be:

		£	£
Cost of goods sold, etc.	dr	100	
Inflation allowance	cr		100
Adjustment of historical cost to current level with factor 110/100			

That is, an extra cost is charged, and an addition to capital is created. The wording of the journal entry avoids infringement of the useful book-keeping rule that links the word 'costs' with balance sheet 'provisions', and 'appropriations' with 'reserves'.

5 See my 'Inflation and partnership rights', *The Accountant's Magazine*. February 1962.

8

The Time-lag Error in Accounting Profit: (B) Specific Price Change

Chapter 7 tried to show how general price change creates a time-lag error in the income statement. Its subject was thus box (1) in Figure 7.1 on p. 80. This chapter deals with specific change; its subject is box (3).

The issues at stake here are just one part of the larger problem—whether the updating of historical cost is best done by applying a general index or by using the specific values of current cost accounting (CCA). Views on this point are divided and likely to become more so. The argument concerns the three familiar areas—the measurement of, (a) asset values, (b) costs for decisions, and (c) income, and thus the time-lag problem.

Measurement of assets, costs, and income

Asset values If asset values are to be stated in current terms, the CCA case is completely convincing. The alternative of updating historical cost with the general index is arithmetically easy; but the resulting values cannot command much respect.

Costs for management decision The costs needed for internal decision budgets (the right-hand column of the table on p. 80) should show the sacrifice from devoting assets to the plan under consideration. Deprival value is designed for this purpose; usually it is replacement cost, and then reflects specific prices. So here too the CCA case is normally overwhelming.

Income and the time-lag error When the argument shifts to income, the case becomes less obvious. The reformer who pleads for correction with the general index now has strong arguments. For our convenience, he will perhaps let himself be called the 'general-index man'; his opponent then becomes the 'specific-index man'.[1]

This chapter concentrates on income and the time-lag error when specific price change differs from general price change.

Capital maintenance objectives and income

We must now hark back to the question discussed on pp. 20–3 i.e. what is the best method, when prices change, of comparing wealth *at different dates* in order to measure its growth.

To a considerable extent, as we have seen, what is here right and wrong depends on the *objectives* of the men concerned: the objective defines cost. The specific-index man assumes a main objective in measurement to be the maintenance by the firm of an effective team of assets. The general-index man assumes it to be maintenance of the owners' welfare—this being defined in terms of power to buy general goods.

The accountant has no right to question the wisdom of other men's objectives. But, as the men who use his statements fall into different groups, he must ask who are his real masters, and what information this group needs to achieve its aim.

Wealth comparison over time

The specific-index man does not explain his case fully if he merely pleads the merits of any given type of current value. Suppose you have a house in France and another in Germany, and you want to compare their values. Using your favourite current value, such as sale price, you find the French house to be worth x francs and the German house y marks. You cannot complete the comparison without an exchange rate.

You face a rather similar problem, if the £'s value changes, when you try to compare your British home's current values at different dates. Your balance sheet compares opening wealth (your capital, etc., at the start of the year) with assets at end. Thus a semi-reformed balance sheet for date 2 might compare the date 1 current value of your house (opening capital) with its date 2 current value (end asset). In times of price rise, this comparison would probably show a holding gain. A fully reformed balance sheet must also 'translate' the opening capital into closing £s, thus comparing like with like—and reducing the gain.

If you use the general index to 'translate' capital, the figure for gain measures your real gain—a useful bit of information.

If you use instead the specific index for houses, corrected capital rises exactly in step with the asset. Gain is zero. In other words, so long as your home has the same physical size the balance sheet cannot measure appreciation. Specific index correction in business accounts shows gain only from 'operation' as distinct from 'holding' (see page 31). This limitation alone would seem greatly to lessen its usefulness to most owners. (Note the complexities of trying to raise capital with several specific indices, where there are several assets.)

A reformed income statement also tries to make £s of date 1 comparable with £s of date 2. Here date 1 is that at which an input is acquired, and date 2 is that at which the corresponding output is sold. Our task is to find how best to 'translate' the date 1 value of the owner's investment into date 2 £s, so that he can compare cost and sale in like terms, and be sure that the profit is genuine growth after the bit of capital invested in the input has been maintained. For the 'translation', the specific-index man relies on the sub-concept of physical capital maintenance; as we shall see, this raises issues that are difficult, and indeed far transcend accounting.

The problem can be seen most clearly if one starts by considering specific change when general prices are stable, i.e. when the change in an asset's price, during an otherwise stable period, has no perceptible effect on the owner's index of general prices—say, because sales of the asset are too small a part of the market's total transactions. So, until it reaches its final pages, this chapter will assume an unchanging general index.

Specific price alters while general index remains stable

Maintaining the owner's capital or physical assets?

The argument of Chapter 7 stressed the aim of capital maintenance, and defined the latter in terms of the owner's investment. The time-lag error then emerged as an unfortunate trick of reckoning that leads to the sapping of his wealth, measured in terms of his ability to buy another bundle of goods (perhaps for private consumption) like the old bundle in desirability, but not necessarily in physical quantity or shape. There was little need to talk of the replacement of particular assets.

In some ways, it would have seemed easier and more persuasive to frame that argument in terms of physical asset replacement. The firm whose accounts are given on p. 86 could be described as buying 1000 kg of a stated type of stock on 1 January, at £1 per kilogram. It sells this stock on 30 June at £1.54; it then pays out £540 as drawings and tax, and retains £1000 to buy a repeat dose of the same goods. But they now cost £1.1 per kilogram, so the firm can replace only 909 kg. Historical cost has failed to maintain the assets at their initial level. QED

In fact, the argument on p. 84 tried to show instead that, with general price change, the historical cost approach fails because it makes the firm less able to maintain the real value of the owner's investment, regardless of physical form. Its stress was on the assets' power to maintain the owner's standard of life, and not on their shape and number.

Numerical example

The problem can be illustrated by again using the earlier figures (see pp. 88–97). These dealt with a capital of £1000, invested in a single input. The new assumption is that the general index stays at 100, but the specific index rises to 110. The physical nature of the inputs now impinges on the argument; they can for instance be envisaged as 1000 kg of stock, bought at a wholesale price of £1 and sold at retail (for £1540) when that price has risen to £1.1.

Balance sheet approach The balance sheets in Table 7.4 can be repeated here without changing the assets. But the wording of the equity section needs revision. Table 8.1 tries to give an analysis acceptable to the specific-index man. He equates capital with 1000 kg; these now cost £1100; so an extra £100 must in effect be added to capital, e.g. as a 'current cost reserve'. In other words, the real holding gain of £100 must be excluded from profit, which is thus reduced to the 'operating profit' of only £440.

To show holding gain in the absence of inflation, opponents of the specific-index man could redraft the equity figures thus:

Date	(1) £	(2) £	(3) £	(4) £
Initial capital	1000	1000	1000	1000
Gains:				
Stock appreciation			100	100
Operating profit				440
Total (accounting profit)			100	540
	1000	1000	1000	1540

So, by this re-analysis, total profit is £540—and conventional accounting is right (provided always that the general index does not change).

Table 8.1 Comparative Balance Sheets, Showing Special Appreciation in Time of General Price Stability

Date	(1) *Opening figures* £	(2) *Stock bought* £	(3) *After price change* £	(4) *After sale* £
Cash	1000			1540
Stock (current cost)		1000	1100	
Capital—defined as the cost of 1000 kg of input:				
Initial cost	1000	1000	1000	1000
Increase in cost (current cost reserve)			100	100
			1100	1100
Trade profit				440
	1000	1000	1100	1540

Profit and loss approach CCA charges input at replacement cost, as in column (2) of Table 8.2. Profit is reduced to £440.

The specific-index man argues that, as the input has appreciated by £100, the current sacrifice from using it up is the replacement cost of £1100. This is true: and the £1100 is a useful statistic. But then should not column (2) tell the full story of the period that it purports to cover—by showing *both* the £100 gain and the £100 cost? Can you logically record the exit of wealth whose entry you have ignored? Column (3) shows both current cost and holding gain, and so ends with a profit of £540.

Sometimes those who use CCA do not show the nature of their costs so frankly as column (2). They reach much the same results covertly, e.g. by using Lifo, or by writing up plant and then charging correspondingly more depreciation.

By the real wealth test, profit is £540, as in columns (1) and (3). If the owner decides to plough back £100 of his profit to finance extra investment in stock, his decision may be wise but does not change the year's profit; the £100, if shown in the income statement, should be put 'below the line' as an appropriation.

Table 8.2 Profit and Loss Account with Cost Corrected by Specific Index

	(1) *Ordinary accounting*	(2) *Replacement cost*	(3) *Replacement cost and holding gain*
Cost			
Historical	1000	1000	
Provision for increased replacement cost		100	
Replacement cost		1100	1100
Revenue			
Sale	1540	1540	1540
Holding gain			100
			1640
Profit	540	440	540

The specific-index case put badly

Perhaps the most revealing way to canvass the pros and cons of the specific-index case is to set this out in its weakest light, and then to see how its advocates would make it more persuasive.

At its crudest, then, the case runs like this. Suppose I make my living as a speculator in stock exchange securities. One of my purchases is 1000 shares in the XY Company for £1000. Later, I sell them for £700, i.e. the specific index has fallen from 100 to 70 (the general index remaining constant). An ordinary trading account for my venture compares the £1000 cost with the £700 sale, and tells me I have lost £300. The specific index theory says that—despite the obvious worsening in my position—I have lost nothing (i.e. profit is zero): for my £700 will buy another 1000 shares in XY, i.e. covers replacement cost, and thus my physical assets are exactly maintained.

Now, why does my exposition sound so weak? A specific-index man can make it sound far more convincing by using an example that differs from mine on several points.

Points favourable to the specific-index case

Cash strain of asset replacement The specific-index man would take, not a discrete venture, but a firm with a stream of transactions from a composite team of assets; failure to replace any asset physically here tends to upset the whole stream, perhaps disastrously. Further, he would suppose that the specific price of the given input is not dropping but rising. Given these two conditions, a change in input price means the firm is faced with an imperative problem of finance. Its officials will long to conserve enough cash to replace the dearer inputs at the same physical level, and thereby keep activity at a pitch that they deem satisfactory. They will gratefully embrace any doctrine that may lead to lower dividends and perhaps tax.

Unchanged future receipts My example glossed over the question of whether or not the fall in the value of my shares heralded a fall in XY's future dividends, etc. The specific-index man does not neglect this point. He concedes that higher input prices sometimes result in higher sale prices and margins. But his favourite example is the firm that cannot pass on higher costs to customers. For it, a rise in input prices spells lower future profits. Admittedly it is glad to hold a store of inputs at their moment of appreciation, but thereafter the rise is an unrelieved misfortune. To count it as income would be absurd.

Distinction between firm and owner The specific-index man keeps apart the firm and its owners. He is happy to let owners measure their personal incomes in whatever way seems good to them (e.g. with general-index adjustment if general prices change). But he accords to the firm the status of an independent body, important in its own right, remote from the tests of personal consumption, and entitled to its own measures of income. Indeed, the accountant's attitude to this matter 'depends on whether one tends to look on a firm from without or from within, and this depends on what one's environment has been'.[2] Logic is thus coloured by one's environment, and 'one's subconscious ideas on for whom or for what accounting systems are maintained', i.e. by whether one looks at the firm's wealth through the eyes of the outside equity-holder or through those of 'the entity itself'.

Consideration of these points

Each of the above points is beset with difficulties. The third point, in particular, raises philosophical issues that a book on accounting must approach with humility.

Cash strain of asset replacement The suggestion that income is changed by the cash strain of asset replacement cannot be brushed aside lightly, especially in a book advocating the view (see p. 25) that an income concept must be judged by its informativeness. Is not an income figure highly informative if it warns owners of the need to restrict dividends in order to finance new assets?

One answer is that we should not rely on the income statement in isolation. A single figure may not be the best means of giving information on varied matters: two or more figures may be clearer. When real replacement costs are rising, the owners may be better served by an income figure that ignores the increase, plus a cash account or forecast, than by an income figure that tries to be maid-of-all-work.

Another answer runs thus. Suppose a factory has for some years made a steady profit of £*x* p.a. Suddenly it is acutely short of cash. A conscientious accountant cannot announce without investigation that income has dropped. If the sole change in the situation is that the firm is now spending heavily on building a second factory, most of us (including the specific-index man) would say that its income is still £*x*—no matter how crippling the cash strain: the income figure of £*x*, coupled with a clear explanation of cash needs, gives better information than a lower income figure.

Plainly the cash need is not the main test. What really matters is whether the cash shortage is deemed to be due to an *expansion* of the assets or merely to their *maintenance*, i.e. the problem hinges on how one defines 'expansion' and 'maintenance'. The definitions of the specific-index man ignore real expansion that is unaccompanied by physical expansion, and so enable him in such cases to blend income measurement with cash conservation.

Asset values and future receipts The link between asset values and future receipts provides more solid grounds for thought.

A rise in the value of an equity investment may be due to a rise in either the given company's dividends, etc., or the market's capitalisation rate for all equities. In the latter case, the investor who consumes the appreciation during the week (see p. 26) is as well off at the end as at the beginning in terms of capital, but not in terms of future receipts; such change in the market's capitalisation rate thus produces a dubious form of income (perhaps justifying the phrase 'capital gain'—see p. 28)—which most of us would, however, deem to bring some degree of benefit.

Where instead the company's rate of dividend rises, the owner can consume the appreciation and still be as well off at the end of the week in terms of both capital and future dividends. Or he can leave the gain invested, and so secure a higher standard of 'well-offness' in future weeks. In either case, the gain meets more of the tests of income.

A comparable analysis can be made of holding gain on inputs. Stock appreciation, for instance, may or may not herald higher future profits. Where the firm can pass on higher costs, and future profits and dividends are likely to rise, holding gain brings unmixed benefit. Where instead the firm cannot pass on higher costs, the appreciation does not herald continuing benefits, i.e. it somewhat resembles the 'capital gain' due to change in market rates of capitalisation; here the specific-index case becomes stronger.

However, it must often in practice be hard to separate the two possibilities with any feeling of assurance. And perhaps the onlooker may without undue cynicism doubt whether many firms are inhibited from passing on costs, in the long run at least. Economic logic suggests that, in an industry where asset prices become high relative to profits, firms will tend at replacement date to switch to other industries, and potential competitors will stay out, until reduced supply forces prices up to a level again yielding normal profit.

Distinction between firm and owner To say that the firm is privileged as a separate entity is, I suspect, to stray on to very thin ice. The notion seems to imply that firms, by virtue of being separate entities, have a right to continued existence and growth, regardless of their economic and social contributions. It thus has obvious appeal to the employees of a firm: and it strengthens the hand of those managers with a paternalist attitude to shareholders and other 'outsiders', enabling them to build up what are (by real-wealth standards) secret reserves.

The entity view was born in a simple way. A Victorian tradesman, keeping his ledger in a style that was still common, might jumble both business and private expenses in the same accounts. In time, however, he might come to see advantage in knowing how much he spent on his shop and how much on his home. So his bookkeeping was rearranged to distinguish sharply between shop and outside. If this modest step deserves a high-sounding name, 'entity theory' will pass muster. But its analysis implies no more than that separate figures are useful, and does not endow business with special status.

In much the same way, the economist is helped in his reasoning when he unravels man-the-firm from man-the-consumer. And the law finds much convenience in its fiction that a corporation is a person.

But the status accorded to the entity by some accounting theorists seems to go much further. It presumably derives mainly from the view that a business is run by more than one man, and that a group of men—working together as, say, a church, gild, or firm—acquires a personality of its own, demanding our special respect. This line of argument leads us into the realm of political philosophy, and far beyond the competence of one who, like me, is trained only as an accountant. Apparently some serious philosophers, as well as demagogues like Mussolini, have attributed 'the red blood of real corporate personality' to the group, asking whether it has a 'personality beyond the persons of its members, and a will beyond their wills'. An opposing view is stated by Ernest Barker. He sees in the group not an extra person, but merely an 'organising idea' (presumably a set of common aims, standards, and loyalties). 'What has happened is that this idea has entered into a continuous succession of persons . . . a new personality has not arisen, but a new organising idea has served as a scheme of composition for existing personalities.' Thus he cuts down the group's status:

> When we talk of real persons, we attach to them an intrinsic value as such, because we feel that all personality has value. At that rate we should see value in the Mafia or Camorra. If one talks rather of ideas, one can keep something more of critical poise . . . one can deflate a bubble idea with a prick of logic.[3]

Clearly an entity theory of accounting should be spelled out with some caution.

Economic and physical quantities

There is a further reason for preferring the owner to the entity. If one fails to do so, one runs the risk of confusing physical with economic qualities. The latter do not depend on number, size, etc., but on scarcity and capacity to meet human wants. 'There is no quality in things taken out of their relation to men which can make them economic goods'; wealth (in the sense of a flow of economic goods)

> is not wealth because of its substantial qualities. It is wealth because it is scarce. We cannot define wealth in physical terms as we can define food in terms of vitamin content or calorific value. . . . So, too, when we think of productive power in the economic sense, we do not mean something absolute—something capable of physical computation.[4]

The specific-index man seems perilously near to forgetting such ideas. Yet it is doubtful if he can without them even decide how to define the physical size that he seeks to maintain. Does physical size mean for instance the *number* of items of stock, regardless of other attributes? Or their weight? Or qualities such as thermal content of fuel stores? With plant, does it mean the machines themselves or capacity to produce a product? Product measured by volume or value? What if the firm decides not to have any replacement? Perhaps most important in practice, what if the replacement is utterly different (e.g. mule teams will be replaced by helicopters)?

Britain's Standard 16 tries to surmount such problems by stressing 'operating capability'. But this phrase hardly answers all the troublesome questions posed above. We may guess that, when acute difficulties arise in practice, the accountant must in the end use human rather than physical tests: he must rely on some rather woolly concept of maintaining an activity level that is satisfactory to various human beings—perhaps the level that keeps workers in jobs, preserves management's morale, and provides customers with their usual purchases.

In this area, however, theory is easier to read than to apply. If for instance a firm starts a year with one ton of opening stock costing £1000, and after a fortunate series of sales and purchases ends with a closing stock of three tons costing £3000, accountants will readily register a gain of £2000; but if closing stock is one ton costing £3000, they are not so sure. Those who follow Lifo think the physical expansion an essential condition for the gain's existence; three tons indicate a £2000 profit, one ton indicates zero. Yet in terms of economic reality the two gains seem equally desirable. With both, the owner is richer by £2000, regardless of the number of tons. With both, he has ploughed back his profit as extra investment—again regardless of the number of tons: the increased value of one ton seems in this sense to be just the same 'expansion' of assets as the increase marked by physical growth. In less simple problems (e.g. where the units are depreciating assets, or the gain is unrealised), the issue is less clear. With them too, however, the accountant must decide whether holding gain on one physical unit is tantamount to profit and its reinvestment, or whether increase in the number of units is a necessary condition. This is the heart of the matter.

Conclusions on the specific-index view

This chapter began by suggesting that right and wrong here depend largely on objectives. If the maintenance of a viable set of physical assets is really what lies closest to the owners' hearts (an implausible assumption where there are many shareholders), we must not challenge their value judgment. But where the hearts in question are those of managers, we may ask whether these men are not too authoritarian in measuring profit in a way that suits themselves rather than owners, and which, moreover, fosters automatic reinvestment, regardless of its fruitfulness, and so may lead to the inefficient use of resources. The democratic alternative is to show real profit, and then leave the owners to opt for expansion or distribution. This is what is done by the franker figures of the general-index method.

All in all, it seems to me that though the specific-index man's treatment of asset values and decision costs is right, he has not yet proved his case where the time-lag error is concerned; and that (in the absence of general price change) income should be found by subtracting historical rather than replacement cost from revenue. His income accounts are normally incomplete, in that they charge out gain whose prior arrival they have ignored. In addition, his method is particularly harmful if it shows no loss in the income statement when input prices fall calamitously; his neglect of price decline is a yawning gap in his exposition.

The only time when the specific-index case appears valid is when input appreciation is not due to change in expected net receipts, but in their capitalisation rate (p. 111). Then the gain is so different from other forms of income that it might well be excluded or at least carefully segregated. But such gains seem likely to be rare, hard to distinguish, and harder to quantify. So we may doubt whether they deserve much space in a reform programme.

Specific change in times of general change

The notion of specific change in a time of otherwise stable prices helps analysis but hardly smacks of real life. In practice, reform must be able to deal with simultaneous and unequal changes in both indices. The arithmetic of such reform may be a trifle laborious, but the principle is simple.

General-index viewpoint on specific change

If one accepts the general-index case, one ignores specific change (in the narrow context of income measurement), and corrects income by converting costs with the general index, as in Chapter 7.

To illustrate, let us once more use our main numerical example. Suppose that I again hold input (costing £1000) from January to mid-year, while the general index moves from 100 to 110; but now let the specific-index at the same time rise to 132, so that replacement cost is £1320. Sales prices are likely to rise in sympathy with costs, say to £1848. Column (1) of Table 8.3 shows the new ordinary accounts.

The specific-index view is that the time-lag error on cost should be corrected by converting the input's historical cost to its current replacement level, as in column (2), i.e. by creating a replacement allowance of (32/100) × £1000 = £320.

The general-index view leads to an extra charge of only (10/100) × £1000 = £100, as in column (3).

The corrected profits of columns (2) and (3) are both more cautious than the uncorrected profit of column (1). In this example, the CCA cost of column (2) happens to yield a profit smaller than that found with the general index; but, when the specific lags behind the general index, CCA's profit will be the less cautious. Where input prices are volatile, the general index must yield a steadier trend.

Hybrid reform: Blending CCA and real income

As we have seen, there are strong grounds for using CCA for asset values. There is a good case too for employing CCA for the costs of the income statement: the use of current costs should be encouraged wherever they may influence decisions; and, where the assets have been revalued, replacement cost depreciation ties in with the balance sheet.

On the other hand, this chapter has suggested many defects in CCA profit; the general-index man's figure seems more defensible.

One can make the best of both worlds with the 'hybrid' or 'ideal' system. This uses CCA values for assets and costs; yet it shows real income—by crediting real holding gain as revenue. Column (3) of

Table 8.3 Accounts Illustrating Specific Change Superimposed on General Change

	(1) *Ordinary accounts* £	(2) *Specific-index correction* £	(3) *General-index correction* £	(4) *Real holding gain and replacement cost shown* £	(5) *Stabilised end-£*
Income statement					
Input					
Historical cost	1000				
Replacement cost		1320		1320	*1440*
General-index correction			1100		
Sale	1848	1848	1848	1848	*2016*
Profit					
Accounting	848				
Corrected with specific index		528			
Corrected with general index			748		
Operating profit				528	*576*
Real holding gain (1320−1100)				220	*240*
Real profit				748	*816*
Balance sheet					
Cash	1848	1848	1848	1848	*1848*
Capital	1000	1000	1000	1000	*1200*
Replacement allowance		320			
Inflation allowance			100	100	
		1320	1100	1100	
Profit	848	528	748	748	*816*
Loss on holding money [(10/110)×1848]					*– 168*
	1848	1848	1848	1848	*1848*

Table 8.2 introduced this device. Column (4) of Table 8.3 shows the same form of correction: it charges CCA cost but credits the real holding gain of £220 (the difference between cost found by CCA and general index correction), and thereby neutralises the extra cost and achieves the real profit of £748.[5]

Stabilisation and CCA

The earlier tables of this chapter, it must be remembered, show merely the minimum changes needed in the ordinary accounts to correct the time-lag error by CCA rules. They do not try to give stabilised figures for, e.g., assets and capital.

Like the earlier tables, stabilised accounts deal with the time-lag error. But their results must vary according to the type of capital that is to be maintained. Thus a stabilised income statement for Table 8.3 could be built on the CCA approach of column (2), or the general-index approach of either columns (3) or (4). In fact, the example in column (5) builds on column (4). It uses the end of the year as base date, and assumes the general index to be 120 then. So it must slightly change all the historical figures of column (4); the end-£ equivalent of the 748 mid-year £s of profit is (12/11) × £748 = £816.

Table 8.3 thus interprets the results in five of the possible ways, (1) as in ordinary accounts, (2) as in accounts where the time-lag error in the income statement is corrected by the CCA method, (3) as in accounts where that error is corrected by the general-index method, (4) as in (3), but with replacement cost and real holding gain shown, and (5) as in (4), with both income statement and balance sheet stabilised in £s at the end of the year.

Value loss raises operating profit

Suppose now that the input's replacement cost falls to £800 while the input is held (sales and the general index remaining as in Table 8.3).

Columns (1) and (3) do not alter. But the fall in replacement cost changes the column (2) income statement to:

	£
Input	
Replacement cost	800
Sale	1848
CCA profit	1048

Thus misfortune *improves* CCA income (though the balance sheet must of course show the holding loss as a deduction from equity). This seems a very odd result.

The hybrid method of column (4) will give a clearer view of the year's ups-and-downs, and end with a more cautious profit. It will now include:

	£
Operating profit	1048
Real holding loss (800 − 1100)	(300)
Real profit	748

CCA: Income statements versus budgets

Accounting makes a great leap forward when it uses CCA in decision budgets. This helps to explain the high esteem in which many accountants now hold CCA—and why they find difficulty in seeing its limitations.

So perhaps it is worth our while to go quickly over the ground again, this time with the help of diagrams. As before, we start by considering holding gain in the absence of inflation.

Constant general prices

Figure 8.1 shows my wealth on the vertical axis, and time on the horizontal axis. My starting wealth is AB; it includes a lottery ticket. At date 2, I am lucky enough to win £50, so my total rises (by ED). At date 3, I give the £50 to my favourite charity; wealth drops by FG to its original level HG (= AB). I am back where I started.

We all agree that (a) my sacrifice at date 3 is £50, but (b) my income account for the whole period from date 1 should show not only this loss but also the earlier £50 gain. The account thus shows that the two

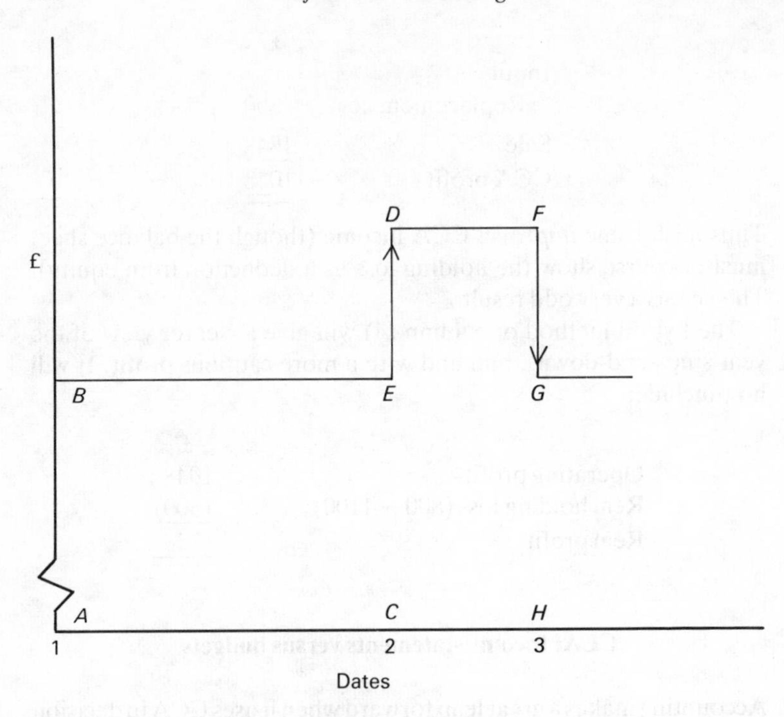

Figure 8.1

transactions have no net effect on my wealth.

Should not the same reasoning hold for business accounts, and where the £50 gain is not in the form of cash? Suppose a firm's wealth is one asset (*AB* in Figure 8.2) that appreciates by £50 (*ED*) while awaiting sale. At date 3, the asset is given up in order to earn revenue of *IL*. Two quite different calculations of gain can be made, each right for its own purpose.

1 A *decision budget at date 3*, to test whether the sale is worthwhile, is concerned only with the short future period (sometimes zero) of the transaction. It compares the sacrifice *FH* (usually the cost of replacement) with the revenue *IL*. Thus it should charge the input by CCA rules, and certainly not at historical cost *AB*. The budget shows that sale brings a further gain of *KL*.
2 An *income statement for the whole period from date 1* looks back

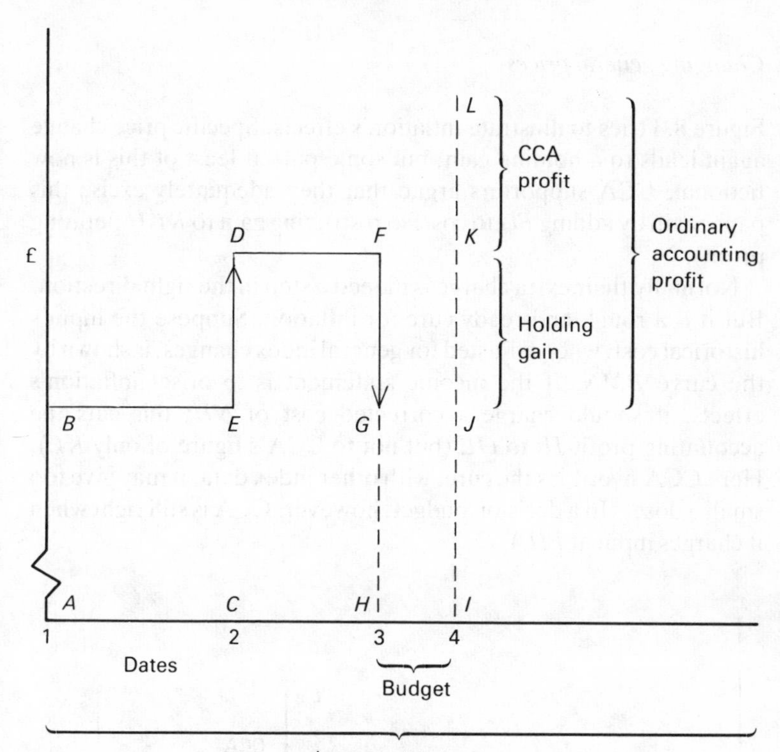

Figure 8.2

at all events (including the £50 gain at date 2) since date 1. Opening wealth *AB* has been exchanged for closing wealth *IL*; therefore the income statement should charge the historical cost *AB* against the revenue *IL*, so arriving at the traditional accounting profit *JL*. If cost is put instead at *FH* (as strict CCA logic demands), the holding gain at *C* is in effect left out, and profit is restricted to *KL* (operating profit); sacrifice is fully stated, but not gains.

Thus CCA would seem to use rules that are right for the short period of the budget, but wrong for the longer period of the income statement.

Changing general prices

Figure 8.3 tries to illustrate inflation's effects. Specific price change again leads to a holding gain; but some part at least of this is now fictional. CCA supporters argue that they adequately excise this paper gain by adding *FG* to cost, so restricting gain to *KL* (operating profit).

Normally their extra charge is indeed a step in the right direction. But it is a rough-and-ready cure for inflation. Suppose the input's historical cost, when adjusted for general index changes, is shown by the curve *BMN*. If the income statement is to offset inflation's effects, it should charge a corrected cost of *NH*; this cuts the accounting profit *JL* to *OL* (but not to CCA's figure of only *KL*). Here CCA overdoes the cure; with other index data, it may give too small a dose. (In a decision budget, however, CCA is still right when it charges input at *FH*.)

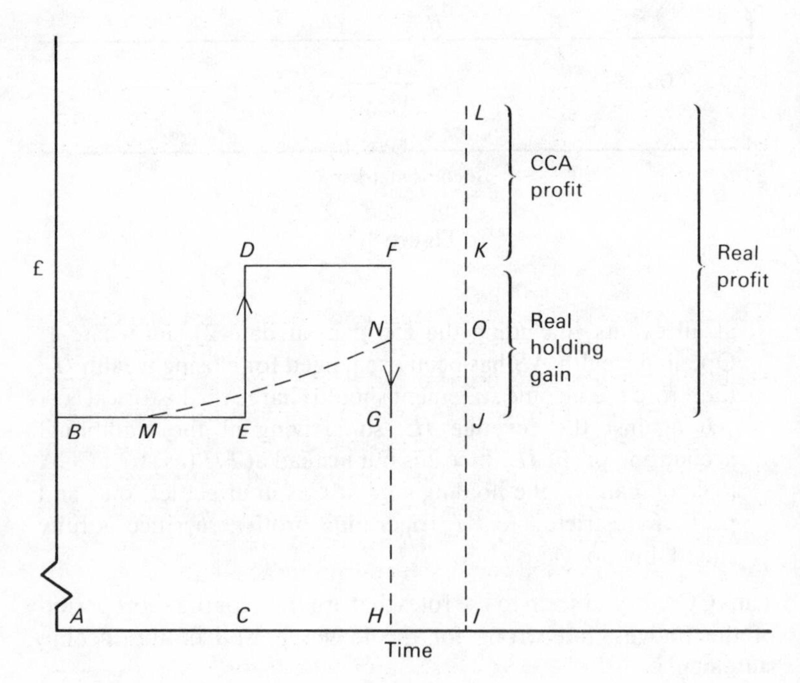

Figure 8.3

CCA is too subjective for tax calculation

The current cost of an input may be uncertain. Often no-one can be sure about the worth of for instance an unusual machine or building; even a skilled appraiser may feel uncertain, and different appraisers may make very different guesses. It follows that CCA charges (e.g. depreciation on the machine or building) may be subjective, with some scope for bias and manipulation.

Managers cannot evade such uncertainty. They must perforce guess current values for their budgets, and pray that their judgment proves sound. But outsiders may reasonably demand that, where income is at issue in a legal contract, less debatable figures should be used. (A strong argument for the hybrid system is that, though it shows inputs at current values, it then takes out the subjective element with its credit for holding gain.)

This reasoning applies to tax on income. Many British accountants hoped that a standard on inflation accounting would serve as a basis for income tax reform. But, by opting for CCA in Standard 16, they have made this impossible. No tax authority could accept such subjective and pliable figures. Thus, in 1975, when the Inland Revenue did give relief for the time-lag error on stocks, it prescribed a somewhat general index (of wholesale prices). Similarly the capital gain reliefs of 1982 use the general index.

Conclusion

The early pages of this chapter suggested that specific values, though excellent for other purposes, do not fit happily into the income statement when general prices are constant. They yield a profit that may be subjective and at odds with acceptable ideas of 'well-offness'.

When there is inflation, the case changes somewhat. CCA usually does have good effect on the time-lag error. The general-index man will of course counter by saying that CCA here succeeds merely because it is a surrogate for general-index correction. Direct use of the general index would be simpler and more accurate.

The next two chapters must look more closely into the argument by studying the two charges most susceptible to the time-lag error, cost-of-goods-sold and depreciation.

Notes and References

1 The phrase was coined by Gynther, R.S. (1966) *Accounting for Price Level Changes: Theory and Procedure*, Pergamon Press. I am in debt to his book (a spirited defence of the specific index) for much of the detail in later pages.
2 This paragraph relies heavily on Gynther, *op. cit.*; the quotations are from pp. *x* and 44.
3 The quotations are from Barker, E. (1930) *Church, State, and Study*, pp. 160–3, Methuen.
4 Robbins, L. (1949) *The Nature and Significance of Economic Science*, pp. 46–7, Macmillan.
5 CCA and the hybrid model have been discussed by (among many others) Sterling, R.R. (1975) 'Relevant financial reporting in an age of price change', *Journal of Accountancy*, February; and Vancil, R.F. (1976) 'Inflation accounting—the great controversy', *Harvard Business Review*, March–April. French, E.A. (in 'Physical capital maintenance in income measurement—an exemplification', *Accounting and Business Research*, Winter 1976) suggests that accountants could do well to study ecclesiastical history. The Church of England has for over a millenium sought to maintain its physical assets. Its attempts have proved harmful, and in the end impossible.

9

The Time-lag Error in Accounting Profit: (C) Stocks

A discussion of stocks may not add much to what Chapters 7 and 8 have already said about principles. But it is needed because the 'cost of goods sold' is a much less simple figure than the costs used so far. Moreover, some of the methods of valuing stocks (i.e. of finding the closing stock for the balance sheet, and the corresponding credit in the income statement) can change the cost-of-goods-sold and thus the time-lag error, and so we must extend the argument to cover valuation too. For simplicity, our examples will deal with the stocks of a merchant; but the argument normally holds also, e.g. for a manufacturer's raw materials, work-in-progress, and finished goods.

Difficulties of defining the historical cost of stocks

Most of the usual methods of valuing stocks make extensive use of historical cost. This is consistent with the accountant's way of valuing other assets; and it sounds objective and easy. Yet, as was pointed out on p. 16, there are great difficulties in finding the historical cost of stocks, as well as further difficulties in justifying it if it can be found. Particularly in manufacturing, these difficulties are often the result of 'jointness'—a given outlay helps to make a pool of stock units, some of which are sold during the year and some left at the end. So the cost figure for closing stock can vary with choice of both *ingredients* (e.g. should overheads be included?) and *sequence* (which unit goes out first?).

The ingredients problem is not important for understanding the time-lag; all that need be said is that a bigger overhead content leads to a bigger stock carry-forward, and thus (when prices change) may result in a bigger time-lag error. But the sequence in which units are handed out decides which units are charged to the income statement and which are left in the closing stock, and different units may have different historical costs; so the sequence affects the cost-of-goods-sold and the error.

Valuation methods: the Ifo family

A firm may price stock issues by, for instance, the *first-in-first-out* or *last-in-first-out* systems (familiarly abridged to Fifo and Lifo). However, these are often a matter of *assumed* rather than actual sequence, i.e. the firm may merely value the units *as if* one or other of the two patterns is followed, regardless of the actual physical flow.[1] A less common member of the Ifo family is *highest-in-first-out* (Hifo); it cautiously assumes that the dearest units are issued first, leaving the cheapest units as closing stock.

None of the family can be defended as more than a convenient makeshift; to link value with a past physical event is an affront to economic logic. The problem would vanish if issues and closing stock were valued at current prices; so long as they are valued by reference to past costs, the latter must be allocated between units by some mere rule-of-thumb.

There are many other methods of valuing stock (some of which are mentioned in Chapter 12). All those using historical cost are likely to create time-lag errors. Fifo and Lifo will serve to illustrate the point, and so this chapter deals mainly with them.

Example of Fifo and Lifo

The simple example in Chapters 7 and 8 (i.e. a pre-inflation cost of £1000 and sales of £1400) still meets our needs when the firm deals in stocks; but the £1000 now becomes the net total of several items—say, stock at beginning plus purchases, less stock at end. Suitable figures are set out in Table 9.1. This supposes that 500 stock units, costing £1 apiece, are always held, and the turnover period is six months. For simplicity, it supposes too that transactions are concentrated into a few busy days: thus all the 500 units of stock at beginning are bought as a single lot on 30 September in the preceding year, and 500 units are simultaneously sold and replaced on 31 March and again on 30 September in the current year. If prices are steady throughout the period (index 100), a year's trading account will run (by both Fifo and Lifo).

Table 9.1 Income Account with Stocks—Stable Prices

			£
Stock at beginning	500	units	500
Purchases	1000	units	1000
	1500	units	1500
Less Stock at end	500	units	500
Cost of goods sold	1000	units	1000
Sales			1400
Profit			400

So the outcome is a profit of £400, as before.

How does inflation change this? As usual, we begin on the assumption that the general and specific indices coincide. Let us again say the index moves up steadily from 100 to 120 between 1 January and 31 December. Our figures will, however, be easier to compare with the other examples if we suppose that the upswing in prices began *earlier* than the start of this year—say, that the index was only at 95 on the preceding 30 September, so that opening stock cost only £475. Another lot of 500 units was bought at 31 March (index 105) for £525, replacing 500 units sold then. A third lot was bought at 30 September (index 115) for £575. The figures are set out in Table 9.2—first as stores records, then as final accounts.

Fifo stores accounts assume an issue to consist of the oldest (and here cheapest) units in stock. Thus the March issue is supposed to consist of the units on hand at 1 January (cost £475); and the September purchases are left as end-stock, which is therefore valued at £575.

Lifo interprets the same data differently. Each 500-unit lot of purchases is supposed to arrive just before a sale, and to be issued for the sale. Thus issues are costed at the higher current prices, e.g. the

Table 9.2 Comparison of Fifo and Lifo

Stores account										
Dr		*Receipts*						*Issues*		*Cr.*
			Fifo and Lifo					*Fifo*	*Lifo*	
		Units	*Price*	£		Units	Price	£	*Price*	£
1 January	Balance	500	0.95	475						
31 March	Purchase	500	1.05	525	Issue	500	0.95	475	1.05	525
30 September	Purchase	500	1.15	575	Issue	500	1.05	525	1.15	575
31 December					Balance	575	1.15	575	0.95	475
		1500		1575		1500		1575		1575
Income statement										
Stock at beginning								475		475
Purchases								1100		1100
								1575		1575
Less Stock at close								575		475
Cost of goods sold								1000		1100
Sales								1540		1540
Profit								540		440
Balance sheet includes										
Stocks								575		475
Profit								540		440

March purchase becomes the March issue, costing £525. The January stock is looked on as an unchanging nucleus; its cost (say, £475) may date from a remote time, yet will be retained indefinitely as the value of a 500-unit balance. (If for instance Lifo had first been used when 500 units cost only £250, and if volume has not since dipped at a year-end to below the original amount, then both opening and closing stock would here be valued at £250.) The essence of Lifo is that appreciation on the stock nucleus is ignored. Physical increment alone justifies value increment.

The Fifo income account confirms what was perhaps to be expected. The time-lag error persists unchanged when there are opening and closing stocks—at any event, if these are measured *à la* Fifo; we have without undue trouble arranged our figures so that the cost, accounting profit, and error are again the same as in the staple example on pp. 87–8.

Comparing the Fifo and Lifo income statements, one sees that Lifo during inflation lowers the closing stock (to a level that may be far less than values of the current year), and thereby raises the cost-of-goods-sold (to something more like current cost). As a result, profit is here less than by Fifo.

Time-lag of the physical flow of stocks

To understand the time-lag error on stocks, one should perhaps think of the two sides of the profit and loss account as if they showed physical movements of inputs and outputs strung out *by date*. Thus the left-hand side might list the successive purchases of stock units (starting at the top with the earliest unit affecting the year), while the right-hand side might list the sales of the same units. Such accounts can be represented as diagrams. Figure 9.1 shows three possible patterns. The left-hand side (*AB*) of each oblong lists the successive inputs as dots, *A* being, say, at 1 January and *B* at 31 December; and the right-hand side (*CD*) lists the successive outputs. Thus *E* may represent one input, and *F* the sale of that unit. The diagram tries to suggest the timing of movements, but not their physical or money sizes.

Where each unit is held for almost no time at all (i.e. purchase synchronises with sale), inputs and sales form horizontal pairs, and can be shown as the horizontal lines of the left-hand oblong (1). Thus

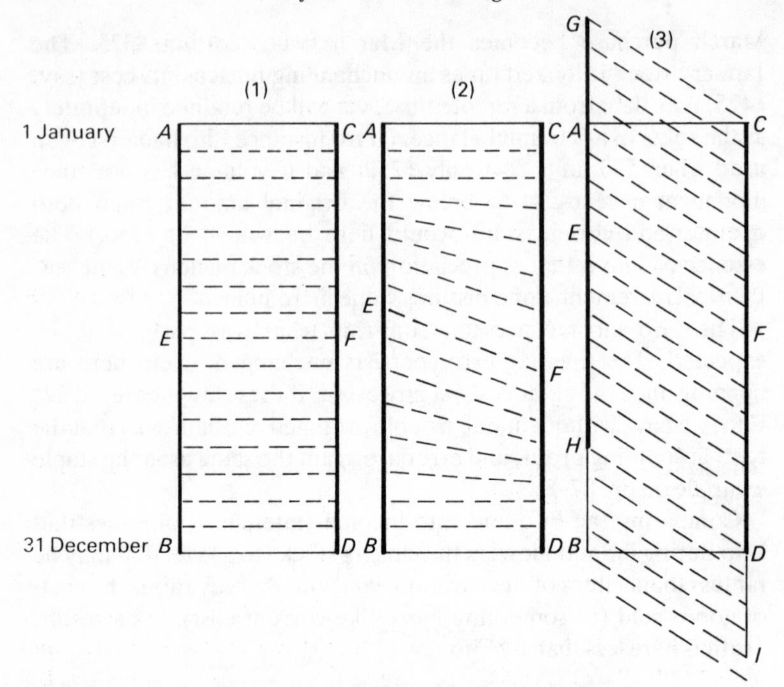

Figure. 9.1 Some patterns of stock turnover. (1) Each stock item is held for a negligible period. (2) Stocks accumulate within year. (3) Stocks are held at start and end of year

E and *F* may represent a pair of transactions in July. There can be no opening or closing stocks in this oblong. Nor can there be any time-lag error.

Where stocks are built up for a seasonal sales peak, one possible pattern is that of oblong (2). This shows more frequent purchases in the top half of *AB*, and more frequent sales in the lower half of *CD*: stocks are bought in the spring for big sales in the autumn, and so the broken lines slope down from the left during the turnover months. If prices change, a time-lag error here occurs within the year (even though there are no opening or closing stocks). In short, any physical undulation of stock may give rise to the error.

Opening and closing stocks are shown in column (3). *GA* is the purchases, made towards the close of the preceding year, that become the opening stock of the current year on Fifo assumptions. *AB* is the purchases of the current year. *HB* is deemed by Fifo to become the current year's closing stock to be sold early in the next year. This leaves *GH* as the cost-of-goods-sold, tied slantingly to the year's sales (*CD*); Fifo cuts away closing stock (*HB*) from the year's costs, and leaves an earlier set of cost £s to be matched against current sales £s.

Lifo's assumptions make the broken lines of column (3) more horizontal. With constant real stocks, it produces an account corresponding to oblong (1). With changing volumes, the pattern cannot be shown in a simple diagram; but the net effect of Lifo is still to link costs with revenues that are almost contemporary.

Fifo

The next step is to analyse Fifo accounts in more detail, and to see how their time-lag error can be corrected.

Anatomy of Fifo

It may be as well to remind oneself of the effect on the income statement of the entries for opening and closing stocks. The accountant seeks to charge the income statement with no more or less than the historical cost of the units sold. But, unless he keeps stores accounts, he does not know this cost figure. His nearest substitute is purchases; so he takes the latter, and trims it by cutting off the units unsold at the end and sticking on those held at the start. Under Fifo (provided all units flow through in regular order, and there are no mark-downs due to spoilage, etc.) his resultant cost-of-goods-sold is the purchases for roughly a twelve-month period starting before the start of the accounting year and ending before its end (*GH* in oblong (3) in Figure 9.1). By subtracting the cost of the later purchases (closing stock) from the cost of the whole year's purchases, he deprives those later purchases of all influence on the year's cost and profit.

Thus in the Fifo income statement of Table 9.2 the cost-of-goods-sold is made up of two lots of purchases—first, goods bought on 30 September in the preceding year, shown as stock-at-beginning and costing £475; and secondly, goods bought on 31 March in the current year for £525, and deemed to constitute the goods sold at 30 September. The table might be clearer if it showed only what

Table 9.3 Income Account with Purchases Analysed on Fifo Assumption

Date	*Index*		*Cost* £	*Sales* £
Previous				
30 September	95	Lot 1. Stock at beginning	475	
Current				
31 March	105	Lot 1. Sold		735
		Lot 2. Purchase of first half-year	525	
30 September	115	Lot 2. Sold		805
		Lot 3. Purchase of second half-year (=end-stock) £575		
		Historical cost	1000	
		Inflation charge	100	
		Corrected historical cost	1100	
		Corrected profit	440	
			1540	1540

happens to these two lots of purchases, i.e. left out the closing stock. Table 9.3 does this. Its arrangement shows—more clearly than the usual form with opening and closing stocks—that the time-lag error arises because the 'cost year' precedes the 'revenue year'. Our minds should link the error with cost-of-goods-sold rather than closing stock; the error can be present even if (as here) closing stock is left out of the account.

Calculation of the inflation charge

Where the physical flows are smooth and simple, it is not hard to find Fifo's exact inflation charge. In the example, one can readily work out the appreciation on each lot:

	Historical cost	*Factor*	*Raised historical cost*	*Inflation charge*
	£		£	£
Lot 1	475	105/95	525	50
Lot 2	525	115/105	575	50
Total inflation charge				100

(Note again that the charge has been found from the cost-of-goods-sold, and without reference to closing stock.)

In real life, the figures run less simply than in our example. Purchases, sales, and stocks-on-hand consist of many items, each with a different date. The goods may not be sold in strict order: thus some of the end-stock items may be as old as items in cost-of-goods-sold; physical groups overlap. Again, physical groups may differ in mix and size, as when seasonal needs bring ups-and-downs during the year (see oblong (2) in Figure 9.1). Such irregularities bring further error, and make correction more troublesome.

So, unless full stores records are kept, one cannot find the exact inflation charge. Some form of approximation is inevitable.

Approximate charges

Several forms suggest themselves:

1 All the cost items can be treated as one big lot, bought at an 'average' date. Likewise the sales can be treated as one big lot. In

the example, we can easily convert the total historical cost (£1000) into £s that match average sales £s in worth: the costs are incurred on average at general index 100, and the sales take place at 110, so corrected cost is 110/100 × £1000, i.e. £1100; the corresponding charge is £100.

2 The many small items can be treated as a few large lots. Thus the opening stock of £475 will normally consist of many small lots, purchased mainly between 1 July and 31 December of the previous year; but, if those purchases were made at a fairly steady rate, they may be looked on as a single lot bought on 30 September, i.e. at an index of 95 'on average'—strictly, a weighted average.

3 The excess of closing over opening stock may be treated as the inflation charge. In some circumstances, such a figure may be fairly accurate. The exact charge is the sum of many smaller charges, each caused by inflation during the turnover of one of the stock items that together make up the cost-of-goods-sold. Suppose that a firm's stock always consists of a single unit, sold at the end of each month and replaced at once. Then twelve small inflation charges will emerge during the year, and their sum is the correction for cost-of-goods-sold. But the sum equals the charge on one unit for a whole year, i.e. the appreciation on one unit between the dates of the opening and the closing inventories. Similarly, where many units are held, the difference between opening and closing stock values is still the year's inflation charge—provided always that there has been no change in the real investment in stock (as shown, e.g. by stabilised values).

   Such stability is assumed in our simple example. So the error can there be found more readily than earlier calculations suggest. It is the appreciation on the stocks between the two valuation dates: £575 − £475 = £100.

   In practice, such stability is most improbable. The more real investment varies, the less likely is the difference between opening and closing stocks to reflect the whole error.

4 More elaborate methods are often needed in practice. The appendix to this chapter explains one such method.

Stocks other than merchandise

For a firm other than that of a merchant (e.g. a factory), the argument runs much the same as above. But purchases are here apt to be only a part of the factory's costs; the other costs, such as wages and depreciation, may or may not be treated as ingredients of manufactured stock values, and carried forward. The facts do not stand out so plainly as in the case of the trader, but the same reasoning holds. And here the firm is more likely to keep stores records, and so may find the cost-of-goods-sold direct from the 'issues' to customers, instead of indirectly by adjusting purchases, etc., with the opening and closing stocks.

Loose tools are often classed in the balance sheet alongside plant, i.e. in the fixed assets section. But their value is usually found by an annual stocktaking; and the figures may well be calculated in much the same way as when goods are valued at Fifo. Where this is so, the treatment for stocks should be applied also to loose tools: the annual charge for their 'using-up' tends during inflation to be understated in the income statement, and should be raised with an inflation charge.

'Inventory profit'

The extra accounting profit that springs from the error on cost-of-goods-sold (e.g. the £100 in the illustration above) is often called 'inventory profit'. The preceding pages suggest that the phrase is not altogether a happy one. It is apt to evoke mental pictures of the inventory sheets that are drawn up at the end of a year, and so to encourage the idea that the error is confined to appreciation in stocks held at the start and end. As we have seen, error can arise too from stock fluctuations *during* the year—which are not reflected in the closing inventory.

'Inventory profit' is thus doubly misleading. The profit is spurious, and its size does not depend on closing inventories. 'Error on cost-of-goods-sold' seems preferable.

Specific change—real holding gain

When the cost price of stock moves but general prices remain stable, the historical cost-of-goods-sold is the correct figure to set against revenue (if the conclusions of Chapter 8 are sound); there is no need for specific index charges. If the price movement is upward, and the firm wants to finance this real expansion from internal sources, it should treat any consequent charges as appropriations, not costs.

Similarly, when real change is superimposed on general price change, Fifo and an inflation charge do all that is needed by the sub-concept of real capital maintenance.

Nevertheless the cost figures in the income statement will be more informative if they are linked with current costs. By using the hybrid model (i.e. by charging current cost but crediting real realised holding gain—see page 116) we can give this information and still end with real profit.

The specific-index man will challenge these views. He insists that the cost-of-goods-sold should be raised to current level, with no credit of real holding gain. His adjustment may take the form of an unconcealed addition to the costs, but is often masked as a method of stock valuation (e.g. Lifo), and then tends to be inaccurate even by his standards.

Specific index example

Suppose all the facts in Table 9.3 still obtain, save that the buying price of stocks rises in September by an extra 23 points—pushing up the specific index to 138 on 30 September, and so raising the cost of the September purchases (unchanged in physical volume) from £575 to £690, i.e. giving a real holding gain of £115 on the goods in stock. Then the trading results are as shown in Table 9.4. Column (1) gives the new ordinary accounts; and column (2) shows the general-index correction—still £100, as calculated on p. 133.

Column (3) puts the CCA adjustment at £215, the figure needed to raise the £1000 historical cost to replacement level. It thus reduces profit to £325, the operating profit. By the canons of the specific-index man, this is the correct profit, and he would rule off the account here. Those who disagree with him can restore the profit to the general-index level of column (2) by using the hybrid model, i.e. adding the £115 real holding gain. This roundabout course gives some useful information. Operating profit (£325) is of course much lower than accounting profit (£540), and is rather low compared with pre-inflation profit (£400—see Table 9.1). This poor result may stem from failure to raise autumn selling prices in step with buying prices. But the realised appreciation (£115) shows the buyer's skill in ordering new stocks (lot 2) before their steep price rise.

Table 9.4 Income Account with Real Appreciation on Stocks

Date	*General index*	*Specific index*		(1) *Ordinary account* £	(2) *General-index correction* £	(3) *Specific-index correction* £
Previous						
30 September	95	95	Stock at beginning—Lot 1	475		
Current year						
31 March	105	105	Purchases: First half-year—Lot 2	525	as (1)	as (1)
30 September	115	138	Second half-year—Lot 3	690		
				1215		
				1690		
			Less Closing stock—Lot 3	690		
			Cost-of-goods-sold (historical)	1000	1000	1000
			Inflation charge (general index)		100	
			CCA adjustment			215
			Corrected cost (general index)		1100	
			Replacement cost			1215
31 March and 30 September			Sales	1540	1540	1540
			Profit—accounting	540		
			operating			325
			real realised holding (215−100)			115
			corrected (real)		440	440

Lifo

Lifo has long been popular in USA. In 1938, it achieved the distinction of being accepted by American tax law for income-tax assessment in a narrow range of industries; and Congress during the next ten years liberalised the rules until all taxpayers could opt for Lifo. A number of provisos were made—e.g. the taxpayer must use Lifo in his own book-keeping as well as in tax calculations, and his decision is irrevocable.[2] The tax benefits were sometimes great, e.g. during the Second World War. Thus for one sample of departmental stores using Lifo: 'the annual reduction in income ranged from 4.2% in 1945 to 17.1% in 1941, a year in which department store prices rose about 15%.'[3]

In Britain, Lifo has so far been unpopular, and the courts have rejected its use for tax purposes.[4] But the Companies Act, 1981 recognises it, and so it may become more common. We shall therefore look at it in some detail.

Lifo's permanent nucleus

To understand Lifo, first take the case where the year's opening and closing stocks are the same in physical size. If the last unit of purchases is supposed to be sold first, then opening stock must be supposed to rest untouched throughout the year. It thus becomes the stock-at-end—still valued at its original cost. It is looked on as a permanent nucleus. No matter how much prices rise in later years, the value of this nucleus stays the same.

Where there are physical 'increments' or 'decrements' during the year, various treatments are possible (and logic cannot help much with the choice). Because of the obvious importance of the US tax rules on the subject, these tend to be dominant; but some non-American firms may nevertheless use other interpretations. Whatever the exact rules, Lifo stock values will tend to reflect remote prices.

General price change and Lifo

Once again, it is wise to start with simple assumptions—that general and specific price movements are the same, and that physical stock is constant. The example in Table 9.2 shows what happens here. In it, Lifo profit is again £440, as when corrected profit was found by Fifo and an inflation charge (see Table 9.3). So here Lifo has taken us to the same answer—by a route that is agreeably short and free from arithmetical hardships. Lifo's net effect is to knock off something from a credit (closing stock), whereas an inflation charge adds something to a debit (cost-of-goods-sold). So long as the two somethings are equal, the two methods give the same result.

Anatomy of Lifo

Lifo's working can be made clearer if the various transactions in our example are shown separately. They are conceived to run as shown in Table 9.5. Comparison of Table 9.5 with the corresponding analysis of Fifo (Table 9.3) shows how Lifo can, in very simple circumstances, circumvent the time-lag.

Table 9.5 Income Account with Stocks Valued by Lifo

	Cost		*Sales*
	£		£
Beginning lot (carried forward as closing stock)	475		
March lot—purchased and sold	525	→	735
September lot—purchased and sold	575	→	805
Cost of goods sold	1100		
Profit	440		
	1540		1540

Specific prices and Lifo

In the example, Lifo transmutes the purchases into cost-of-goods-sold, i.e. charges the latter at replacement cost. This effect becomes more obvious when specific price diverges from general price. The data of Table 9.4 can be rearranged to suit Lifo (see Table 9.6). As in column (3) of Table 9.4, cost-of-goods-sold is 1215, and profit is 325. Thus Lifo acts like a CCA adjustment rather than an inflation charge; at least in the conditions assumed by this example, Lifo profit is 'operating profit' (see p. 30) and so leaves out all holding gain (here the £115 of real stock appreciation), even though this gain is both real and realised. This holds wherever physical stock stays constant, but elsewhere can be upset.

Changes in physical volume

There is some dispute among the votaries of Lifo over the proper treatment of physical changes (and the point can hardly be resolved by appeal to economic logic, since the latter must regard physical sequence as beside the point—see p. 126). But accretions in any year (i.e. expansions of the basic quantity) tend to be valued thereafter at a historical cost of that year; and this cost is excised if the volume falls again.[5]

When physical stock is constant, as in the examples, one can state that Lifo fits in with the sub-concept of physical capital maintenance. Where physical stock changes, this statement ceases to hold precisely, though the imprecision would seem slight enough to be forgiven. With such change, too, Lifo may not produce a cost-of-goods-sold that exactly equals replacement cost. But its tendency will still be to cut profit down to operating profit (and so suppress holding gain). It still acts more like a replacement cost provision than an inflation charge.

Popularity of Lifo

The examples suggest rightly that in many normal situations (i.e. where physical stocks are fairly constant, and general and specific prices do not diverge excessively), Lifo is superior to simple Fifo for dealing with inflation, and is a plausible rival to Fifo plus an inflation charge. The latter calls for the insertion of an awkward and alien figure; the former is hardly noticeable. The latter can be justified only by reference to fundamentals; the former can be explained

Table 9.6 Income Statement—Lifo and Real Appreciation

Date	*Index*		*Cost* £		*Sales* £	*Lifo profit* £
Previous						
30 September	95	Stock at beginning	475			
Current						
31 March	105	Purchase of first half-year	525	→	735	210
30 September	115	Purchase of second half-year	690	→	805	115
			1690			
		Less Closing stock	475			
			1215		1540	325

readily in the specious terms of physical or cost flow. Thus one need not be surprised at the enthusiasm with which Lifo is advocated by many reformers.

Defects of Lifo

When Lifo has such practical advantages and political allure, anyone who quarrels with its use may seem pedantic. However, it has in my view many faults, notably the following.

First, Lifo is unlikely in practice to give exact correction (general or specific). It will tend to be inaccurate (even by the canons of CCA) when physical increments and decrements affect closing stock. And where there are fluctuations *within* a year, i.e. not reflected in the opening and closing stocks, a method of correction that relies exclusively on these two figures cannot be accurate. Perhaps the most vivid way to see the point at issue is to imagine an extreme case in which a trader each year lets his stocks sink to nothing by the end of December and starts to build them up again in January; plainly, Lifo here fails entirely. And, though few real firms reduce their stock to nothing, many (e.g. retail drapers) reduce it substantially, and tend to choose a business year ending at the date when stock is at its nadir. A cure built on such a low figure will not offset the error of busier times. If, on the other hand, the stocks are unusually high at the start and end of the year, Lifo may overshoot the mark, acting in much the same way as too big an inflation charge. If the business year ends when stocks are at their 'normal' size, Lifo has its best chance to function well.

Secondly, Lifo sounds simple (compared, for instance, with Fifo plus an inflation charge), but it is often not so simple as it sounds. Many of its early users were firms handling raw materials (meat packers, non-ferrous metal mines, etc.); their stocks consist of a relatively limited number of physical types whose nature does not vary much over time, and thus comparison of the opening and closing quantities of each type is not unreasonable. With most other firms, however, the nature and mix of types can vary fast; e.g. a grocer may decide to switch from one make or size of soap tablet to another, to hold less tea and more marmalade, or to add a very different line. This difficulty has forced the friends of Lifo to relax their primitive and literal rules (which could apply only to firms handling standard types of goods), and to substitute fairly elaborate calculations, often based on index numbers. (Someday, perhaps the historians of accounting will distinguish between 'paleolific' and 'neolific' ages.) The current cost of the 'pool' of varied goods that makes up closing stock is deflated with the help of an index approximately to base-date level (like stabilised figures). A department store may have to use a different index for each department.

Thirdly, increases and decreases in physical volume must be valued by some arbitrary rule. And they can have odd and unwelcome effects on profit. If stock sinks during a year, the 'decrement' is removed from end-stock, and so in effect charged as cost-of-goods-sold—at perhaps the low acquisition rates of many years ago. Costs are, therefore, small compared with Fifo, and profit large. This is particularly true if stock sinks to below base volume, as happened in many American firms during the lean years of the Second World War; the resulting profits were so high that in 1942 the US Congress was cajoled into granting special tax relief to firms hit in this way.[6]

Fourthly, it seems desirable, for the sake of clarity and comparability with other firms, that the income account should show the size of important price-level adjustments; but Lifo in effect deducts a hidden provision from stock-at-end. Further, the balance sheet is more helpful and realistic if stock is shown at current cost (which Fifo is near to), rather than as a more mixed figure whose core is valued in remote £s.

Finally there is plausible evidence that Lifo's need for stable stock figures (if its tax benefits are to be maximised) may interfere with the buying policies of firms, and even upset markets:

> If you have too little inventory compared with your Lifo base, you buy up stock; when six or seven companies are trying to do the same thing you run the market ragged. Should you be too high on certain goods in comparison with your Lifo base, you cut prices to move out goods. Thus operating decisions are coloured by the operation of the accounting system.[7]

So the Lifo tail may wag the business dog.

One could perhaps avoid the above list by saying merely that Lifo, like CCA, takes physical capital as its benchmark, and so is subject to the shortcomings of the physical sub-concept. Both Lifo and CCA are hostile to all forms of stock appreciation, and omit them from the income statement. But CCA does at least reveal the appreciation in the balance sheet; Lifo suppresses it completely.

Lifo versus inflation charges

We may conclude from these arguments that Lifo is on less sure ground than Fifo plus an inflation charge. Instead of adding a calculated and defensible charge to costs, Lifo-users put an unduly small stock-at-end on the other side of the income account, and hope this error will cancel the unexplored time-lag error. Their income theory is implausible, their profit may be inaccurate even on their own premises, and their method covers up important figures.

Whether these objections will in fact prove strong enough to discredit Lifo is another matter. If we concede that any remedy must in real life be rather rough-and-ready, perhaps we should not condemn Lifo too harshly. It is already in wide use, is fairly well understood, and may be more acceptable politically than a direct and intelligent method. These are not inconsiderable merits.

Other aspects

Tax relief

The peak inflation of 1974 caused a liquidity crisis for many British firms. As a result, the government was forced in 1975 to give belated tax relief for the error on both stocks and depreciation. After various stop-gap rules had been tried for stocks, the Finance Act, 1981 brought in a system that avoided CCA (because of its subjectivity and other defects) and geared relief to an 'all stocks' index.

When inflation fell, this relief was unfortunately withdrawn (1984).

Stabilised accounts and the error on cost-of-goods-sold

In its attempt to lay bare the error in the clearest way, this chapter has used ordinary accounts as its examples, and merely updated the cost £s to make them match the revenue £s. This limited correction is another example of the 'first-aid' mentioned on p. 87—as distinct from stabilisation of all the items in both the income statement and balance sheet. Stabilisation also corrects the error. But its curative action does not stand out plainly, and so it seems less suitable for a first exposition. In particular, the stabilised accounts may not show which of the possible corrective methods is in use: the accountant cannot stabilise without first choosing between, e.g. the maintenance of real and physical capital, and this choice should be obvious.

For an example, let us look again at Table 9.4, and stabilise its figures—in the £ of 31 December, when the general index (GI) has reached 120 and the specific index (SI) 140. Several types of stabilised accounts, analysing profit by different criteria, suggest themselves. The one used in Table 9.7 springs from column (3) of Table 9.4 (cost corrected with SI , income with GI). It assumes that opening capital (equal to the stock) was £475.

Column (2) lets readers at 31 December see all the results in contemporary £s. It has the further advantage of showing (in this format, in the balance sheet) the real holding loss on stocks between September and December (when the SI rose less than the GI), and on cash between March and December.

Falling prices

This chapter would be incomplete if it left out price decline. In particular, it must look at the 'lower of cost or market' rule; and it must compare the behaviour of Fifo and Lifo in bad times.

Lower of cost or market When current values of any stock items fall beneath historical costs, caution suggests that the lower figures should be substituted—the 'lower of cost or market' rule (here shortened to Coma). Thus the Fifo cost of closing stocks may, in bad times, be changed into a market value of the year-end (net realisable value). The rule is applied separately to each item; so this 'pick and choose' system results in a mixed total of old and new values. So far, the US tax authorities have resisted pleas for the rule to be stretched to Lifo; but this need not stop a firm from using both rule and Lifo in its own accounts.

Table 9.7 Example of Stabilised Accounts with Stocks

				(1) *Ordinary figures cost correct with SI and income with GI £*		(2) *Stabilised version of (1) end-£*
Income statement	GI	SI				
Previous						
30 September	95	95	Lot 1. Opening stock	475		
Current			Purchases			
31 March	105	105	Lot 2	525	×120/105	*600*
30 September	115	138	Lot 3	690	×120/115	*720*
				1215		
				1690		
30 September	115	138	*Less* Closing stock, Lot 3	690		
			Cost-of-goods-sold			
			Historical cost	1000		
			Replacement charge	215		
			Replacement cost	1215		*1320*
			Sales:			
31 March	105		Lot 1	735	×120/105	*840*
30 September	115		Lot 2	805	×120/115	*840*
				1540		1680
			Profit			
			Operating	325		*360*
			Real realised holding	115	×120/115	*120*
			Corrected accounting	440		*480*
Balance sheet						
31 December	120		Cash	325		*325*
			Stock	690		*700*
				1015		1025
			Capital	475	×120/95	*600*
			Inflation allowance	100		
			Real profit—Realised	440		*480*
			Unrealised[8]			*–20*
			Loss on holding money[9]			*–35*
				1015		*1025*

Example of falling prices Our usual example can help again. Table 9.8 shows the new twist. To make the figures harmonise with those in earlier tables, one must envisage a year set in a longer stretch of falling prices. Columns (1) and (2) use Fifo. They assume opening

Table 9.8 Income Statements—Falling Prices and Various Valuation Methods

Date	Index General	Index Specific		(1) Fifo £	(2) Fifo and Coma £	(3) Lifo £
Preceding						
30 September	105	105	Stock at beginning	525	as (1)	500
Current						
31 March	95	95	Purchases: first half-year	475		475
30 September	85	62	second half-year	310		310
				785		785
				1310	1310	1285
31 December	80	57	*Less* Closing stock	310	285	500
			Cost-of-goods-sold	1000	1025	785
30 June	90	90	Sales	1260	1260	1260
			Ordinary profit	260	235	475
			Add Deflation credit	100	100	
			Corrected profit	360	335	

stock to have been bought for £525 when general and specific indices stood at 105; the Lifo figure is, say, £500. Lot 1 of the purchases is bought at 31 March, when the indices are at 95. Lot 2 (the end-stock) is bought for £310 at 30 September, when the general index is at 85 and the specific index has tumbled to 62. By the end of the year, the two indices stand at 80 and 57, and the Coma value of the end-stock is only £285.

Column (1) of Table 9.8 puts ordinary Fifo profit at only £260. If Coma is superimposed, i.e. if the account recognises unrealised holding loss, closing stock must be written down to (57/62) × £310, i.e. to £285 (column (2)); thus ordinary Fifo profit is now only £235. Because of Lifo's insensitive way of valuing stocks, it fails to recognise holding loss realised during the year, and so Lifo profits do not respond quickly to price fall. Column (3)'s profit of £475 is much higher than both the Fifo versions (but could be cut to £260 by using Coma).

Correction for deflation Can Lifo's extra profit be defended as a correction for the general fall in prices? The answer is that it is a move in the right direction, but may not be accurate by the general index test.

The inflation argument must here be reversed. Inflation calls for an extra cost (e.g. the £100 charge in Table 9.4); deflation calls for a deduction from cost. In column (1) of Table 9.7, we must re-express an early cost (£1000) in the later and more valuable £s of sale date; the cost is incurred on average at general index 100, and the sales take place at 90, so cost should be reduced by $[(100-90)/100] \times$ £1000, i.e. the 'deflation credit' is £100. Fifo profit, column (1), is raised to £360; if we judge by real capital maintenance, things are not so bad as historical accounts say. Coma's deflation credit, column (2), may not unreasonably be £100 too. (But a purist might argue that December's stock write-down of £25 (= £310−£285) should be corrected to £s of sale date, i.e. to £28; then column (2)'s deflation credit would be reduced to £97.)

Appendix: Approximate inflation charges

It may be useful to illustrate a simple way of finding approximate general (or specific) index charges when real stock-on-hand is not constant.

Table 9.9 shows the income statement for a calendar year with many purchases. The turnover period is some three months; the stock in a balance sheet is thus (on Fifo assumptions) bought at about 15 November, and the mid-point of the 'stock year' is about 15 May. The specific index is assumed to rise faster than the general index,

Table 9.9 Income Statement with Complex Stock Changes

Date	*Indices*			£
	General	*Specific*		
Preceding				
15 November	95	95	Opening stock (Fifo)	950
Current year			Purchases	4350
				5300
15 November	99	110	*Less* Closing stock (Fifo)	1320
			Cost of goods sold	3980

and physical stock to grow somewhat, so that the total investment in stocks grows considerably.

The approximation method assumes that the extra physical stock is bought as a single lot in the middle of the stock year, so that the error consists of: (a) appreciation on the opening stock for the first half of that year, plus (b) appreciation on the expanded stock for the second half. (a) can be found by calculating appreciation on the opening stock, and (b) by discounting the closing stock. Let us say that the general and specific indices stand at 96.5 and 101 on 15 May. Then the calculation is:

Period	*Stock*	*Appreciation* *General*		*Appreciation* *Specific*	
	£		£		£
November–May	(Opening) 950 ×	$\frac{96.5-95}{95}$	= 15 ×	$\frac{101-95}{95}$	= 60
May–November	(Closing) 1320 ×	$\frac{99-96.5}{99}$	= 33 ×	$\frac{110-101}{110}$	= 108
	Approximate charges for year		48		168

So uncorrected profit should be reduced by £48 (general-index test) or £168 (specific-index test).

This method will become more inaccurate if the sales do not centre on the middle of the business year, or the stock transactions on the middle of the stock year (although this fault may be lessened by choosing more representative dates). And, as it depends on opening and closing stocks, it cannot allow for peaks within the year.

References

1 Some accountants speak of the flow of costs rather than of physical units. Viscount Simonds described how this approach is used with Lifo:

> It must in the first place be explained that Lifo does not mean that the metal last to be received into stock is in fact the first to be processed and sold. On the contrary the actual physical flow of the raw material is regarded as irrelevant: that which was purchased in previous years and was in stock at the opening of the relevant financial year or that which was purchased during that year may have been processed and the products sold during that year: this is of no account. It is to cost that Lifo looks, and in the simplest terms it means that the cost per pound of the metal most recently purchased and added to stock is the cost per

pound of metal content to be charged against the next sale of processed metal products. It is the necessary corollary of this that to the stock which is in fact in hand at the end of the year there must be attributed the cost of metal which has not yet been exhausted by the cost attributed to metal consumed; this has been called the unabsorbed residue of cost. *Minister of National Revenue* vs *Anaconda American Brass Ltd.* [1956] 2 W L R at pp. 35, 36.

This has an agreeable air of sophistication, and makes the argument sound better. But it still has all the faults inherent in value theories based on cost; and it hardly seems to prove that any given sequence assumption is better than the rest.

2 A full description of Lifo (covering history, technique, statistical results and tax rules) is given by Butters, J.K. and Niland, P. (1949) *Inventory Accounting and Policies*, Harvard University Press.

3 *Ibid.*, p. 37.

4 *Minister of National Revenue* vs. *Anaconda American Brass Ltd.* [1956] 2 WLR 31; [1956] 1 All ER 20. The basestock method was likewise rejected in *Patrick* vs. *Broadstone Mills Ltd* [1954] 1 WLR 158; [1954] 1 All ER 163. Thus the principle of 'lower of cost (Fifo) or market' now seems to reign in British tax practice. See Edey, H.C. [1956] 'Valuation of stock in trade for income tax purposes', *British Tax Review*, June.

5 The methods laid down by the US tax regulations are: (a) in the year of adoption, all opening inventory units are valued at average cost; (b) any physical increase in a year is valued at its cost (earliest, average, or latest of the year), and this sum is carried forward in subsequent years; (c) any physical decrease ('liquidation') leads to the omission of the latest items in the preceding inventory, valued at whatever historical cost was chosen at stage (b) and then stage (d) (*Internal Revenue Code*, section 472).

6 Zannetos, Z.S. [1954] 'Involuntary liquidations of Lifo inventories', *Accounting Research*, October.

7 A comment quoted by Butters and Niland. *op. cit.*, p. 121.

8 Real holding loss on closing stock between 30 September and 31 December:

	£690	(120/115 – 140/138)	= £20

9 Loss on holding money:

31 March–31 December	£210 ×	(120 – 105)/105	= £30
30 September–31 December	115 ×	(120 – 115)/105	= 5
	£325		£35

The workings of Fifo and Lifo were explained algebraically in the first edition of this book, page 91.

10

The Time-lag Error in Accounting Profit: (D) Depreciation

Chapter 13 will discuss possible ways of improving the stereotyped 'depreciation methods' by which accountants write down the historical cost of depreciating assets. This chapter takes the methods as given, and asks how far their charges are subject to the time-lag error.

The error, as we have seen, occurs when any input is charged in £s whose value does not match that of the corresponding revenue £s. The argument would seem to apply with equal force to stocks, depreciating plant, and any other asset that 'circulates' through the income account (e.g. an intangible asset that is written down).

'Primary' and 'secondary' assets

In discussions of depreciation, it is useful to speak of the *primary asset* and *secondary assets*. The former is the depreciating asset that is being studied. The latter are the extra assets acquired as a result of charging depreciation. (The charges reduce profit; reduced profit tends to restrict dividends; the firm can use the retained cash to invest in extra assets.) The secondary assets accumulate over the life of the primary asset, so offsetting its fall in value and maintaining total wealth.

'Secondary assets' are not necessarily 'current assets'. True, when goods are sold, it is normal for liquid assets to be received in return. In time, however, if such assets are retained to offset depreciation, they will be invested in whatever ways seem most rewarding, and thus become diffused throughout the asset structure, e.g. as stocks and even other depreciating assets.

General price change

We shall, as usual, start with general price change alone. We shall suppose that the price of a new depreciating asset moves in step with the general index; and that the prices of all the firm's other assets do the same—which implies its net money assets to be zero.

Bookkeeping for general-index adjustments

Once again, the simplest way to correct the profit and loss account is to supplement the normal cost (i.e. historical depreciation) with an inflation adjustment.

If correction becomes part of the double-entry system, the adjustments can be credited to the inflation allowance, and shown in the balance sheet as part of the equity. (If they are instead subtracted from the original price of the asset, along with normal cumulative depreciation, the net balance may soon become incongruously small or even negative.) At the end of the asset's life, the accumulated credits in the inflation allowance should not be touched. They are a lasting re-expression of the owners' capital, etc., to be kept permanently unless a fall in the price level justifies transfers of 'deflation credits' back to the income statement.

Example Let us adapt our staple example by turning its annual cost figure (£1000) into a charge for depreciation. Suppose that a capital of £4000 has just been invested at general index 100 in a machine with a four-year life, and that a historical charge of £1000 is each year being written off under the straightline system of depreciation. Inflation sets in, and general prices rise by 20 points per year, i.e. by 10 per cent at average sales date of the first year. Corrected profit is paid out as dividend. If the ordinary accounts of the year are given 'first-aid' correction for the time-lag error, they run as in Table 10.1.

The error's pattern over the asset's whole life

The size of the time-lag error on any given input depends on the size of s/c (see p. 88), which, during inflation, grows with the length of

Table 10.1 Accounts Showing General Index Correction of Depreciation Charge

		Ordinary figures corrected
Income statement	£	£
Sales		1540
Depreciation:		
Historical	1000	
Inflation charge £1000 × [(110/100) − 1]	100	1100
Corrected profit (= dividend)		440
Balance sheet		
Primary asset		
Historical cost		4000
Less Depreciation on historical cost		1000
		3000
Secondary asssets (1540 − 440)		1100
		4100
Capital		
Legal		4000
Inflation allowance		100
		4100

time between the cost and the resulting sale. Thus one can expect the error to rise as the input's 'turnover period' lengthens. Many depreciating assets have long lives; the inflation charge on such an asset may therefore in late life be high relative to the historical-cost charge.

Suppose, in our example, that the inflation continues throughout the four-year life of the machine, with the index mounting by 20 points a year. Table 10.2 shows the charges over the whole life. Column (3) gives the historical-cost charges. Column (4) gives the inflation factor, reflecting the increase in prices between the purchase date of the year's input and the average sale date of the

Table 10.2 Depreciation over Asset's Whole Life

(1)	(2)	(3)	(4)	(5)	(6)	(7)	(8)	(9)	(10)
			Yearly correction			*Equivalents in end-of-year 4 prices*			
Year	*General index*	*Historical cost charge* £	*Factor*	*Inflation charge* £	*Total (i.e. current prices) (3)+(5)* £	*Factor*	*Historical-cost charge (3)×(7)* £	*Inflation charge (5)×(7)* £	*Total (8)+(9)* £
0	100								
0.5	110	1000	10/100	100	1100	180/110	1636	164	1800
1.5	130	1000	30/100	300	1300	180/130	1385	415	1800
2.5	150	1000	50/100	500	1500	180/150	1200	600	1800
3.5	170	1000	70/100	700	1700	180/170	1059	741	1800
4	180								
		4000		1600	5600		5280	1920	7200

resulting output. Each successive historical charge is, in terms of buying power, more inadequate than its predecessor; so the inflation charges rise as in column (5), until in the fourth year they reach 70 per cent of the historical charge. In most countries, the rate of inflation has been slower than the example suggests. On the other hand, many machines last far longer than four years, and so the deficiency of the final historical charges may reach or surpass this degree of shortfall.

Need earlier provisions be adjusted for 'backlog'?

Looking at the £100 inflation charge calculated with the June index of the first year, one may ask whether it is big enough, since by 31 December the index has risen past 110 to 120. Should not a further charge be made against income, to raise this £100 to £200 at the year-end? The answer seems to be that £100 is the right sum, i.e. it is what is needed to maintain the purchasing power of the original capital. In purchasing power, 1100 mid-year £s are the same thing as 1200 end-£s; so our charge of only £100 raises the depreciation provision sufficiently, and no subsequent topping-up charge against profit is needed. A revaluation of the secondary assets may well support this view. Revenue normally flows in throughout the year, on average, say, at mid-year; the firm can thus invest surplus revenue in non-money secondary assets while their price index is still on average at 110. Because of the general rise in prices, secondary assets worth £1100 at June become worth £1200 at December; real wealth is intact.

Similar reasoning answers another question that is often put. The initial investment of £4000 (at index 100) has the same buying power as 7200 of the £s current at the end of year 4 (index 180). Even the augmented charges that column (6) envisages (£1100 in year 1, £1300 in year 2, and so on) will not provide anything like such a high figure; in fact, column (6) adds up to only £5600. Must we each year not merely augment the historical charge of £1000 with an inflation charge, but also look back and top-up still further all the accumulated provisions of earlier years? (And 'top-down' if the index ever sinks?)

Such 'backlog' revisions are not needed. The question betrays the confusion spread by historical accounts. To see things clearly, one must turn from the figures of columns (1) to (6) to their stabilised counterparts, columns (7) to (10). These retell the whole story of the cumulative provision in terms of year 4's end-£s. They explain how the earlier figures have in real terms grown in pace with inflation. Column (10) shows that the final values of the depreciation charges add up to 7200 end-£s, i.e. maintain capital exactly. In effect, topping-up has already taken place automatically and invisibly. Or, looking at the question from the asset side of the balance sheet, one can suppose each year's depreciation provisions to be invested in whatever secondary assets the firm thinks most suitable; if these are non-money (as our analysis has so far assumed), they should thenceforth tend to appreciate with the inflation, and so maintain their real value.

In fact, non-money assets may not be bought at once, nor are they likely to appreciate with such textbook precision. But any variance should be ascribed to the faults or merits of the firm's financial and investment policies, and not to the reckoning of the depreciation charges. If the cashier absconds with secondary assets, this does not show that depreciation has been wrongly calculated. So long as each year's charge allows for current depreciation, managers have done this part of their job in full, and need not bother further with the old entries.

However, analysis is not action: management has merely exchanged one burden for another. It must still take pains to see that the real value of the secondary assets is maintained, and make good any shortfall, e.g. by restricting dividends. This is another reason why the careful measurement of asset values is important.

Specific price change

Next consider the situation in which general prices are fairly constant, but the replacement price of the primary asset changes.

Here the specific-index man will charge CCA depreciation. His first step is likely to be the revaluation of the primary asset (either by appraisal or use of a specific index). For instance, if the firm in our example believes in revaluation, and the replacement price of the machine rises 5 per cent just after purchase, the gross book-value would be put up from £4000 to £4200, as in Table 10.3. A revised depreciation charge—£1050 instead of £1000—follows as a byproduct. Income is cut by £50.

Table 10.3 Accounts Showing Specific Revaluation (General Prices Constant)

	(1) *SI model* £	(2) *Alternative model* £
Income statement		
Sales	1540	1540
Cost (depreciation calculated on replacement price of £4200)	1050	1050
Operating profit		490
Add Realised holding gain (1050 – 1000)		50
Total profit (= dividend)	490	540
Balance sheet		
Primary asset		
Current value (new)	4200	4200
Less Depreciation	1050	1050
	3150	3150
Secondary assets (*Less* Dividend)		
1540 – 490	1050	
1540 – 540		1000
	4200	4150
Capital	4000	4000
Revaluation gain on primary asset:		
At revaluation date	200	
After subsequent depreciation		150
	4200	4150

The reasoning of Chapter 8 is again relevant. It suggests that (there being no inflation) ordinary historical accounts here yield a sounder profit—£(1540 – 1000 = 540). It recognises that the CCA charge of £1050 is the better measure of input sacrifice; column (2)'s arrangement—somewhat akin to the hybrid model—shows this charge, but also the £50 of realised appreciation, and so keeps profit at £540.

Columns (1) and (2) both raise the asset value by £200 to £4200, and thereafter write off this increased figure like ordinary depreciation. In column (1), the £200 credit is kept as a permanent addition to capital. Column (2) treats it as a form of (unrealised) income—which it is, if real capital is used as a benchmark; when slices of it are deemed to become realised, they are transferred from the balance sheet to revenue (e.g. £50 in the table).

The specific-index viewpoint

The specific-index man does not permit the £50 addition to revenue. He supports his view (see p. 109) by pointing to the troubles that will beset some firms if they do not save the full amount needed to replace an old machine with another of the same physical capacity. These troubles are real enough. The counter-argument does not deny the wisdom of putting aside the extra sums for replacement, but considers these to be not costs but voluntary appropriations to pay for what is really expansion.

This point can be made more vivid with the 'Rolls-Royce won in a raffle' approach. If you pay 5p for a raffle ticket and win a £70 000 car, should your friends congratulate you on your luck, or commiserate with you because your depreciation costs will now go up? The commiseration view is sound enough so far as it goes: you will indeed suffer loss in future years as your car wears out, and your profit and loss account could well charge extra depreciation. Why then does commiseration strike you as nonsense? Because it recognizes your *loss* of wealth, but not your *prior gain* of that wealth: it calls for debits in your profit and loss account, but ignores a potential credit. To give a full picture, each year's account should show both depreciation and original gain realised; over the whole life, the cost and gain cancel, and you are back where you began, i.e. you have exactly maintained your original capital of 5p. If you decide to replace your Rolls at the end of its life with a second one, then you are bent on expanding your assets (compared with their original size), and must seek the extra finance as best you can. And this view would still seem to hold where there is real appreciation in the value of a machine bought in the ordinary way (though here the lesson is not rammed home by the advent of an extra physical asset, and so is less obvious). Real depreciation thereafter goes up, but only because the firm first makes a real gain from the appreciation of its assets; over the years, the two real movements cancel.

Replacement cost can be intolerably high

If the specific index rises sharply, the replacement cost charge for the current year could be high. Moreover, if replacement-cost accounting is not to fail in its aim, presumably the provisions of former years must be topped up to current level, i.e. the situation is no longer so comfortable as that described on p. 156 where general price change automatically raised the former provisions.

Indeed, should not this year's provisions attempt to meet the estimated *future*, not the current, replacement cost? Where inputs can be replaced at once—as with stocks—current cost is the same thing as replacement cost. Where they will not be replaced for a long time—as with most depreciating assets— current cost may prove a very poor guide to ultimate replacement cost, and can be defended only as a shortcut that avoids guesswork about remote prices.

One way and another, the charges could reach an embarrassing size, and indeed might cut profit to a level at which no dividend could ever be paid. Only a very stern breed of owners would wish to save on this heroic scale: most men would instead make post-replacement plans for working on a lower physical level of activity, or for financing the same physical level by raising fresh capital from outside (as with any other kind of economic expansion).

Other aspects of the specific-index case

The specific-index case has obvious allure for firms seeking an excuse to pass on increased replacement costs to others, e.g. a monopolist who must justify his high prices before a government commission. If (in the absence of inflation) he is allowed to charge depreciation in excess of historical cost, then his unfortunate customers must make him a present of the expansion of his business.

However, prices can fall as well as rise. Indeed, real fall is very likely with machines, because of improving technology. Then an owner who charges only the falling replacement-cost depreciation will have good cause to doubt whether he is maintaining his capital in a satisfactory sense. And what happens when a firm decides not to replace the asset? Is depreciation here zero?

Real change combined with general change

This last stage in the argument must deal with the position where both general and specific indices change, but to differing degrees. Here the mechanics become a trifle more intricate, but the principles stay the same.

Unravelling general and real changes

In this true-to-life situation, the total holding gain in a year's input (i.e. the excess of specific-index depreciation over historical-cost depreciation) should for clear understanding be split into two parts, (a) that part found with the general index—the inflation charge on pp. 153–4), and (b) the remainder, i.e. real holding gain (or real 'cost saving') on the asset during its 'turnover'. If the argument of earlier pages is valid, the inflation charge is still the proper means for correcting income; the real gain merely adds extra information to both sides of an income account.

Example To illustrate this matter with our main example, let us say that both general and specific indices start the year at 100; that in the next few days they rise to 110 and 115 respectively; and that they rise no further. Thus the year's input grows in money value by £150, but in real value by only £50. By the test of real capital maintenance, the income statement should still end like that in Table 10.1, with corrected income at £440. If the accountant wants to spell out the whole story (stopping short of full stabilisation), he needs something on the lines of Table 10.4. This charges depreciation at CCA level, but also credits the £50 real gain.

Table 10.4 Depreciation Charge Adjusted for General and Real Change

	£	£
Income statement		
Sales		1540
Depreciation		
Historical cost	1000	
Inflation charge	100	
Real realised holding gain	50	
Current replacement cost		1150
Operating profit		390
Realised holding gain		50
Corrected profit (= dividend)		440
Balance sheet		
Primary asset—revalued at 115		4600
Less Depreciation		1150
		3450
Secondary assets (1540–440)		1100
		4550
Capital		4000
Revaluation gain on primary asset (3450 – 3000)		450
Inflation allowance		100
		4550

Other matters

Records of date

To calculate inflation charges, etc., one must know all the relevant dates. Therefore, adequate plant records are needed; and published reports could helpfully show both cost and depreciation figures for all disposals. A firm with many depreciating assets should, for easy calculation, group them according to purchase years; the same index factor can then be applied to the total historical cost of each group.

Mid-year or end-year depreciation charge?

If they use a one-step price rise, both CPP and CCA examples evade an important issue. In the income statement of Table 10.3, for instance, the £1150 cost is in effect measured in mid-year values, and yet ties in neatly with an asset value of balance sheet date. But what if the index goes on rising after mid-year, so that mid-year and end-year £s differ in value? Should the year's depreciation charge then tie in with the mid-year or end-year index?

Suppose the input consisted of a single unit of stores, all converted into product and sold at mid-year, and not replaced. Here the logic of charging the input at the price of mid-year (rather than end-year) seems plain; the mind is not distracted by a figure in the end balance sheet. Why then should the logic change when similar assets are still held at balance sheet date? If this view is right, the year's depreciation charge should reflect the prices of input date (approximately mid-year in most cases).

Unfortunately, such a charge cannot tie-in with revalued figures in the balance sheet. In the example of Table 10.3, suppose the price of a new asset continues to rise between July and December, to £5000. Then, though the charge should stay at £1050, the value of the (one-quarter worn) asset is £3750, i.e. its depreciation is shown as £1250.

	(1) *SI model* £	(2) *Alternative model* £
Balance sheet		
Primary asset		
Current value (new)	5000	5000
Less Depreciation	1250	1250
	3750	3750
Secondary assets	1050	1000
	4800	4750
Capital	4000	4000
Revaluation gain	800	750
	4800	4750

Because the balance sheet writes up the non-existent one-quarter asset, it must also raise depreciation by an equal amount. Both movements aim solely to give more information in the balance sheet, and do not affect income.

Accelerated depreciation allowances

In general, accounts recognise the gravity of the time-lag error, but dislike to abandon traditional methods. So they may try to meet the depreciation shortfall by speeding up the normal process of writing off historical cost. Thus, they may adopt a depreciation formula that makes heavy charges in the early part of the life of the asset (perhaps justifying this by pointing to abnormal physical activity in the early years); or they may write off an arbitrary initial allowance in the first year. There may well have been a tendency to switch from the straight-line to the 'fixed percentage of the declining balance' and (in the USA) the 'sum of the digits' and 'double-rate, declining balance' methods.

All such tricks for speeding up depreciation are useful during inflation. Thanks to them, the firm can set aside receipts earlier than it would do otherwise, and so is more able to buy new assets before their price has risen much. However, so long as any part of the asset's cost is not written off shortly after purchase, historical charges are bound to be inadequate. The only satisfactory course for those who regard historical cost as sacrosanct is to write off 100 per cent depreciation as soon as the asset is bought. From this angle, the unfashionable method of allowing for costs by charging renewals instead of depreciation may in some circumstances work well.

Tax concessions

Tax authorities in countries where inflation is mild tend to disallow inflation charges, etc., in computations of income for tax purposes. But they have been more generous about accepting the accelerated methods.

As a grudging concession to rising prices, British tax law in 1945 began to make various arbitrary arrangements that boosted capital allowances (and so reduced tax) in the early years of an asset's life.

These concessions have been continued; they reached their highest level between 1975 and 1984, when there were 100 per cent first-year allowances for most machinery and plant.

Replacement when there are many depreciating assets

Though it seems right to take a single asset as the starting-point for a study of replacement, one should be wary about generalising from such simple arithmetic.

In practice, the flow of depreciation funds can become an intricate pattern; often it can be comprehended only in terms of complex formulae. A firm may have many assets, with uneven life spans; it can choose between several depreciation methods (and in particular can adopt accelerated methods); it gets tax concessions on new assets; and often its total plant is growing. Only a rash person would dogmatise on the net effect of all these factors. But there are some grounds for thinking that a growing firm, using accelerated depreciation methods, can meet replacement burdens (even during inflation) with less strain than our one-asset example would suggest.

Depreciation and borrowed money

Some types of reform (e.g. the gearing adjustment of SSAP 16) presume ties between loan and depreciating assets. This seems unfortunate, for two reasons:

1 Probably in logic it is unsound to link a given asset with either loan or equity. These should be looked on as jointly providing a financial pool; in the long run, all assets are financed from this merged source.
2 A clear analysis of profit must (see page 95) measure and show separately both (a) the whole inflation adjustment for depreciation, and (b) the whole gain on owing. Any offset blurs important facts.

The time-lag error and the trade cycle

So far, we have considered only the error's effects on a single firm.

But the error will be repeated, at much the same time, in a great many firms. So we must ask whether it may not have had wider social effects, notably by influencing the traditional trade cycle.

When prices rise on the upswing of such a cycle, the error overstates profits in innumerable accounts; when prices fall, it understates them. Such mass alternations seem likely to aggravate the ups-and-downs of the cycle. They could do so in particular by affecting investors' expectations. Cheerful profits make businessmen hopeful, and thus tempt them to expand. Gloomy figures make them cautious and unventuresome.[1]

Over the months of a trade cycle, the depreciation errors will tend to move with a rhythm that loosely reflects the movements of prices above and below their average. Error will be positive (and boost profit) while prices are above, and negative (and depress profit) while they are below; it will distort most when prices are at their peak and nadir. The stock error would seem to depend more on the steepness of price change; if so, it boosts profit most when prices are rising fastest, and (particularly if reinforced by the lower-of-cost-or-market rule) depresses profit most when prices are falling fastest; thus it may change course ahead of the peaks and troughs.

If these notions are sound, they add a powerful—though seldom heard—argument to the case for reform. They suggest that the accountant must bear some of the blame for the major social ills of boom and slump—a rhythm that was of great importance prior to 1939, and may well reassert itself at some future time.[2]

Stabilisation

To show the effects of the time-lag error as simply as possible, this chapter has confined itself to 'first-aid' correction of the ordinary accounts. Full stabilisation (of all the figures in both income statement and balance sheet) would of course also cure the error; the appendix gives an example.

Appendix: Illustration to various types of price-level reform

A simple example may help to contrast some of the alternative reforms that have been suggested for depreciation accounting.

Data

A new firm's transactions are:

19x0	31 December	Receives £1000 capital and uses it to buy a machine. General and specific indices = 100.
19x1	1 January	General index rises to 110, and specific index to 115; thereafter they stay at these levels.
	30 June	£550 rents are received for hire of machine.

Possible treatments

Some alternative versions of the half-year accounts are given in Table 10.5. They are:

(A) *Ordinary accounts*. (Column (1).

(B) *Accounts with time-lag error corrected (but without asset revaluation)*. In column (2), cost is adjusted with the general index, i.e. income is found by the real-capital sub-concept.

Column (3) uses the same income sub-concept as (2), but cost is adjusted with the specific index, and the resulting £5 real gain is credited.

In column (4), income is found by the physical sub-concept, i.e. cost is adjusted with the index but the £5 is not credited.

(C) *Stabilised accounts, in end-£s*. As a further elaboration, the corrected figures of columns (2) and (3) can be stabilised in various ways. Thus all the historical figures of the balance sheet can be raised with the general index; column (2) then turns into column (5), and equity and non-money assets go up by 10 per cent. Again, the asset can be raised with the specific index (the full hybrid system); column (3) then turns into column (6).

Notes and References

1 The trade-cycle effects have been explored, in particular, by K. Lacey: see, for example, his *Profit Measurement and Price Chang s*, Pitman,

Table 10.5 Various Forms of Price-Level Adjustment for a Depreciating Asset

	(A) *Ordinary accounts*	(B) *Correction of time-lag error*			(C) *Full stabilisation*	
	(1)	(2)	(3)	(4)	(5)	(6)
Type of capital maintained		*Real*	*Real (current cost shown)*	*Physical*	*Real (CPP)*	*Real (Hybrid)*
	£	£	£	£	*end-£*	*end-£*
Income statment						
Depreciation. Historical	100	100	100	100		
Adjusting charge		10	15	15		
Total charge	100	110	115	115	*as*	*as*
Rent	550	550	550	550	*(2)*	*(3)*
Operating profit			435			
Realised real appreciation			(115−110) 5			
Profit	450	440	440	435	*440*	*440*
Balance sheet						
Asset—Cost (new)	1000		Details as in (1)		*1100*	*1150*
Less Depreciation	100				*110*	*115*
	900				*990*	*1035*
Cash	550				*550*	*550*
	1450				*1540*	*1585*
Capital	1000	1000	1000	1000	*1100*	*1100*
Allowance—inflation		10	10			
replacement				15		
Profit—realised	450	440	440	435	*440*	*440*
unrealised						*45*
	1450	1450	1450	1450	*1540*	*1585*

1952. They are discussed in Haberler, G. (1941) *Prosperity and Depression,* pp. 49–50, Columbia University Press; Schiff, E. (1933) *Kapitalbildung und Kapitalaufzehrung im Konjunkturverlauf,* pp. 113–34, Wiener Institut für Wirtschafts und Konjunkturforschung, and Ray, D. D. (1960) *Accounting and Business Fluctuations,* University of Florida Press (which argues that the error's effects are slight).

2 The above paragraphs summarise an argument that is set out more fully in the first edition of this book, Chapter 11.

11

Accounting Opinion and the Error

For shortness and clarity, this book has so far concentrated on its own line of reasoning, and thus has not done justice to views held elsewhere. It must now consider the rival approaches, and especially those embodied in Standards.

Early debate

Rather surprisingly, an early debate on CCA was caused by *deflation*. Many US railroads were built soon after the Civil War, at a time of peak prices. Later in the nineteenth century, regulatory commissions (setting the rates charged to users) insisted on considering the lower current cost of assets; the railroads naturally argued for historical cost. After prices rose in 1914, commissions and railroads veered around.[1]

One or two theorists began to write about inflation accounting at the end of the First World War, and F. Schmidt (professor of business administration at the University of Frankfurt) produced notable work after the 1923 German inflation. Earlier pages of this book have paid tribute to the works by Sweeney (1936) and Edwards and Bell (1961). In recent years, there has been a flood of articles and books.[2]

A census of these writings would (I suspect) reveal a majority in favour of CCA rather than CPP—not only in asset and cost measurement (where I agree with them), but also in income measurement (where I disagree, for reasons set out in previous chapters).

The defence of historical cost

Practical accountants have been much divided on the time-lag error. They hardly recognised its existence till after the Second World War. The stiff dose of inflation in the late forties made it big and conspicuous, particularly when it prompted businessmen to say harsh things about their accounts and to demand tax reform. The complaints stirred up warm—even heated—debate on whether accounts could contain error. For long, opinion among accountants tended to be incredulous of this charge, and hostile to any reform; but the continuance of inflation, and lively criticism in financial journals, gradually won many converts.

Accounting is often described as 'conservative'. Now, this can mean many different things—some good, some not. For instance, the accountant is conservative when he uses methods that paint a firm's results in cautious hues and discourage reckless dividends; but he is also conservative when he uses methods that no longer work well but save him trouble. In the past, both forms of caution have tended to point to the same methods, and one could not tell which form was the stronger. With inflation, they point in opposite ways; cautious conservatism asks for reformed methods to maintain business capital, while sleepy conservatism supports the old methods that erode it. The outcome of the argument will show which strain of conservatism is dominant.

Inflation charges as costs or appropriations?

The accountant had several reasons for disliking and misunderstanding the case for reform. The very ease with which historical costs can be gathered in a ledger gave him something of a vested interest in such figures. Again, he probably was confused by the intermixing of general with specific price change; this clouded the problem by raising questions of whether inflation charges are costs or appropriations.

In the days when company accounting was taking shape (say, 1850–1914), few accountants had cause to worry over general price change. The only kind of price change that entered into their theory was specific change. They decided that such movement in asset values is often irrelevant to income measurement; and that, where the financial difficulties of replacing dearer assets led to the gesture of transfers to reserve, the charges in income account were not costs but appropriations, and so must be put 'below the line'.

In the context of specific price change, this procedure may well (as Chapter 8 argues) be logical. Unfortunately when accountants at last came to face general price change, many of them applied the old logic to the new facts. The adapted argument therefore ran: inflation raises asset values; a firm that wants its accounts to allow for this increase in the money value of inputs is no doubt wise; but it must treat the extra charge as an appropriation and not a cost. Charges against income must be confined to historical cost.

Stewardship record or up-to-date photo?

The above argument was reinforced by the view that accounts are not meant to give a current picture of assets and inputs, but are instead a record of stewardship. Thus the balance sheet's duty is to show what moneys have been received as capital, etc., and how they have been spent on assets. (This was no doubt one of the original aims. But, though a historical record has its uses, to add or subtract £s of different dates is to invite confusion. And, if we now want to revise the balance sheet's duties, surely we may do so.)

Organisations and orthodoxy

Corporate groups of accountants, like individuals, have varied in their reactions to the time-lag error. But in general the accounting bodies were for many years hostile to reform. Perhaps it is salutary to recall—particularly as accountants now pin such high hopes on Standards—how near-sighted some of the collective pronouncements on inflation have proved.

The Institute of Chartered Accountants in England and Wales first dealt with the topic in Recommendation XII (1949). This statement by the Council summarises the arguments of the reformers and the conservatives. For example, the latter 'claim that not only is the suggested change wrong in principle, but also that it strikes at the root of sound and objective accounting because of the practical difficulties of assessing the amounts which would be treated as charges to revenue if the new conception were adopted'. Then follows the Council's own analysis of the problem, and its conclusion in favour of historical cost.

The accounting press welcomed this document, but outside comment was less favourable and indeed derisive. Possibly the Council realised that Recommendation XII was tending to bring accountants into discredit, for in 1952 it published Recommendation XV on the same subject. This is more cautious. Though it ends by backing historical cost accounts, it concedes their limitations and encourages experiment.

The American Institute of Certified Public Accountants also stood stoutly by historical cost. Its attitude was in part a reaction to excesses during the boom of the twenties, when some companies raised asset values to an extent that later seemed scandalous.[3]

Standards

In the late sixties, resistance to reform started to crumble. At least the leaders of accounting bodies became convinced of the need for change. They succeeded in issuing a series of Standards on inflation; these show both the leaders' determination and their difficulties in choosing an acceptable type of reform.

The Accounting Standards Committee (representing the main British bodies) was set up in 1969. It has issued a number of somewhat conflicting pronouncements on inflation. These are listed below. The space given to them may seem unduly small. This is not because they were unimportant—far from it—but because the various issues at stake can be analysed more systematically in separate chapters. Further, the pronouncements form a continuing saga, and a long discussion of the current Standard may well soon be obsolete.

Provisional Statement of Standard Accounting Practice No. 7 (1974)[4]

This recognised the gravity of the time-lag error, and sought to correct it with general-index factors. It called on quoted companies to include a CPP statement as a supplement to their published reports. The supplement consisted of a stabilised income account and balance sheet, and a note reconciling the historical and stabilised profits.

In retrospect, these proposals seem admirable as first steps to reform. But unfortunately the infant Standard was abandoned almost as soon as it was born. The government did not take kindly to the proposals, presumably because reformed income statements would have strengthened the case for not taxing unreal profits. So it quickly set up its own (the Sandilands) committee, to see what fresh minds could make of the problem.

They gave short shrift to the general index, and backed physical capital maintenance (CCA) instead. As a corollary, they argued that loss or gain on money should be ignored—an odd conclusion in a study of inflation. They adopted the notion of deprival value (explained and recommended in the next chapter) as the basis for asset value. Their report is impressively long and well written, but on balance has (to my mind at least) done great harm.

The government welcomed these views, and told the accounting profession to take steps to put them into effect. The accountants, instead of sticking to their guns, jettisoned CPP, and formed another committee to implement the CCA proposals.

Exposure Draft 18 (1976)

The new committee set about its work at a great pace. It soon split up into various sub-committees, each charged with the task of reforming one bit of accounting, e.g. the fixed assets. The separate proposals were tacked together as ED18. The completed model was both complex and ungainly, and perhaps introduced more reforms—good and bad—than was wise as a first step.

ED18 was launched with unwonted publicity. For some months, it aroused little opposition. Then, as the time drew near for its adoption as a Standard, two private members of the English Institute put up a motion that members 'do not wish any system of current cost accounting to be compulsory'. Rather surprisingly, the motion was adopted in a big poll. This in effect killed ED18. We could long debate whether the objectors were deplorable reactionaries or men too wise to swallow a half-baked scheme.

The Hyde Guidelines (1977)

After this rebuff, the ASC set up yet another committee, to draft less ambitious proposals. These were still based on CCA, but had the advantage of being fairly simple. They excited less opposition, and after a trial period were incorporated into a more formal scheme, Standard 16. It was adopted.

Standard 16 (1980)

This requires larger companies to publish (either as a supplement or part of the main accounts) inflation-adjusted figures, using CCA throughout.

The new balance sheet shows assets at current values. The basis seems not unlike deprival value; but, presumably to disarm opposition, the phrase 'value to the business' is used instead. Appreciation is credited to a 'current cost reserve'.

The new income statement starts with the historical-cost profit. This is then subjected to four CCA adjustments. The first two aim to reduce trade profit to CCA level. The others try to allow for inflation's ill effects on money owned, and good effects on money owed.

The four adjustments are:

1 *Depreciation*. To raise the historical charge to replacement level.
2 *Cost of sales* (COSA). To do the same for stocks consumed.
3 *Monetary working capital* (MWCA). To allow for loss on cash and debtors, less gain on creditors.
4 *Gearing*. To allow for the gain on long-term liabilities.

In each case, the opposite side of the double entry is in the 'current cost reserve'.

Comment on the adjustments

Adjustments 1 and 2 are not unlike the first-aid corrections of earlier chapters, and so have the merit of simplicity. The usual arguments for and against physical capital apply to them (see

Chapters 8, 9 and 10). They are likely to be popular with firms whose input prices rise faster than the general index, but unpopular when the cat jumps the other way. Accountants and auditors will in some cases have great trouble in defining 'replacement' and in revaluing fixed assets.

The adjustments for monetary items are complex and more controversial. A Standard that is wedded to physical capital must face difficulties when it tries to allow for the £'s decline; after all, the physical number of banknotes, etc., does not shrink. Its solutions to this problem are remarkable for their ingenuity if not their logic.

Adjustment 3 for loss on 'monetary working capital' argues thus: debtors are closely connected with sales of stock; creditors are closely connected with purchases of stock; some minimum cash float is needed for dealings in stock; so, to measure the erosion of these three items, treat them as if they really were stock—i.e. use the stock index of adjustment 1.

The resulting charge will sometimes be quite different from what is commonly regarded as inflation's effects on money. Thus the firm's stock index can vary from the general index; and the definition of minimum cash float—a highly subjective matter—may exclude a big cash surplus from this adjustment (as where the firm holds a 'cash mountain'). And many firms have insignificant stocks (e.g. banks and insurance offices); presumably they must perforce use the general index. One cannot but suspect that there will here be scope for plenty of cosmetic calculations, and that the final 'income' will be much too subjective for legal and tax purposes.

The above three adjustments aim to maintain the firm's 'operating capability'—a phrase that may help to make the notion of physical capital less vague. Surplus after these adjustments is named 'current cost operating profit'.

Adjustment 4 to show how inflation has lightened the burden of long-term debt—uses an impressively convoluted device. It raises profit by a fraction of the other three adjustments. The fraction is that of debt to (debt plus equity).

Thus the Guidance Notes to the Standard suggest the following four steps:

1 Find the loan (L). This could be the average of the net borrowing in the opening and closing balance sheets, or a weighted average.

2 Find the equity (S). This should again be an average, of shareholders' funds including preference shares and minorities, as they would be calculated in a revalued balance sheet.
3 Find the gearing fraction, $L/(L + S)$.
4 Multiply the three current cost adjustments by this fraction.

The usual example puts L at £800 and S at £1200. Then the fraction is 800/(800 + 1200) or 40 per cent. If the three other adjustments total £300, the gearing adjustment is 40 per cent × £300 = £120. So profit is raised by £120.

As Chapter 6 emphasised, gain on loan is important. But this form of gearing adjustment—is hard to explain, justify, or calculate with precision. It has at least three major faults. It does not directly recognise the inflation rate. It must be small in size when the other three adjustments are small (e.g. for firms such as investment trusts that do not own machinery or stocks, but may be highly geared). And, despite the Standard's claim to the contrary, it takes credit for gain (exactly comparable with appreciation of land) that normally will not be realised for many years.

The reception of SSAP 16 has been very mixed, but most of the big companies seem to be adhering to it loyally. It is to be reviewed after a trial period.

An arithmetical example is given in the appendix to this chapter.

The American Standard

Most other English-speaking countries have issued inflation standards. But the American version is the most interesting.

Its story parallels that of the British Standard in a rather odd way. First a non-governmental committee, the Financial Accounting Standards Board (FASB), in 1974 issued an exposure draft that backed the general index: companies were to supplement their reports with a second set of accounts expressed in constant $ units. Then the government (in the shape of the Securities and Exchange Commission (SEC)) quickly killed this plan: in 1975 it required large companies to show instead replacement costs (in notes, and for a limited set of items only).[6] The FASB was thus forced to draw in its horns, and to devise a Standard that would not clash with the SEC rules.

It solved the problem adroitly in Standard 33. This is in many ways more reasonable and tentative than SSAP 16. It requires large companies to use *both* CCP and CCA. Various experimental formats (in a supplementary statement) are permissable; they must disclose costs and incomes by CPP and by CCA. Gain or loss on net monetary items is shown separately. The statement need not include revised balance sheets, but must disclose the CC amounts of stocks and of property, plant, and equipment, and real gain on these.

Appendix

Comparison of Various Methods

Problem

Data

		£
1 January	Machine (new) with four-year life	40
	Stock of inputs: 100 units at cost	100
	Trade debtors and cash float	60
		200
	Capital	120
	Loan	80
		200

2 January	General index rises by 20% to 120
	Machine price falls by 10% to £36
	Stock price rises by 25% to £1.25 per unit
31 December	Stock: 100 units at £1.25, £125
	Debtors and cash (before dividends), £60 − £250 + £300 = £110
3 January to 29 December	Prices constant
	Purchases: 200 units at £1.25, £250
	Sales: 200 units at £1.5, £300

Solution

Income statement	A *Historical cost*		B *CPP*		C *Hybrid*	D *SSAP 16*			
Stock at start	100		120						
Purchases	250		250						
	350		370						
Less Stock at cost	125		125						
Cost of sales	225		245	200 @ £1.25	250				
Depreciation	10		12		9				
Total costs	235		257		259				
Sales	300		300		300				
Trade profit	65		43		41	As in **A**			65
Realised holding gain						Adjustments:			
Goods sold				250−245	5		225−250	−25	
Depreciation				9 − 12	−3		10−9	+ 1	
Monetary working capital		(20/100)×60	−12		−12		(−25/100)×60	−15	
								−39	−39
									26
						Gearing		15*	15
Net profit (= dividend)	65		31		31				41

Balance sheet

Debtors, etc, *less* Dividend	45		79		79			69
Stock	125		125		125			125
Machine, net	30		36		27		+3	27
	200		240		231			221
Loan	80		80		80			80
Unrealised real gain: money		(20/100)×80	16		16	'CC reserve'	→	21
machine				27−36	−9			
Capital	120	×120/100=	144		144			120
	200		240		231			221

$$* \quad \frac{1}{2}\left\{\frac{80}{200}+\frac{80}{221}\right\}=0.38; 0.38\times 39=15.$$

Required Final accounts based on the above figures.

A Ordinary form (i.e. historical cost).

B CPP form (= general index only), with full stabilisation.

C Hybrid form, combining current cost charges and values with real income.

D Standard 16 form.

Assume the profit of each form is paid out as dividend and tax.

Here the CCA profit is bigger than the CPP version. The former includes the gain on loan; the latter puts this into the balance sheet as unrealised real gain. The gap between the two profits could be still greater if specific and general indices had moved differently.

Notes and References

1 Boer, G. (1966) 'Replacement accounting: A historical look', *Accounting Review*, January.

2 This early ferment is reflected in the papers on 'Fluctuating Price Levels in Relation to Accounts', read at the Sixth International Congress of Accounting. 1952. K. Lacey's book, *Profit Measurement and Price Changes*, Pitman, 1952, was a British forerunner. A broad survey of the pioneers is included in Mattessich, R. (1982) 'On the evolution of inflation accounting: With a comparison of seven major models', *Economia Aziendale*, December (in English). Some of the articles are reprinted in Zeff, S.A. (ed.) (1976) *Asset Appreciation, Business Income, and Price-Level Accounting*, Arno Press.

3 For these early reactions, see e.g. American Institute of Certified Public Accountants (formerly American Institute of Accountants), Accounting Research Bulletin No. 43, 1953. However, the Institute also sponsored some able publications with contrary views, e.g. Alexander, S.S., Bronfenbrenner, M., Fabricant, S. and Warburton, C. (1950) *Five Monographs on Business Income,* American Institute of Accountants. Sprouse, R.T. and Moonitz, M. (1962) proposed somewhat radical changes in the *A Tentative Set of Broad Accounting Principles for Business Enterprises,* American Institute of Certified Public Accounts. And this attitude is also found in the Institute's *Research Study No.* 6, 1963.

4 Reproduced in the first edition of this book.

5 Summarised in Tweedie, D. (1979) *Financial Reporting, Inflation, and the*

Capital Maintenance Concept, ICRA Occasional Paper 19, University of Lancaster.

6 For the history of this period, and an excellent treatment of the whole problem, see Fabricant, S. (1978) 'Accounting for business income under inflation: Current issues and views in the United States', *Review of Income and Wealth*, March.

12

Asset Revaluation

Price change brings demands for current values in the balance sheet. So we must now face up to all the problems of whether and how to revalue assets and liabilities.

Such revaluation may be limited to certain items, or cover almost the whole balance sheet. It may be treated as a once-and-for-all step, or as a periodic routine. It may or may not be part of the more thorough going reforms discussed earlier, e.g. full stabilisation. It may or may not be part of the formal process of measuring income—though, where it is not, any gain or loss on revaluation must tend to give much the same impression as figures that are labelled income; and therefore the overtones of income measurement always seem relevant.

A discussion of revaluation must consider the aims of revaluation, not only to decide whether revaluation is worthwhile, but also because the aims influence the choice of methods.

The firm's value versus the sum of the net asset values

A preliminary point deserves attention. Sometimes one must value the firm as a whole (e.g. to find a suitable price for a takeover bid). Then one should normally use the *ex-ante* concept of p. 14, i.e. try to estimate the present value of the future cash flow (of dividends, etc.) that an owner can expect from the firm. The statement that would most help the valuer here would be the firm's cash budget (not its balance sheet). And the market value of the whole firm is most unlikely to be the same as the balance sheet's net total of assets less liabilities (despite the fashionable view that accounts should provide predictive data for investors' decision models). For one thing, the value of the whole must tend to fluctuate, like share prices, with every change in the firm's prospects and market sentiment, whereas assets tend to be inert.

Where the prospects are reasonably good, the whole's price is likely to exceed the sum of the net assets. For instance, one can imagine a valuer deciding that the expected flow of dividends and final capital proceeds is worth £100 000, when the net assets add up to only £80 000. Does the £20 000 gap between the two figures necessarily mean that the separate asset values have been estimated wrongly, or that some shadowy £20 000 asset has been omitted from the list, or that the separate values are useless? I think the answer to all three questions is no. If two values are calculated by different concepts, a gap is entirely proper. Even if methods of valuing each asset are reformed and refined out of all recognition, some gap should still persist.

What good are asset values?

A more pertinent question is whether, if the balance sheet contributes so little to the fundamental *ex-ante* calculation, revaluation of the assets is worthwhile—and perhaps even whether the balance sheet is worth publishing. A wise man will answer rather hesitantly. But it seems not unreasonable to hold that the balance sheet, with all its faults, provides a kind of information that the human mind still needs. The *ex-ante* calculation gives one kind of picture; a list of the existing resources gives another; both can be helpful. If the balance sheet is weak on prediction, it is strong on achievement to date. It provides a neat conspectus of the firm's present size and structure. And, as the next section will suggest, it can give at least indirect help to the investor who is sizing up the firm or its shares.

Imperfect information is often better than no information. Certainly we should recognise all the imperfections of the balance sheet: but to dismiss it as worthless seems too clever by half.

Pros and cons

The case for revaluation

People turn to the balance sheet for an impression of the firm's general nature, size, and ownership structure; they look to it also for help with more detailed problems of asset strength, liquidity, etc. Thus the argument for updating it is that managers, investors, etc. rely on it when making important judgments, and are misled if it fails to reflect the current facts. So far as possible a balance sheet ought to be a realistic model of the firm. But historical costs, even when the general index rests stable, must sooner or later cease to indicate current values. Over the years, the prices of some assets are likely to rise, and those of others to fall. If general prices also move as far and fast as has been normal since 1914, the gap between historical cost and current value may become wide indeed. Then a conventional balance sheet of all save the newest firms is no longer a realistic photograph.

The balance sheet may help with at least five areas of activity.

Investment in shares Decisions on investment in a company's securities can be influenced by the values of its assets. To be sure, the overriding consideration is the estimate of future cash benefits (dividends and final proceeds); the stock exchange price of a share may be remote from the 'asset value per share'. But asset values are useful secondary evidence: normally they give at least some notion of the earnings potential, the nature and efficiency of the asset structure, and whether there will be any break-up receipts if things go wrong. As one company chairman has put it: 'True, net assets do not produce profits any more than mere possession of the tools automatically enables a man to exercise a craft. But a company which possesses enough good "tools" in the form of assets can recover more quickly from bad times and expand even further in good times than concerns with more limited resources.'[1] Further, money values are the only common denominator by which one can compare or appreciate diverse lists of 'tools'. It is easy to sneer at journalistic phrases like 'Fire at £10 million factory', but the words may convey a useful impression. Value totals will inevitably be used to compare the size of different companies, etc. and to find the 'asset cover' for loan or preference capital. Even the man who speaks slightingly of the separate assets would probably think several times before investing in a company with attractive earnings but unusual asset values.

The balance sheet enables an analyst to use ratios (e.g. of current assets to current liabilities) and turnover rates (e.g. of stock). In particular, many investors and managers treat ratios of *earnings to capital employed* as useful guides. Again, a person studying the efficiency of a whole sector of the economy (industry X *versus* industry Y, big *versus* small firms, foreign subsidiaries *versus* home-controlled companies, and so on) often seeks help from these ratios. Possibly their usefulness is overrated.[2] But, without asset revaluation, they must inevitably lose whatever virtue they may otherwise possess. They will then lead to false comparisons between companies whose assets vary in age and type. They will tend during inflation to flatter a company with old assets; its earnings and dividends may look high when compared with its antique book-values, yet be low compared with current values. (The ratio will mislead still more if the time-lag error is also large.) Here the shareholders and financial press are lulled; even the managers may believe that they are doing a sound job, and can rest on their oars; and the seemingly high return on capital may prompt trade unions to demand a larger share of such easy money.

Takeovers and proxy battles are relevant here, because they give such powerful evidence of the extent to which historical figures deceive. Big takeovers could hardly evoke shocked headlines if investors were not ignorant of the values at stake. It is surely wrong that the high current value of assets should come as a surprise; that, deceived perhaps by a seemingly adequate ratio of earnings to assets, managers should for years allow the performance of their firm to lag behind its full potential, to the detriment of both shareholders and consumers; and that shareholders who happen to sell just before the bid should get a price much lower than that obtaining afterwards. Doubtless some of the struggles have tinges of sharp practice, and are harsh to staff. In general, however, we can hardly object to the transfer of assets from less to more fruitful uses.

Nowadays the opposite fault—historical costs that are too high—is not often met. But there have been times, notably during the depression of the thirties, when it was a source of complaint in the USA. New share issues (the allegation ran) could be floated on the strength of fixed assets valued at a cost price that was excessive compared with current value.[3]

Thus a balance sheet based on historical cost fails to give important information to actual and potential shareholders, to the analysts who advise them, and to managers. Their decisions will therefore tend to be less sound than if current values were used. This harms us collectively as well as individually; because we lack clearer pictures of the relative prowess of different firms, industries, and regions, the nation's flow of new capital may be misdirected.

Creditor protection Creditors constitute another kind of 'investors'. A traditional aim of the balance sheet has been to tell them about the firm's ability to meet their claims, i.e. how far the claims are covered by the value of the assets. Plainly, up-to-date figures meet this aim better than old ones. Or, looking at the matter from the firm's standpoint, one can say that sound current values will help to obtain longer credit and fresh loans.

Managers' appraisal of progress and new projects The task of managers is made harder by lack of current values. Without these, it is hard to size up the past profitability of ventures. Where for instance a firm owns several divisions, etc., its manager will have trouble in comparing their performances unless their assets are valued in a consistent and up-to-date way. Bad figures may impair the efficiency of many firms—and therefore of the whole economy.

When managers are weighing up proposed new projects, valuation may be important for their decision budgets. Assets to be bought specially for the project will be costed at the price to be paid for them, i.e. their current value. If assets already owned (e.g. stores) are to be devoted to the project, they too should be costed at their current value; their historical cost may be a very poor measure of the sacrifice involved (as most managers quickly realise when prices begin to rise fast). A good manager must treat bygones as bygones, and cost all inputs in current terms; yet, where historical figures persist in the accounts, the bygones tend to creep into even sophisticated budgets.

Management accountants, like outside investors, make much use of the *ratio of earnings to capital employed*. This ratio is expected to help alike with internal studies of a given firm[4] and with inter-firm comparisons, with post-mortems and with decisions on future ventures. But old asset values can reduce the ratio to nonsense.

Insurance It is hard to believe that insurance cover is kept at the right level if managers have no idea of current values.

Laxness in the matter of fire insurance brings such obvious perils that one may perhaps be pardoned, where managers profess to have no up-to-date values at their disposal, for feeling some incredulity.

Income measurement Out-of-date figures in one part of the ledger are apt to lead to out-of-date figures in another; thus low values for plant go hand-in-hand with low charges for depreciation, and so foster the time-lag error. And the lack of figures for real appreciation (or loss) on assets robs 'income' of one of its dimensions.

Incidental benefits

The process of revaluing may yield certain incidental benefits. Thus, because it will in some cases require managers to think about the best future role of assets, it will draw attention to replacement needs; to consequent problems of finance; and to the possibility of re-developing assets, or (sometimes very important) of selling them when their market values have risen above the values of their services.

Up-to-date asset values may be particularly useful to firms whose costs are subject to public scrutiny. Where the state buys goods from monopolistic suppliers (e.g. munitions, drugs for the health service, etc.) at agreed prices, such values can help investigators to decide whether the profits are a normal return on capital employed. The same may hold where the state regulates public utilities.

There are sometimes legal, as well as economic, grounds for using current values. In the UK, shares qualify as trustee investments (under the Trustee Investments Act, 1961) if *inter alia* the company has an issued and paid-up capital of at least one million pounds. Some companies below this status-line could with propriety revalue and then issue enough bonus shares to qualify.

Opposition to revaluation

Though the case for revaluation is so strong, the majority of small firms do not revalue. Thus the counter-arguments must be strong too. The main ones are, (a) revaluation is troublesome and costly, (b) it opens the door to guesswork and deception, (c) it would displease shareholders when prices fall, and (d) it offends against principle.

Argument (a) cannot be lightly dismissed. Revaluation must bring extra work, some of it by senior staff or expensive consultants. Moreover it is not likely to be a once-and-for-all affair; price change is always with us, and so further work will be needed to keep the values up to date. Where the firm and the price change are small, this objection may well be conclusive. Where they are big, it is less so: once we grant that large-scale investment must necessarily lead to absentee ownership, then we must grant also that good communications between firm and owners will be troublesome and costly; the provision of useful statistics for the owners is part of the price to be paid for bigness and remote control. And careful planning can here, as in most other accounting work, point the way to many economies and shortcuts.

Argument (b), that revaluation involves too much guesswork, is also worthy of respect. But accounting is more and more finding that in some areas (notably management decision) figures cannot be both sure and informative. We must give up some sureness if we are to get more information.

Precision and sureness are good things, but they are less so in some contexts than others. Where for instance tax assessment depends on an income figure, they are important since they affect the size of cash payments; and therefore a straitjacket of rigid rules may here be defensible. But does the same apply where the aim is to give readers of a balance sheet a general impression of the assets? Most readers will prefer figures that are helpful though mildly unsure to ones that are misleading but precise.

Revaluation admittedly brings a risk of window-dressing and even dishonest manipulation. But this risk can be kept low by the use of suitable internal checks and new audit methods.

Argument (b) is not something to be disposed of in a couple of paragraphs. This whole book is in a sense a reply to it—a plea for cautious experiment, with plenty of checks, to see whether current values can be used safely.

Argument (c), that write-downs during slumps would displease shareholders, is less serious. Some companies, notably British investment trusts, already show current values that have during slumps fallen steeply; and, under the 'lower-of-cost-or-market' rule, companies dealing in raw materials, etc., must sometimes report heavy falls in stock values. In such cases, the shareholders seem able to take the bad with the good. And probably most investors would agree that topical figures, even when gloomy, serve them better than historical costs.

Argument (d), that revaluation violates principle (of historical cost, conservatism, etc.), has featured in pronouncements by various writers (some eminent) and accounting bodies. Thanks to the educative power of inflation, it is nowadays being used more sparingly in Britain, though it still commands some distinguished support in the USA. To my mind, it is far less weighty than the other objections. Our historical cost 'principle' is really not much more than a belated rationalisation, thought up by theorists anxious to justify a procedure that in fact just grew from the book-keeper's daily routine. This procedure became widespread because it was well suited to the needs of former times. There seems no good reason why we should not now adapt it to present needs.

The accountant has not in fact applied the historical-cost principle consistently. His 'lower-of-cost-or-market' rule for current assets is a clear breach. On occasion, he may revalue fixed assets; thus in a consolidated balance sheet he frequently deems it sound practice to revalue individual assets of a newly acquired subsidiary. Some American companies in the volatile 1919–34 era wrote assets up and down freely (perhaps too freely). Since 1945, many countries that have suffered from severe inflation have used tax rules permitting revaluation (notably Brazil); and these breaches of principle seem to have been welcome and beneficent. The inflation Standards of both Britain and the USA require big companies to show revalued figures, at least as supplementary statements. If today we knew nothing about accounting, and had to think out a system *ab initio*, is it likely that we should prefer old to new values on grounds of principle? Surely the overriding principle in statistical matters is that the more informative is preferable to the less informative.

How do we revalue?

If we accept that we must revalue the assets and liabilities, we must next consider the best way of doing so. We may of course entrust the whole task to an outside appraiser, or change the old figures blindly with an index. But critical users of the accounts will then ask what (if anything) the results mean. If the job is to be done properly, the accountant must give thought to the nature of value, and also to the fundamental rules of accounting; and then he will soon see how sketchy some of these rules are, even in times of relative price stability.

For most assets, there are several possible values, corresponding to the concept chosen (see p. 13). So a valuer should first explore the principles, and decide which concept to use. Even when he has chosen his concept, however, he can still have trouble in applying it, e.g. in finding the needed figures. Thus revaluation may not be easy. With physical measurement, one can reasonably suppose that technical skill will sooner or later yield fairly precise figures, and that they will obey familiar principles. With values, this may not hold. Values stem from human wants, and so must be elusive. We should approach our task with limited expectations and some pessimism.

The next few pages explore the principles, and thus try to find a not inadequate concept for revaluing. Thereafter the chapter shows how far this can be applied to various types of assets and liabilities; but depreciating assets are such a big subject that they are left to Chapter 13.

The principles

A valuer must choose between concepts

If a biologist was told to find the 'growth' of rats, he might reasonably start by asking whether the most revealing unit of measurement would be one of weight, or length, or something else. For valuation problems, likewise, one should choose the most revealing kind of value (historical, current, etc.) for the given task. So, when a professional appraiser is told to make a valuation, he must first ask what it is for. Unthinking clients are apt to be startled by the question, and even to suspect that it has shady overtones. It need have none. The appraiser is entirely right to use one concept for, say, business assets that are to be sold piecemeal, another if they are to be sold as a going team, a third if the valuation is for fire insurance, and so on. In accounting, the main reason for valuing is of course to find figures for annual reports.

Earlier chapters, in dealing with the different concepts of capital and income, suggested that the user of the figures should choose the concept that most adequately answers his questions—that there is no better test of the concept's 'truth' or 'rightness'. Much the same applies to the valuation of separate assets. An unprejudiced valuer will choose, from the long list of concepts (see Chapter 4), the one that gives the best information to the particular user. For accounts, 'best information' is apt to mean the figures that are most helpful for economic decisions.

Difficulties of picking the best value concept

When the values are for use in a balance sheet, the trouble about choosing between the concepts is that the demands of the users of the balance sheet are varied and sometimes vague: it should give them a general picture of the assets' nature, should show the 'size of the tools', should tie in with income measurement, and so on. Moreover, the chosen value should so far as possible be objective, verifiable, and found readily from common transactions. And it should give maximum information not only when each asset is viewed separately but also when the separate figures are summed in a grand total. None of the obvious values stands out clearly as the fittest for such multiple requirements. Obviously the successful candidate in this competition will not be as good as we could wish, and will suit some assets less well than others (e.g. since work-in-progress is remote from market transactions, its link with market prices must be thin). We are here in a no-man's-land between accounting, economics, and appraisal, and cannot expect much help from any of them.

One suggested solution is to show *several* values for each asset, i.e. to issue multiple accounts.[5] There is much to be said for this plan, costly and complicated though it might be. But it would still leave important problems of choice: someone would still have to decide that one set of figures was the best for a given purpose, e.g. the measurement of taxable income.

Individual asset values and their total

These matters can be put rather differently, by saying that the best candidate must meet two tests, the first concerned with any given asset viewed separately, and the second with the total of these separate values.

Separate assets Managers are more likely than outside investors to make decisions about individual assets. Thus the case for a given value concept is greatly strengthened if it has proved its helpfulness for practical purposes within the firm, i.e. if its figures form part of a manager's calculations on the best use of the asset. Some assets—notably those that are often bought and sold—lend themselves readily to this requirement; others are less obliging.

Sum of the separate asset values The sum of the separate values (i.e. the total net assets) should if possible constitute a meaningful figure in its own right—the 'aggregation' or 'additivity' test. As was pointed out on page 182, this total cannot usually equal the value of the firm as a going concern; but it could for instance be the likely total proceeds from selling off the assets piecemeal, or alternatively the total capital that could justifiably be used to buy an equivalent set of assets piecemeal, e.g. if the firm were to set up another branch of the same size. Otherwise we can hardly claim that the balance sheet shows the 'size of the tools' in any helpful sense, or treat its yearly increase as income.

Viewed in this light, some 'assets' (notably intangibles such as research) hardly seem to contribute to a meaningful total. As we shall see, this is one of the most awkward problems in accounting.

Sometimes the two tests may point in conflicting ways. Then one must perforce choose between them. On the whole the second test is perhaps the more telling.

Market price versus personal assessments of worthwhileness

In thinking about these things, it is very important to distinguish between market price and the figure at which a given person might deem a given transaction to be worth his while. This applies to decisions alike on consumption and production. Thus when a householder is considering whether to buy an extra pound of sugar, or whether to sell his antique clock, he compares the price with his satisfaction from its ownership (marginal utility) to see whether the transaction would be worthwhile. When a manager is considering whether to buy a new machine, he compares its price with its likely future contribution (marginal revenue production) by way of higher revenue or lower costs, and so judges whether the purchase is worthwhile. Every buyer and seller has a private set of values that he contrasts with market value to decide to what extent (if any) he will buy or sell—a matter described at length by textbooks on economics. So we must here distinguish strictly between these two meanings of 'value'—market price and subjective estimates of cash flows or utility ('personal value').

Where the good, etc., can be finely subdivided, we may go on buying extra units until personal value of the last unit hardly exceeds market value. Where the good cannot be finely subdivided, there may be a wide gap between the two values. This seems a likely situation with fixed assets. For instance, the village taxi-driver may pay £10000 for his one-and-only taxi because he gauges its contribution at £15000, but may decide not to buy an additional taxi because he gauges its extra contribution at only £7000. He might maximise his profit if he could buy one-and-a-fraction taxis, but their indivisibility makes this impossible; his best plan may be to hire an extra taxi for short periods.

A consumer's estimates of his marginal utility must plainly be highly subjective, and will often lack the crispness of money figures. A manager's estimate of contribution (e.g. in discounted cash flow budgets for judging the worthwhileness of new equipment) employs money figures, and so may look coldly factual. But here too the figures must often be conjectural, particularly where the asset will last a long time: though they take the form of money figures (sales of product, maintenance costs, etc.), they must depend on very personal and changeable views on dates, quantities, probabilities, discount rates, etc., and so may well have much the same subjective and unsure quality as estimates of utility.

Finding market values

When an appraiser estimates the market value of an asset, he is trying to guess what its price would be if a sale really took place. He is greatly helped if he knows of actual dealings in similar assets. For then he can compare the given asset (which we may call the 'unknown') with a similar asset (the 'known'); and he can ask how far the actual price of the 'known' is a guide to the potential price for the 'unknown'. Thus to estimate the sale value of a house, he should know the sale prices of similar houses at recent dates.

Various difficulties can beset him. One is that there may be no exactly similar 'known'. When for instance a house is to be valued, it may differ somewhat from neighbouring houses in size, design, appeal, etc. Even here, however, the valuer should probably work from the known to the unknown; he must in effect combine several knowns, instead of relying on a single one. He presumably begins by finding the price at which a not-too-unlike house has been sold at a not-too-remote date. Treating this as his starting point, he next tries to allow suitably for the variances between it and the unknown. If for example the unknown differs in area, he may argue that market prices work out at so much per square foot, and use this rate to assess the variance. If he is valuing unquoted shares, he may find the price of shares in comparable quoted companies, and then adjust this suitably—subtracting something to allow for adverse variances such as the poorer market in the unquoted shares, and adding something if there are favourable variances. But these 'somethings' may not be the subject of clear market dealings, and so may be debatable: thus the price of a known share may have risen when it got a quotation, but how far was this due to getting the quotation and how far to other new forces? The variances must often be concerned with subtle matters. In particular, how does the market allow for different degrees of risk? And all the knowns will tend to fluctuate quickly and often, with the general tone of the market. (Where securities are to be valued, it is of course easier to twist 'price' around into the market rate of interest or earnings.)

The idea of a known and unknown can often clarify difficult steps in accounting valuation. Suppose for instance that unquoted shares are the subject, and there is doubt over the suggested price because the company is highly geared. The sensible procedure must surely be to ask whether the known shares were in companies with comparable gearing, and, if not, how much the variance should be.

A good valuer has a wide knowledge and intuitive judgment of market prices; even so, his synthetic figures must often be arbitrary and unreliable. When he lacks a clear known, he must peer into markets of his imagination to find a hypothetical price—the sum that might be paid if such an asset were in fact on offer; like the judge who had to value unquoted shares, he 'must enter a dim world peopled by the indeterminate spirits of fictitious or unborn sales'.[6]

Difficulties of defining market value[7]

Sub-divisions of the market A good can well have more than one market value for a given person, since he may deal in what are, for practical purposes, different markets, and on different sides of the counter. Thus he may buy cheap at wholesale and sell dear at retail. Or his markets may lie in different lands linked by slow and costly communications.

If he both buys and sells in the same market, his buying price may or may not be near his sale price. Sometimes the two are separated only by a small brokers' commission, etc.;[8] a wheat merchant may have access to an almost perfect market, and then the sale and purchase prices of his stocks will indeed be almost the same. At the other end of the scale, the market can be small, the units unlike, and marketers ill-informed. Such defects are particularly likely where the asset is 'specific' to the given owner. For instance, there is probably a big gap between the buying and sale prices of your toothbrush, dentures, spectacles, etc.; these seem to be very specific. A manufacturer who needs a highly specialised machine must usually have it made to order; if he wants to sell it thereafter, nobody else may have much use for it, and it may fetch only a small fraction of its replacement cost.

The gap can arise from another cause. Before the asset can fetch the best sale price, it may need an overhaul, etc. Or it may need to be adapted or changed in some more fundamental way. Under this head should probably be put the cost of uprooting and transporting it. Plant may be embedded in cement foundations. Crops or minerals may lie in a remote store. If an oil refinery stands in a desert, the costs of dismantling and taking away the parts may reduce their net sale prices to paltry sums.

Where there is a range of possible prices, the chosen one must (to give serviceable information) be that for which the firm would opt in actual transactions. Buying price must be the lowest available, and similarly sale price must be the highest.

Single units or groups? Sometimes goods can be sold either as single units or by the gross, etc.; or indeed the whole stock can be sold *en bloc*. Likewise a machine can be sold as a whole or split into separate components; or all the machines in a plant can be sold together, with or without spares and other stores. An oil company can keep an asset account for each well drilled, or for a group of wells; with separate accounts, a dry hole must be written off at once, and so depresses current profit—a matter that has caused furious debate in the US oil industry.

What should be the unit for valuation? Accounting's attempts to answer this question show up the inherent weakness of any asset-by-asset approach; our rules on the point are vague. The least unsatisfactory answer is that the chosen physical unit must feature in the firm's common dealings and calculations, and must reflect the most advantageous scale of marketing. Thus if buying price is taken as value basis, and the firm has found that its best plan is to buy a gross of articles at a time, the buying price per gross seems the right choice (and, where a lesser number remain on hand, they should be valued as a fraction of a gross); if the best plan is to buy a machine rather than its parts or a whole team of machines, the price per machine seems the right choice.

Units in their present state or after transformation into product? When sale and purchase prices are contrasted, usually one assumes that both relate to the asset in its current physical state. Thus 'the sale price of our factory's raw materials' suggests the resale of those materials, without physical change, in the market for raw materials. But the most rewarding course with such assets may well be to turn them into finished goods. Then their 'sale price' could mean something far from raw-material price, namely the net realisable value of finished products less future costs of manufacture, etc. The same may hold for work-in-progress. Why stop here? Almost all the assets in a firm (e.g. depreciating machines) can be valued as contributions to output (either extra revenue or cost savings), and may in fact be most unlikely to be sold in any other form. Clearly 'sale price' may be highly ambiguous. If we are to draw a firm line between current values and the *ex-ante* approach to cash flows of the whole business, we must look at an asset's present state only.

For various reasons, then, 'market value' demands a clear definition of the market, of whether the asset is deemed to be bought or sold, and of the unit size; and the definition of 'sale value' must have regard to the asset's state of completeness.

We must next look more closely at the different kinds of value, to decide which of them is most likely to be the best 'standard' for the balance sheet.

Sale price as standard

Sale price (net of selling costs, etc.) is in some ways an attractive candidate for the role of valuation standard. Some influential writers have adopted it—in particular, Professor R. J. Chambers in his system of 'continually contemporary accounting' (CoCoA).[9]

There are several arguments in its favour. Thus the total of potential receipts from the piecemeal sale of all assets is a statistic that creditors may well deem important (and 'creditors' also covers, for example, the policy-holders of an insurance office and any government department that acts as their watchdog). Again, the advocates of sale price argue that a manager wants to know how much money he could marshal for new projects, i.e. how much he could at a pinch raise by selling off assets piecemeal. Valuation at sale price gives him this figure, and may also give him a rough notion of how much he could raise from creditors, mortgagees, etc. Further, it can draw attention to assets that the firm would be wise to get rid of (because their sale price is high relative to their earnings in the firm). In the same way, the sum of the sale prices has meaning as the minimum potential proceeds from going out of business and selling all the assets piecemeal; it may thus be the benefit forgone by staying in business, and so an ingredient in the most momentous budget of all. And it can be useful for other decisions. For example, in budgets for showing whether or not a machine should be replaced by a new model, the old machine should usually be put in at sale price. In short, 'the single financial property which is uniformly relevant at a point of time for all future actions in markets is the market selling price or realisable price of any or all goods held'.

This is all very true. On the other hand, the chances that a healthy firm will scrap the assets needed for everyday production are hardly big; and so their sale prices are not likely to feature in everyday decisions. The latter are far more often concerned with normal production and investment, for which different values are needed. Admittedly the ability to raise cash for new projects is to some degree linked with the sale prices of the assets; sale and lease-back is an excellent example. But otherwise one can scarcely imagine a manufacturer selling off chunks of his plant to finance its output: only a crisis or fundamental change of role would justify such dismemberment. An extra venture is usually financed from the more liquid assets only, or by borrowing; and potential lenders and investors tend to be impressed even more by the prospect of high and sustained earnings than by scrap values (though certainly these can be comforting background information).

Moreover 'sale price' can cover a range of urgency, from a leisurely sale in the ordinary course of business to sale in a distress situation at almost any price. If assets will not in fact be sold in any probable circumstances, then surely (one is tempted to suggest) a valuer should envisage the improbable circumstances. But what would be the least improbable circumstances that would cause a wholesale scrapping of fixed assets? The near-bankruptcy of the firm? And is this conceivable unless there is a general crisis and slump, with a consequent collapse of sale prices? Once a valuer is forced to work on artificially gloomy assumptions, there seems no end to the spiralling catastrophies that he must envisage. I might argue that the most plausible sale price of my piano is what it will fetch as firewood during the next ice-age; and yet that price hardly seems to add much information to my current balance sheet.

With highly specific assets, moreover, sale price may be far below purchase price; and then it is a bad measure of 'size', and leads to an excessive earnings: assets ratio. It may lead also to absurd results if it is linked with income measurement: where the firm must at once write off the difference between a new asset's cost and sale price, the accounts may show a loss if the firm buys useful but specific machines, and a profit if it buys unsuitable machines with a high resale value. This seems a major objection to use of sale price.

There is some case for valuing stocks at sale price in the rare situation where the excellence of the market guarantees that the firm can sell its whole output without trouble or uncertainty. This probably justifies plantations and mines in valuing stocks at net realisable value. In general, however, sale price hardly seems a good standard, save when assets are on their last legs or the firm is on the brink of liquidation.

The *retail method* of valuing stocks, at sale price minus average gross profit margin, does not seem to fit into this section. It usually is better looked on as a shortcut to valuation at approximate historical cost.

Contribution to net revenue as standard

Another possible candidate is the 'personal value' of page 192—i.e. not a market value but the asset's future contribution to net revenue (by raising receipts or lowering outlays). This is sometimes called 'economic value'—a handy but inept term, for surely market values are equally 'economic'.

Such a figure can be of great service in some kinds of calculation, e.g. in the 'capital budgets' (often using discounted cash flows—DCF) for showing whether the initial purchase of a given type of asset is worthwhile. But that does not make it a strong candidate for frequent use in the balance sheet. Most of us expect the latter to give much the same information as we should get from an ordinary inventory of our assets; and we also expect such an inventory to use familiar and reliable values, usually linked with market prices. Personal value is often a matter of wild guesswork, sometimes about complex possibilities in the remote future; further, it may be warped by momentary optimism or gloom. The other value standards may involve at least some element of guesswork (e.g. on the future life of a depreciating asset); but a large element would be unsuitable in routine accounting, particularly if it entailed elaborate budgets for each of many assets. Only where the other values clearly fail to fit the facts should we use personal value.

There is another objection. If personal value is used for all the assets in turn, if often offends the additive test (p. 192) by making the sum of their separate values absurdly high. Consider a firm whose value as a going concern does not by any useful method of assessment exceed £20000. Suppose it has two assets, A and B, both essential to production and both hard to replace. If A is destroyed (say, by fire), the owner may in desperation decide that its contribution justifies payment of a very high price, perhaps approaching £20000, for quick replacement. If B instead is destroyed, he feels the same about it. But the total of these values, nearly £40000, far exceeds the value of the whole. And the more links there are in the chains of assets, the more enormous and useless the total becomes.

These views on personal value may suggest misguided hostility to DCF budgets, etc. But in fact, as we shall see, thoughtful use of comparative budgets is what justifies one's choice of value candidate in any given set of circumstances—and normally disqualifies personal value.

Replacement cost as standard

Later pages will suggest that replacement cost (i.e. current buying price) has strong arguments in its favour, and fewer defects than sale price or contribution (personal value).

But there are times when it too does not seem suitable. In particular, the owner may think the asset not worth replacing—because its contribution has declined (e.g. a machine becomes out-of-date, merchandise becomes unfashionable), or its replacement price has grown too high, etc. Sometimes replacement is 'impossible' (e.g. because a given model is no longer made); but here the argument will be simpler if it is couched in terms of a forbiddingly high price rather than physical shortage.

'Deprival value' as standard

If the reasoning of earlier pages is sound, what is needed for the standard is a concept that normally uses replacement cost, but on suitable occasions substitutes a lesser value. We shall call this *deprival value*. (It has other names too, e.g. Standard 16 uses 'value to the business'.)

Such a *selective* standard is grounded in common sense. If for instance a works manager is drafting a budget to compare the costs and revenues of a proposed job that will use up material already in store, normally he can reason: 'When the stores are issued, I'll have to order more of them. So the sacrifice caused by their use is their replacement price.' But sometimes the stores will not be worth replacing (e.g. because they have become obsolete); and then he will rightly argue that the sacrifice is less than replacement cost.

Or we might make the issues more vivid by imagining some melodramatic situation. For instance, if a thief threatens to make off with one of your assets, but offers to refrain if you pay enough, what is the highest sum that he can prise from you? Usually your ceiling will be replacement cost—i.e. this is here deprival value. But sometimes you will stick at a lower figure, because you do not deem the asset worth replacing; here the lower figure takes over as deprival value. Or insurance compensation may serve as an analogy. If an insurance company offers you compensation for an asset that is lost by, say, fire, deprival value is the sum—replacement cost or less, according to your opinion of the asset—that will in your own eyes seem just as good as the asset, i.e. will 'make you whole'.

Thus the concept has a negative twist: it hinges on loss from deprival rather than (as is usual in our notions of value) gain from acquisition.[10]

The concept was probably first discussed in depth by Professor J.C. Bonbright of Columbia University. It has been tacitly adopted by the British standard-writers, but is sadly neglected in the USA.

Deprival value and alternative cash budgets

Usually the easiest way to find deprival value is to draw up alternative budgets (in one's head or on paper) showing the future cash flows that depend on the possession of the asset. The valuer thus adopts the economist's 'what difference does it make?' approach, and compares alternatives.

Since the owner has already taken the step of acquiring the asset, the 'difference' does not here turn on the advantages of its acquisition but *on the disadvantages of its loss*. His two alternative possibilities are that he will (a) cease to possess the asset, e.g. deprive himself of it by using it up on a job, or lose it by theft, etc., or (b) continue in possession. The valuer must draw up cash budgets for each of these two scenarios. Plainly the owner's future cash flow will normally be worse under (a) (say, because he will have to pay for replacement) than under (b). The gap between the alternatives is the cash advantage of ownership, i.e. the value of the asset by this concept.

The value will vary greatly with the circumstances of the particular asset. If a deprived owner's best policy would be to replace the lost asset, replacement price must clearly loom large in the budgets. Indeed, one may then be able to say without more ado that replacement cost measures the value of the asset exactly, and that there is no need to draft the budgets; here the valuer's task is made simple. However, it is the reasoning of the budgets that gives logic to even a simple valuation, and budgets become essential when the facts are complex, e.g. when a half-worn asset would be replaced by a new and very different model. So we must look at the budgets with some care. I propose, for shortness, to call their two columns the

Have not and *Have* budgets. To begin with, we shall suppose that replacement (with an exactly similar physical unit) would be worthwhile.

Illustration: alternative budgets where replacement is worthwhile

As a simple example, suppose that an item in a shopkeeper's stock is expected to sell for £8 (net of future selling and delivery costs), can be replaced for £4.8, and is so profitable compared with other lines that the shopkeeper would (if it were lost to the shop, say, because he took it for home consumption) replace it with an exact duplicate. A possible way of calculating its value is given in Table 12.1; this may look unduly pompous for such straightforward facts, but sets out the essentials in what seems the clearest manner. Column (2) shows what the relevant cash flows will be if the asset stays at the owner's disposal and he sells it in the ordinary way. Column (1) shows what they will be if instead the asset is lost but then replaced and sold. Here the owner, if deprived of the asset, can and will 'make himself whole' by buying a duplicate for the replacement price of £4.8. This sum

Table 12.1 Alternative Budgets to Show the Role of Replacement Cost in Finding Deprival Value

	Future cash flow if the asset:	
	(1)	(2)
	is lost and replaced ('*Have not' budget*)	*stays at owner's disposal* ('*Have' budget*)
	£	£
Outlay:		
Replacement cost of duplicate	−4.8	
Revenue:		
Sale proceeds	8	8
Net receipts	3.2	8
Difference (= advantage of owning asset)		4.8

emerges as the difference between the two columns, and is the 'differential' or 'deprival' value of the asset. So we are here in the simple situation where replacement cost meets our need.

Because the asset or its replacement both sell for £8, that figure appears in both columns (1) and (2) in Table 12.1—and so does not affect the answer, and might just as well have been left out. This is an important point: items common to both columns are irrelevant. Usually it is revenues that are common.

Importance of replacement cost

The above budgets seem fairly typical. We may reasonably suppose that, for the great majority of assets, replacement cost is the basis of deprival value.

Sometimes the role of replacement cost is less obvious. What do we mean if we say enviously that a neighbour's house has appreciated in value, and is now worth £x? We are hardly thinking that it will give him more enjoyment (and he himself may grumble that appreciation means more insurance costs, property taxes, etc.). He does not mean to sell his house, so increased sale price is of secondary importance. But he does mean to go on living in such a home; so, as he already has this one, its ownership saves him the need to spend £x. 'Replacement cost obviated' is here the soundest justification for our statement.

Where the asset is not worth replacing

The above paragraphs dealt with assets whose replacement is worthwhile, e.g. whose revenue exceeds replacement cost. But sometimes the asset is not worth replacing. This may be because replacement price has risen (at the extreme, to the immense height at which one says the asset is 'unobtainable'); or the contribution may have fallen, e.g. merchandise may have become unfashionable.

In such cases, deprival will not result in the owner buying an exact replacement. Indeed, he may already be planning to get rid of assets of this type as fast as possible. So here the cost of an exact replacement should not be put in the budgets. Deprival robs the firm not of this sum but of whatever the asset can still contribute (in its best use) to the firm's cash flow. In other words, *when the contribution is less than replacement cost, it becomes a relevant part of the deprival budgets*. We now see where personal value (the 'recoverable amount' of Standard 16, and 'contribution' above) fits in: it sets a lower limit to deprival value.

The argument can be boiled down to a diagram:

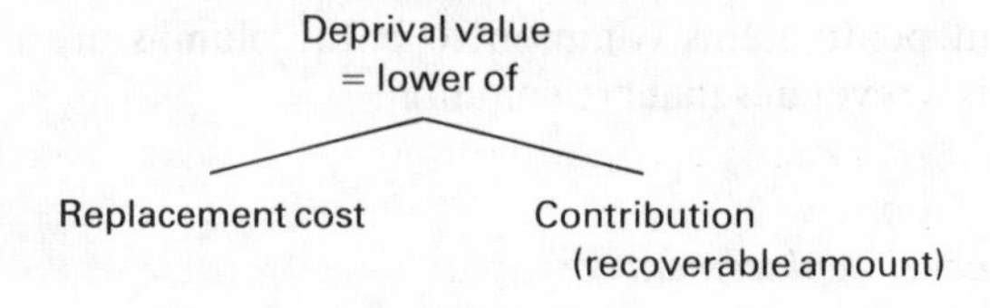

The contribution can take one or other of two forms: (a) the net revenue from the asset's early sale, or (b) use (or 'economic') value—normally the cost savings from keeping and using the asset, but sometimes future revenues (e.g. from hiring out the asset). Let us look at these possibilities in turn.

Net realisable value as deprival value Where the disappointing asset is stock intended for sale (e.g. an article in a shop), the highest contribution will usually still come from sale. Then deprival value is sale price less any future costs of completion, selling, etc.—i.e. is net realisable value.

Table 12.2 Alternative Budgets to Show the Role of Net Realisable Value When This is Below Replacement Cost

	Future cash flow if the asset:	
	(1) *is lost and not replaced* (*'Have not' budget*)	(2) *stays at owner's disposal* (*'Have' budget*)
	£	£
Revenue—net proceeds	—	4
Difference (= advantage of owning asset)		4

So here the asset's deprival value is its resale price as scrap, £4.

Suppose for instance the asset of Table 12.1 does not sell when priced at £8, and the owner decides that his best course is to sell if off at a price of only £4. After the sale, he will not pay the replacement cost of £4.8 for a duplicate that may also sell for £4 or less, i.e. he will not replace; and likewise if he is deprived now he will not replace. Thus the replacement cost of £4.8 has ceased to be of interest, and should be left out of both columns, as in Table 12.2.

Use value as deprival value Sometimes deprival value lies in a zone between replacement cost and net realisable value. The asset is not worth replacing, but is still worth keeping because its contribution (e.g. future cost savings) is worth more than net realisable value. Here the contribution is the deprival value.

As an example, take a new machine that was expected to save £1600 of wages, but now seems likely to save only £500. Its replacement cost is £600, so the owner will not replace it. He can get only £400 by selling it now (and nothing later on). The formal budgets are:

Table 12.3 Alternative Budgets to Illustrate Zone Between Replacement Cost and Scrap Price

	Future cash flow if the asset:		
	(1)	(2)	
	is lost	*stays at owner's disposal and is to be*	
		(a) *Sold*	(b) Used
	£	£	£
Gains: Scrap proceeds	—	400	—
Wage saving	—	—	500
	—	400	500
Difference between between (2b) and (1) (= advantage of owing asset)			500

The cash flows in column (2b) are better than those in (2a), i.e. the owner's best plan is to keep the asset in use. So budget (2a) can be ignored. Comparison of (2b) with column (1) shows that the benefit of owning the asset, i.e. the desired value figure, is £500.

We can now expand the diagram on p. 204 to:

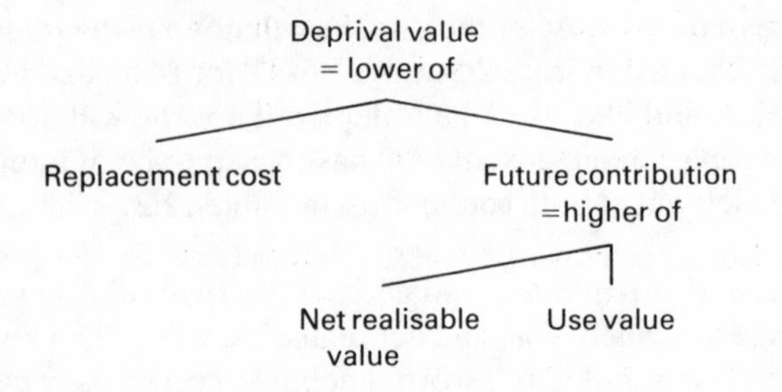

So far, we have assumed the potential replacement to be an asset more or less identical with the present one. The reasoning must be modified where replacement would be different.

Where the asset will be replaced by a different type of asset

An asset can differ from its potential replacement in many respects. Thus the demands of customers or the methods of the firm may have changed in ways that call for a changed kind of asset, or (particularly where technology is improving fast) the model on sale today may bear little likeness to the model bought some years ago. This is apt to seem a major stumbling block to the calculation of value. But in fact it is not, though admittedly it may make the valuer envisage a more elaborate series of figures. Provided deprival would trigger off a series of consequential cash flows, one can still compare *Have not* and *Have* budgets, and thus find a deprival value for the existing asset. The comparison of two sets of cash flows is what matters, even where the *Have not* column envisages a very different 'replacement'.

Suppose the existing asset is priced at £600, and its use value is £700. The £100 surplus would justify replacement; and so replacement price gives the deprival value of £600. But now a better model is invented—price £650, use value £900; the £150 increase in surplus makes it the potential replacement.

What effect has the invention on the vaiue of the old asset? Clearly the latter's attractiveness (relative to its potential replacement) has sunk. Everyday speech might describe it as semi-obsolete. So we may well expect its value to have fallen; deprival budgets confirm that it has, and have the merit of explaining the reason (Table 12.4). So deprival value is cut from £600 to £450, i.e. by the £150 extra surplus that the new model confers. And the invention of still better models would cut the value further.

Table 12.4 Alternative Budgets Where the Replacement has Improved

	Future cash flow if the asset:	
	(1)	(2)
	is lost	*stays at owner's disposal*
	£	£
Use value	900	700
Replacement price	(650)	—
	250	700
Relative advantage of owning asset (deprival value)		450

Note that simple diagrams—like that on page 204—may become unhelpful if the new and old assets differ. There are three reasons.

1 Replacement *cost* ceases to be the same as replacement *price*. Cost is now price adjusted for change in benefits.[11]

2 Suppose a series of new models, each better than its precursor, comes on the market. At some point, the owner of an old asset will decide that it is obsolete, and should be replaced.

If he were deprived now, he would lose not use value but net realisable value (e.g. scrap proceeds or trade-in). Net realisable value here provides a floor to deprival value.

3 Sometimes the changes consequent on deprival would be so great that the word 'replacement' hardly fits ordinary speech. For instance, the cheapest 'replacement' for a little-used machine may be the occasional hire of another machine, or the use of more labour; deprival would make the owner pay more rent or wages. So deprival value is here the 'cost obviated' on a remote and perhaps unexpected factor.

An asset's value can vary though its own prospects are unchanged

Table 12.4 illustrates an important point. When an asset's value is defined as a gap between budgets, its size must vary not only with any change in the asset's own budget, but also with change in the budget of the potential replacement. If for instance the replacement's budget improves, then the value of the asset drops—even though its future contribution still looks as good as ever. As financial journalists say, market values move 'in sympathy'.

Thus the value of our asset A depends partly on the net benefits from its rivals B, C, D. 'Every valuation is a comparison; we have no conception of an absolute utility or an absolute standard of utility. The notion of value is meaningless except in relation to alternatives of choice.'[12]

The formal set of deprival budgets

It may be helpful if (at the risk of repetition) I slightly rephrase my description of the deprival-value arithmetic.

One should perhaps start by visualising the full set of budgets on which deprival value rests—though often the valuer can reach the right answer with a single mental step or few columns.

The 'deprival method' tells the valuer to ask (a) how can the undeprived firm best deal with the given asset (shown, if the answer is not obvious, by alternative columns in the *Have* budget), and then (b) if deprival occurred, should the firm replace (something shown, if the answer is not obvious, by alternative columns in the *Have not* budget), and finally (c) how much is the difference between the courses indicated by (a) and (b). This difference is the loss on deprival, i.e. the asset's value.

Why the contribution to future cash flows is often irrelevant to deprival value

The hardest bit in the deprival reasoning seems to be the relevance or otherwise of future contribution (to revenue or cost saving). When and why should it be excluded? So, at the risk of labouring the point, let me restate the argument. And I must warn you that many distinguished theorists reject my view; in particular, some of them hold that a depreciating asset should be valued by discounting all its future revenues or cost savings.[13]

If a deprived owner would in fact replace an asset, and its contribution is common to both the *Have not* and *Have* columns, the contribution cannot be part of his loss on deprival. Replacement cost is enough to restore his position in full. A purist would maintain that both economy of style and marginal logic demand the exclusion of the contribution from the two columns.

In other words, so long as the contribution exceeds replacement cost and is the same in both budgets, it is irrelevant, and *deprival value can then be found without reference to the asset's future earnings or cost savings*.

This view often accords with everyday reasoning. If your living depends on your having a car, and the car is stolen, you do not ask your insurance office for say £1 000 000—the present value of all your future earnings to age 65. You are content to ask for a more modest sum, the car's replacement cost: with this, you can replace promptly, and still earn your full income. The £1 000 000 does not depend on ownership of this car but of a car.

But contribution is of course relevant where it differs in the *Have not* and *Have* scenarios. Table 12.4 gives an example. Again, the annual cash flows of a depreciating asset sometimes change in its later years (e.g. cost savings); here the fall budgets must compare the future flows of the old asset and its younger replacement—a matter illustrated in the next chapter on depreciation.

In such situations, the valuer faces all the troubles of the capital budgeter, and may have to probe into present values of dim anticipations. But these situations are perhaps less likely than the simple one. If a single tool in an assembly line wears out, or the office clock becomes unreliable, the firm's sales rarely dry up; given normal foresight and replacement facilities, the ill-result of the asset's failure is limited to payment of replacement cost.

Acquisition budgets versus value budgets

It may further clarify the argument if we contrast budgets in which contribution is essential (e.g. normal capital budgets) with deprival budgets. Probably the former will be used when the firm is deciding whether to acquire a new asset; the latter will be used when it has owned the asset for some time and wants to value it.

1 *Capital budgets*. These may show that, say, extra land costing £1000 will raise revenue (or cut costs) by equal annual sums whose DCF value is £1500.
2 *Deprival budgets*. If on the strength of this finding the firm goes ahead and buys the land, the £1500 contribution becomes 'fixed'; it can be omitted from both the *Have not* and *Have* columns of later budgets that assume the continued use of this or an equally productive plot. So the £1500 is irrelevant to deprival value; for instance, £1000 will normally be enough compensation if the state expropriates the land to widen a road, and the firm can for £1000 buy another plot yielding £1500.

In short, different figures are needed for studying different sets of alternatives—in capital budgets (for studying 'an asset versus no asset'), and in deprival budgets ('this asset versus its replacement').

Circumstances envisaged by deprival budgets

Loss by deprival must vary with circumstances. For example, when the deprived owner is in desperate haste to replace, he may pay a price far higher than when he can buy in leisurely style. Therefore, if 'deprival value' is not to cover a whole spectrum of possible figures, we must try to decide on a suitable background of assumptions, i.e. to set out the circumstances envisaged at a general revaluation. If the figures are to help with normal investment decisions, etc. they must reflect normal circumstances. Earlier pages have tried to meet this point by envisaging a firm depriving itself of assets during its everyday activities, as when a manager prices stores, etc. for use in production. The 'willing buyer and willing seller' of the appraiser may also be helpful.

Perhaps we can list the main points thus.

Assumptions should be reasonable and likely The budgets should be drafted on reasonable and likely assumptions—about the particular owner, the particular asset, and the particular circumstances.

Owner will try to minimise loss If the two columns of a deprival budget are to be helpful, they must show what will happen on realistic assumptions. They must suppose that the owner will make the best of his chances in each of the two sets of circumstances, by picking the course that offers the best cash flow prospects (after discounting for time and risk). Each column in the above tables may thus be the best of a wide range of possible budgets. The *Have not* column may picture the least costly of many ways in which a deprived owner could make the best of a bad job; the *Have* column may picture the most profitable of many ways of using the asset.

Sometimes one gets a clearer picture by including several of these extra budgets in the table. For instance, column (2) in Table 12.3 is split into budgets (a) and (b) to show the results of two alternative courses open to an undeprived owner; the deprival value emerges from a comparison of column (1) with the higher of columns 2(a) and (2b)—in fact column (2b).

Plenty of time is available As was pointed out above, if an owner has to replace an asset in haste, replacement cost may be higher than if he can approach the task with ample time. On dramatic assumptions, then, he can revalue his assets at high figures. Such figures conflict with our aim of showing the 'size' of assets in a way that helps business judgment in ordinary circumstances—enabling us (for instance) to compare the resources of one firm with those of another, or to form some idea of how much money a new firm would today need to build up a collection of like assets at a realistically economical pace. Given this aim, we should assume that the asset can be replaced without any suggestion of haste or duress. We are seeking the prices that will obtain when the firm makes its typical investments in assets.

As an example, suppose that a blizzard isolates a factory at balance sheet date. The fuel stock is running low. So long as the snow lasts, the value of fuel should surely be exceedingly high for purposes of decisions on short-term usage. But the same high figure in the annual accounts would be unhelpful. The replacement price at times of easy delivery will give a better view of the assets, when the accounts are read by normal readers at normal dates.

Plenty of cash available Difficulties could arise, similarly, in *financing* replacement where an owner really was deprived (e.g. fire loss not covered by insurance). He might not have enough ready cash, and therefore might need to borrow at high rates of interest or to pinch his other activities. Here, then, is another possible constraint that may push up the value of an existing asset and lead to dramatic figures that do not fit our picture of placid and efficient working. So we must assume the firm to have access to enough cash to replace the old asset in the most economical way (e.g. buying an expensive new machine where this will in the long run prove more economical than a worn one).

Time discount A valuer who recognises that value depends on comparisons will try to show that a £ due some years hence is less attractive than a £ already in the till. So, where the figures are high enough and the times are long enough to be material, he will discount future receipts and payments in his alternative budgets, at the firm's appropriate rate.

Conclusions on deprival value

One might summarise the above section as follows. The owner of an asset will aim to reap whatever benefits it can contribute in its best role (as shown perhaps in a capital budget justifying the acquisition of an asset of this kind). But, if he is deprived of it he does not necessarily go without these benefits. Where the benefits exceed replacement cost, he will limit his loss by buying or making a replacement; and thus replacement cost measures value to the owner. Where the benefits are less than replacement cost, the latter drops out of the picture. The benefits themselves here constitute value to the owner, i.e. he must estimate the future contribution of the asset to the cash receipts to be won or the cash payments to be obviated. So, to value an asset, one must play a game of make-believe, and imagine the various consequences of deprival. Valuation is a selective process, with three possible answers: (a) replacement cost; (b) net realisable value; and (c) cost savings.

Deprival value has the great advantage of being the right figure for many everyday management decisions: if the decision is on, say, whether or not to do a job (the stores example above), the manager should cost inputs already owned by asking what bad effects their using-up will have on the future cash book. If thoughtful managers already employ this approach in deciding how best to deploy their assets, perhaps it is a sound guide too for appraising each asset at revaluation time. At any rate, it is practical, subject to a clear logic, and increasingly familiar (thanks to the fact that it—or a close relation—has been backed by inflation Standards).

It was suggested on p. 192 that the best standard of value would meet two tests. The first test is that the figures must be helpful for decisions on the use of the separate asset; deprival value meets this test. The other test is that the standard must show the 'size' of the total assets in an informative way. Deprival value seems to meet the second test too: it yields figures whose total shows how much the firm would (given adequate earnings prospects) feel justified in paying for an equally productive set of assets—if, for instance, it were (for some reason such as a fire) deprived of its existing set and had to start afresh, or if it wanted to start a duplicate business in another area. (But of course this does not mean that the net sum of the deprival values is the same thing as the *ex-ante* value of the whole firm. The latter, as was pointed out on p. 182, is likely to exceed the sum of the separate asset values, however found. Where the *ex-ante* value is less than the sum of the separate deprival values, this sum still serves a useful purpose in pointing to the skimpiness of the receipts relative to the 'tools', and perhaps to the desirability of going out of business—either at once or when some costly asset needs renewal.[16])

Assets hard to value

There are some assets that seem ill-fitted for valuation by the deprival or probably any other method. Their links with the market are too weak to provide the needed price data. Obvious examples are the work-in-progress and finished goods of some factories, long-term contracts, and intangibles. A wise man will admit that his chosen method for valuing such assets is merely a makeshift.

In recent years, company law and Standards have somewhat narrowed the range of permitted valuation methods in published accounts. But that range is still broad enough to afford plenty of scope for reasoned choice. And it is good for the mind to ask what the choice should be in the absence of official limits, e.g. for the internal accounts of managers.

A factory's work-in-progress and finished goods

Stock in particular can be valued in many ways. Indeed this wealth of possibilities is itself evidence that any guiding logic is hard to find.

Methods used The stocks of a factory may be valued at historical cost. But then, as was pointed out on p. 126, the firm must link cost with some physical *sequence*, supposed or real, i.e. must choose between Fifo, Lifo, etc. It must also decide on the *ingredients*—whether to restrict cost to direct charges, or to include overhead (and, if so, how many items, found by what method of allocation). Thus a historical value is arbitrary in the extreme.

Attempts to find current values A value based on current prices would seem far more defensible than a historical cost. Such a value (one might suppose) could be based on prices in the outside market, or on the current cost of replacement within the factory. But in fact neither of these possibilities may yield an easy answer. Where each factory makes its own differentiated product, market dealings in work-in-progress may be rare, i.e. such assets may have neither a buying nor a sale price; and finished goods may have no buying price. We shall consider internal replacement below; but its values too must be very arbitrary.

Accountants are not alone in finding that current value is elusive here. We might innocently suppose that the expert whose job it is to appraise the value of stocks (e.g. to assess compensation for their loss by fire) could come to our rescue. But he too cannot make bricks without straw. He will probably tell us that he assesses compensation by whichever method the firm itself uses to value stocks in its own accounts. So all that we should learn from our quest for help is to look with care at the wording of the insurance policy and to pay for generous cover.

Let us ask ourselves why the stocks are regarded as wealth. Two of the answers are:

1 The existence of the stocks makes for smoother operating; it thus may lead to sales that otherwise would be lost, and to a good reputation for quick delivery. But accounts cannot evaluate this advantage.
2 In the absence of the stocks, future manufacturing costs would be higher. Here we seem back to the more tractable problems of deprival value.

A deprived firm would have to incur the extra cost of replacing its stocks. Direct costs of material and labour are obvious figures, and may seem easy to measure. But even here there may be doubts.[17] Thus labour cannot usually be hired and fired by the hour, and so the labour cost of a few product units may be as much a fixed cost as (say) rent. Replacement's effects on other factors could be of almost any size, according to the circumstances envisaged; the replacement of one unit in slack times might bring almost no extra outlays, whereas the replacement of many units in busy times might bring not only big outlays (overtime pay, etc.), but also general disruption. If a manager had to cost such assets for a decision budget, he would have to weigh all the circumstances of the moment. Such a complete review would be out of the question at a routine stocktaking. The first test on p. 192 (price found by everyday dealings in the asset) is of little use here.

Can the second test come to our rescue, i.e. can we measure the stock's contribution to the firm's 'size' by estimating how much capital is needed to finance all the stocks? Such an estimate would be crude and hypothetical; but it might none the less give quite a helpful view of the resources of the firm, and offer an adequate way of dealing with the difficulties. The argument would presumably run thus: to furnish itself with a comparable total stock, a new or deprived firm would have to buy raw materials and also pay wages and overheads during the time period needed for manufacture of the whole stock. The 'replacement cost' of the stock can thus be interpreted as the total expense for that period. An approximate figure could be built up by valuing each item of stock at average total cost, i.e. loading it with all overheads. However, the valuer could assume that the firm would work at the most efficient level of activity, and so he could charge overheads at the low rates of such a level; thus the rates would somewhat resemble those of full standard costing. Unsatisfactory items that the firm would not replace would be written down to scrap value, etc. often zero.

This method differs from those in common use mainly because of its stress on overheads. It must therefore offend theorists (as it seems to involve allocation of fixed costs) and practical men (as its values are higher and thus less cautious than is normal). But overhead is the core of the problem—and is likely in future to gain in importance with every increase in mechanisation, etc. The overhead rate in the electronics industry can already exceed 500 per cent of labour. To value at direct cost may soon be to value almost at zero. Indeed, any discussion of principles should, to be satisfying, deal adequately with the extreme case where *all* the cost is overhead. The method suggested above does at least meet this test.

Long-term 'unique' contracts

In a contracting firm, a partly finished building, ship, etc., is another kind of work-in-progress. It is one that is likely to constitute a big part of the firm's 'size'; so the valuation method can greatly affect the year's profit. But here again valuation is hampered by the lack of market dealings.

One can suggest only that the aim should be to use a deprival value, and that the latter should normally be interpreted as replacement cost at today's prices for the work done so far, but with an eye to the savings that hindsight can detect. Most of the inputs are here likely to be direct and obvious. Overheads should be added, on the same grounds as for factory work-in-progress. Deductions should be made for progress payments, and for loss (where this is likely).

However, contracting firms have in recent years tended to raise the asset values in a different way—by each year adding on a slice of the expected profit on the whole contract. This method clearly breaches the usual cautious rule against taking credit for gain before it is realised (here, by completion of the contract). Many accountants denounce the breach. Their chief objection is of course the danger of counting chickens before they are fully hatched. Until completion, the final cost of a long contract—perhaps lasting six or seven years—may be impossible to estimate at all closely, especially if there is a risk of strikes, wage increases, technical pitfalls, etc. For that matter, even after completion the contractor may still be liable during a guarantee or maintenance period of perhaps two more years. Therefore profit estimates must often be upset by later events.

But the practical grounds for recognising some profit during the contract are strong. Where a firm's activities consist of several big ventures—putting up tall buidlings, making costly machines, etc.—the group of ventures that happens to end in a given year may differ greatly in number, size, and profitability from the groups of other years. Thus successive annual totals of profit on completed ventures may bob up and down capriciously. Such figures give poor information. So there is a strong temptation here to throw the usual rules overboard, and to smooth the figures by recognising interim profit.

If the firm decides to do this, it must choose some rather artificial way of allocating final profit between the years (perhaps the 'percentage of completion' method, by which the estimated total profit is split in the proportion that each year's cost bears to total cost).

In this area, then, caution clashes with expediency. It will be interesting to see which wins (and whether a conceptual framework can resolve the clash). The relevant US Standard, FASB 56, permits both methods. Britain's Standard, SSAP 9, backed 'cost plus any attributable profit'. Embarrassingly, the Companies Act, 1981 seems to make this illegal.

Intangibles

Accounting interprets 'tangible assets' broadly, so that the phrase covers not only physical assets but also rights (e.g. claims on debtors) that can be enforced at law. 'Intangibles' is correspondingly restricted.

Should intangibles be looked on as assets? It is hard to suggest rational rules for intangibles ('dangling debits'). By what tests should one decide whether outlays on advertising, research, etc., give birth to an asset? And, where the existence of the asset has been recognised, at what dates and rates should it be written off? Here once again we see that a list of separate assets is an imperfect device for measuring wealth.

Much the same problem faces the economic statistician who is compiling figures on national resources. He knows that, where country A invests heavily in physical assets and country B in education, comparison of figures for physical capital alone gives a false picture. But he knows also that to measure human capital is difficult. So he may reasonably decide to find the physical figures only, and leave his readers to allow for B's superior education as best they can.

A simple mind could hardly entertain the notion of intangible assets. In a child's tales, wealth is castles, land, flocks, gold—i.e. physical things. It is a long step forward to realise that the essence of wealth is the prospect of benefits, not their physical source. The accountant is thus showing his maturity if he ceases to use the physical test for deciding whether outlays fall under the heading of 'asset' or 'expense'. The correct test, he then argues, is whether or not the outlay improves the firm's prospects (when the outlook at the year's end is compared with that at its start). Tangibility has nothing to do with this test; he applies it alike to the cost of a lathe and an advertising campaign.

But, alas, physical attributes do help with valuation. Most tangible assets can be traded on the market; they also lend themselves to the notion of deprival. Intangibles are less helpful: in what sense can one speak of the sale or replacement of last year's advertising, and how can a firm deprive itself of the benefit of its preliminary expenses? Physical attributes may at least set limits to the asset's life. And often the valuer can visualise and predict the cash flows of physical assets more surely than those of intangibles. In short, valuation of intangibles is apt to demand superlative judgment plus prophetic gifts that none of us can feel sure of possessing. As like as not, moreover, the decision on whether to 'assetise' expenditure on intangibles (for instance, to capitalise the cost of research and development) will need to be made when the company is going through a bad patch, i.e. when the pressure to improve the profit figures is highest and cool judgment is hardest. Yet bad judgment can here spell disaster, since it may enable a company to report reassuring profits throughout a lean period that ends in bankruptcy (e.g. Rolls-Royce in 1967–71).

The deprival concept is no help here: the notion of depriving a firm of all knowledge won by past research, etc., hardly makes sense. The sale-price concept would have at least the merit of providing a clear if extreme solution, since many intangibles are by their nature incapable of being sold and so would have to be valued at *nil*. Some such complete ban on intangibles (save perhaps where they are property in the legal sense, e.g. patents) would provide a workable rule, and might prevent the deception of creditors and shareholders; the ban would also make balance sheets more intelligible. But it would be an intolerable constraint on many sound companies during a development stage.

American accountants have decided that research and development must be written off at once (FASB 2), but that other intangibles should be treated as assets and 'amortised over estimated future life' not exceeding forty years (FASB 44). In Britain, the ASC has decided also (Standard 13) that research and development should be written off at once (with an escape hatch for development whose good results seem assured); it has yet to pronounce on a wider range of items.

'Goodwill' Normally the balance sheet concerns itself with separate asset values, and ignores the going-concern (*ex-ante*) value of the whole. If, however, a whole firm changes hands, the buyer's book-keeper may need to make entries that first split up the price between the separate assets acquired, and then somehow insert any remaining surplus as an extra debit: an awkward balancing figure thus emerges because two incompatible methods of valuing have become entangled.

Our experience of the physical world suggests that the whole must equal the sum of the parts—that, if our measurement of physical things belies this, we must have gone wrong somewhere, e.g. we may have overlooked one of the parts. But we should be wary about applying this experience to the realm of value. To treat the balancing figure as an extra asset (still more, an asset linked with popularity) is an error. It is not an extra asset;[18] it is the gap between the answers found when two quite different things—in the economic sense—are measured. This is obvious where the whole and the parts are valued on different bases (e.g. the whole firm at its current price and the assets at the historical costs of earlier dates). But even if both the whole and the parts are valued on the current basis, a gap is likely: where, because of market or technical or other difficulties, a set of parts cannot readily be acquired and built up quickly into an effective whole, the market will tend to prefer the whole and to pay more for it. (It is instructive to compare a set of golf clubs with a rare Dresden shepherd and shepherdess.) The extra price is for the extra benefits that the whole will yield.[19] To ascribe them to one hidden part is naive.

Suppose that a connoisseur is willing to pay £10 apiece for separate china figures, and £50 for a matching pair. The extra £30 suggests that he gets extra pleasure from the pair, and not that there is a third figure lurking in the background.

But, by calling the debit 'goodwill', accounting has unfortunately fostered the notion that an extra asset does exist. In consequence, there have been some valiant efforts to appraise the asset directly (e.g. by the once-popular 'super-profits' method[20]). Where, however, a figure is born as a discord between two primary figures, it hardly seems suitable for direct valuation. We should treat articles on 'the valuation of goodwill' with several grains of salt.

Once the 'plug figure' gets into the ledger, logic cannot help much with its treatment—except perhaps the urge that one should get rid of the alien intruder, and the sooner the better. (In Britain, the Companies Act, 1981 requires companies to write off goodwill over a 'period chosen by the directors' but 'not exceeding useful economic life'—whatever that means. In America, the rules for other intangibles apply.)

It seems desirable that the balance sheet should describe the debit with some full and clear phrase, e.g. 'Excess of price paid for whole firm as a going-concern over the net sum of the separate asset values'. (In a consolidated balance sheet, words such as 'Excess of price paid for shares in subsidiary over the separate values of the subsidiary's assets' are now accepted usage for describing an analogous figure.) When we instead use 'goodwill', we confuse readers. What is worse, we betray confusion in our own thought.

Balance sheet treatment In the absence of any clear solution to the problem of intangibles, we must accept that it will be dealt with in various unsatisfying ways. We can at least say that a balance sheet ought to separate tangibles from intangibles in a style that will alert readers to the more arbitrary nature of the values of the intangibles. Perhaps the balance sheet should class as assets only the intangibles that are backed up by legal rights (patents, copyrights, etc.), and should show the rest as deductions from the owners' balances until they are written off.

Where the price paid for a going-concern is *less* than the net assets, the shortfall could best be shown as a deduction from their total. This would be more informative than arbitrary cuts in the value of one or more fixed assets, or the creation of a 'capital reserve'.

Revaluation of intangibles If intangibles are (for better or worse) included in a revalued or stabilised balance sheet, how should the figures be updated during inflation? Presumably one could think up some special index for, e.g. advertising or research costs. However, on the assumption that such items are better looked on as explanations of past cash outflows than normal assets, the general index would seem more appropriate.

Assets that yield cash directly

In part as a preface to a discussion of long-term liabilities, it may be worthwhile to spell out the steps in the valuation of the corresponding assets, e.g. holdings of long-term loans, etc. Here these are called 'assets that yield cash directly'.

To find deprival values for such assets, one must again ask how the owner should measure them for his decision-budgets. The occasions when he will draft such budgets may in some cases be rare; but one can for instance envisage him getting an offer for his unquoted shares, and asking himself (as a guide to the minimum price to accept) what difference their loss would make to his cash flows.

The benefit of ownership

In simple cases, the reasoning must presumably be like that for other assets. There will be three possible figures.

Where replacement is worthwhile Suppose that the asset in question is called A_1, and the owner expects his holding to yield £x a year as interest or dividend plus a lump sum of £y at redemption date; that he likes this package so much that he will, if deprived of it, try to buy a similar one; and that, for £90000, he can buy a holding of another security, A_2, so like A_1 (as regards interest, redemption, risk, etc.) that we can conveniently call its price 'replacement cost'. Plainly, *Have not* and *Have* budgets would show that the value of A_1

is £90000, since the receipt of £90000 enables him exactly to make good the loss of A_1. (The face values of A_1 and A_2 are of no relevance.) Deprival value is once again replacement cost.

In other words, the asset should be valued with the aid of known prices of similar assets. For convenience, these 'prices' are of course twisted round and stated as market rates of interest.

Where replacement is not worthwhile But sometimes the owner's opinion of A-type assets will have fallen since he bought A_1, so that he is disinclined to replace it with A_2. Thus he may now see other investment possibilities that promise a higher rate of return—after allowing for risk—than A-type securities. He now has two possible courses:

1 He may decide that his best plan is to sell as soon as possible. If his holding will fetch £85000 (£90000 less the 'dealer's turn', etc.), then this smaller sum is now deprival value.

   With many types of cash-yielding assets, the gap between replacement cost and sale price will be less than is suggested in this example, e.g. it will be trifling in a highly-developed market such as that for government securities. But in some circumstances the gap could be greater. Thus there may be no willing buyers for the obligations of a small company, particularly if its record is poor; and the gap will increase if the seller has to pay capital gains tax.

2 Where there is a big gap, another type of receipt is likely to become more relevant than net realisable value: the receipts to be got by keeping the asset (cf. use value) may now seem more desirable than those from prompt sale. Here value is the discounted present value of the receipts from holding the asset for the best future period—say, the £*x* per year and £*y* at redemption. If the firm can borrow readily, the market rate of interest indicates the discount rate; then present value and replacement cost must be almost identical (£90000 in the example). Where the firm has not ready access to the market—the 'capital rationing situation'—it must use the rate of return on its own marginal ventures. This may be high; and presumably the valuer must somehow adjust it to allow for variances in risk on the security and the firm's ventures.

The deprival formula

The deprival value of cash-yielding assets can thus (in simple cases at least) be defined by slightly adapting the argument of p. 204. Now 'use value' changes to 'future receipts' (interest and ultimate proceeds). Thus the deprival value of cash-yielding assets is the lower of (a) (if the owner could and would replace on deprival) replacement cost, and (b) (otherwise) the higher of (i) net current sale price, and (ii) the present value (at his appropriate discount rate) of future receipts, according to whether his best plan is to sell the asset at once or keep it.

Difficulties

In practice, it may well be impossible to value cash-yielding assets with any sureness, because the variances between the 'unknown' and the nearest 'known' assets are so great (e.g. the valuer must try to allow for differences in factors such as gearing and cover). Even if the cash flows from both purport to be fixed sums of money (as with debts, debentures, etc.), there may be variances in timing and risk. Where the size of the flows is also likely to vary (as with equities) the difficulties increase still further.

There are plenty of other problems to test the judgment of the valuer. A simple debt may be subject to unpredictable delays. Loans to associated companies may secure trade benefits (over and above such obvious receipts as interest) that are well-nigh impossible to quantify. Moreover general price change must tend to affect the owner's discount rate. During inflation, he will expect equity investments to yield rising money receipts, i.e. to earn at a rate that is influenced by both (a) time and risk in the absence of inflation, and (b) the fall in money's value. He should therefore discount receipts at a rate higher than that appropriate in times of stable prices.[21]

Liabilities and provisions

If there is a good case for evaluating the cash-yielding assets, consistency suggests that there must be an equally good case for revaluing the liabilities (and here we shall stretch the word to cover all fixed-money obligations, e.g. preference shares). The aim of a revaluation may be to aid scrutiny of the firm's resources; it may also be to aid income measurement (e.g. by finding unrealised change in value); for both these ends, the negative items in the balance sheet would seem just as significant as the positive ones.

'Relief value' of long-term liabilities

With liabilities, the phrase 'deprival value' may be inept. Logical symmetry suggests that we must now switch from the benefit lost by deprival to the benefit that the firm would gain *if it were relieved of a burden*; so 'relief value' is perhaps a more suitable term.

There may not be many occasions on which a manager must calculate such a value for decision purposes. But we can imagine him doing so when, for instance, a would-be buyer of one of the firm's departments, etc., offers to relieve the firm of a loan as part of the consideration.

The measurement of a burden

A long-term liability usually saddles the borrowing firm with a burden such as the payment of £x per year as interest and a lump sum of £y at redemption date. What is it worth to be rid of the burden?

This value seems often to be harder to envisage than the value of assets. But again there are likely to be three possible figures.

Replacement loan Let us first suppose that the firm's best plan, if it were relieved of existing loan, would be to borrow afresh in much the same way; and that it could today raise £90000 (net of cost) in return for its undertaking to pay £x a year and £y at redemption date. By following this plan, it would still face unchanged future cash outflows, but gain £90000 at once. So the benefit of relief is £90000, i.e. is the amount of the potential 'replacement loan' that can be serviced with the given future cash flows.

If the loan's 'price' (restated as the market interest rate on the given type of loan) has changed much since issue, a relief value such as the £90000 may be rather far from the conventional balance sheet figure.

But the firm may be unwilling (if relieved) to raise a fresh loan. Thus it may consider the terms too unfavourable (e.g. lenders may now regard the firm as very risky, and offer only a small sum in return for the future flows of £*x* and £*y*); or the firm may now foresee greater dangers in high gearing. Two new values suggest themselves.

Repayment cost The firm's best plan may be to get rid of the loan, by paying it off or buying it in the market and cancelling it. This may involve costs such as a premium on early redemption. Relief value is the total 'repayment cost obviated'.

If the transaction can go ahead easily in a good market, relief value here must lie close to the size of a replacement loan. But various snags seem possible. In particular, the loan contract may lay down awkward redemption terms, such as a prohibitively high premium. (And that would cause a further difficulty: could and would a replacement loan now be raised with these same terms in the new contract? If not, such loan ceases to be one of the valuer's simple options; here he must allow for an unusual variance.)

Present value The firm may decide that it will make the best of a bad job by sticking with the liability, i.e. continuing to face the future payments of £*x* and £*y*. Relief from the loan would here mean obviation of these future payments. So 'relief value' must be their present value. As with comparable assets, the discount rate will be the lower of market rate or rate of return on the firm's marginal investments. (Or is there another snag here? The market charges a rate that allows for the risk of non-payment by the firm. But does the firm itself normally anticipate its own collapse? If not, it seems to have grounds for valuing the burden at a figure above that of the outsiders.)

General valuation rule

It is not easy to suggest any convincing and simple formula when the problem is so complex, and so much depends on the degree of capital rationing.

The valuer must in theory go through a budgeting process analagous to that for assets. He must ask, (a) what is the best way for the firm to deal with the liability (i.e. the *Have* budget shows whether to repay or retain), (b) whether—after the hypothetical relief—loan replacement would be worthwhile, and finally (c) how much is the difference between the courses indicated by (a) and (b). This difference is the benefit of relief, and so the measure of the burden.

However, the above views do not get much support. Value theorists probably argue even more hotly about liabilities than assets.[22] Fortunately 'it is difficult to visualize how, in a rational capital market, the three values used in the algorithm would deviate greatly from one another, so perhaps the problem is not worth great emphasis'.[23] Quite right; but the problem returns when the firm cannot look to a rational market.

Arguments for and against revaluing liabilities

Even where the three current values do not differ much from one another, sometimes they will all be very different from the par values of historical accounts. This will clearly be the case where there have been big shifts in market interest rates since the loan was issued.

Then revaluation must surely be helpful. Current values are the logical figures to use in studies of capital gearing. Further, they give some evidence of the company's skill at borrowing; for instance, a decline in the market value of the debentures suggests that the managers borrowed at a good moment, and so have served the equity-holders well. (Does loyal service to the equity-holders imply disloyalty to the holders of preference capital, loan, etc.? My feeling is that holders of fixed-money claims have opted to speculate on the money unit, and must be left to win or lose. To show their holding at current value would at least let them see how their speculation has fared.)

The argument against revaluing money liabilities (and also money assets) is that the gains or losses are common knowledge and sometimes small; if the balance sheet were to set out the few important facts (interest rate, date and terms of redemption, and—best of all—quoted market price), it would tell the reader everything he normally needs in order to form a judgment. Further, the gain or loss on redeemable securities tends to evaporate as redemption date draws near.

Despite these comforting arguments for accounting inertia, the fact remains that good analysts often do find it worth their while to revalue prior charges. An informative balance sheet might well do the same for the general reader.[24]

Example of revaluation of liabilities

Suppose that a company starts (at general index 100) with £4000 of equity capital and £1000 of debentures, and invests the £5000 in land. In the years that follow, the general index trebles, the land rises in step, but the relief value of the debentures sinks to £700. Trade profit is paid out at once as dividend. The closing balance sheet (ordinary figures) is shown in colums (1) of Table 12.5. The revalued figures of column (2) show that the equity has gained 300 from the debenture holders. But column (2) has not told the whole story. To avoid real loss, the claim of the debenture holders would now need to stand at £3000; inflation has switched £2000 of this (on top of the £300) to the equity. On the other hand, the equity has made no real gain on the land. The stabilised figures of column (3) reveal these facts.

Table 12.5 Balance Sheets Illustrating the Revaluation of Liabilities

	(1) *Ordinary figures* £		(2) *Revalued* £		(3) *Stabilised figures* £
Assets	5000	×300/100	15 000		*15 000*
Ordinary shareholders:					
Capital	4000		4 000	×300/100	*12 000*
Gain on revaluing assets			10 000		
Gain on revaluing liabilities			300		*300*
Gain on owing money					*2 000*
			14 300		*14 300*
Debentures	1000		700		*700*
	5000		15 000		*15 000*

Provisions and allowances

If an old provision, etc., is meant to show that a particular asset is overvalued, presumably it should usually be revised in much the same way as the asset itself (e.g. with that asset's special index). Thus an accumulated depreciation provision should keep step with change in the gross value of the asset (a matter that Chapter 13 will discuss at some length). A provision for maintenance (e.g. of furnaces for making steel) ought to mirror expected costs at the rates likely to obtain when the repairs will be done.

Provisions for loss on money assets (e.g. for bad debts) fall in real value during inflation. But then so do the money assets. There is thus no need to restate the provisions.

Fortunately tax liabilities are not indexed, and so do not need restatement.

Equity

If a balance sheet were revalued whole-heartedly, the equity items would have to be up-dated (as in stabilised accounts). Such a revision would stop the mixing of unlike £s; it would thus reveal the relative sizes of the various contributions by the owners—possibly several issues of capital, and a long series of yearly gains. The general index seems the best tool for this revaluation (page 51).

Where (as is usual) revaluation stops short of the equity items, a composite surplus (e.g. the 'current cost reserve') must be put among them. It means little.

Accumulated gains, etc.

If accumulated profit is revalued during inflation, the older parts may rise considerably. As an example, suppose a company started with £1000 of capital, and used this to buy land (at general and specific indices of 100). In succeeding years, the general index went up to 300. Undistributed trade profit is £220; it came from the rent of the land, and so includes no time-lag error. It accumulated during the company's early years, when the general index stood at 110. The

Table 12.6 Balance Sheets Illustrating Stabilisation of Accumulated Gains

	(1) *Ordinary figures* £		(2) *Ordinary balance sheet with assets revalued* £		(3) *Stabilised figures* £ *at index 300*
Land	1000	×280/100	2800		*2800*
Investments	220	×300/110	600		*600*
	1220		3400		*3400*
Capital	1000		1000	×300/100	*3000*
Profit (trade) accumulated	220		220	×300/110	*600*
Gain on revaluation of assets:					
In money terms: Land			1800		
Investments			380		
			2180		
In real terms: Land					*−200*
	1220		3400		*3400*

corresponding cash was promptly used to buy investments (cost £220), which then appreciated in step with the general index, so that their end-value is £600; but the value of the land did not quite appreciate in step, and rose from £1000 to only £2800.

The closing balance sheet (ordinary figures) is shown in column (1) of Table 12.6. Column (3) shows the stabilised figures; both capital and old trade profits rise substantially, but the £200 real loss on land is made obvious.

Various compromises between columns (1) and (3) are possible. Column (2) shows the usual one; it retains orthodox capital and trade profit, and therefore must announce an unreal gain of £2180. And, where this 'reserve' also includes time-lag adjustments, it becomes a queer jumble.

New legal concepts on profits available for dividends?

Columns (2) and (3) suggest that the shareholders' balances exceed those shown by ordinary accounts, and that the latter figures should be raised. But if some such revaluation becomes usual, important new problems will emerge. In particular, directors and shareholders will begin to ask where the legal ceiling on dividends now lies; 'mixed' totals, like the £220 of the example, will no longer seem convincing. How should the law decide such novel questions?

By raising the other parts of the equity, stabilisation lessens the unrealised gains. It thus is inimical to the distribution of such gains, and reinforces the prohibitions of the EEC Second Directive and Britain's Companies Act, 1980.

Restated trade profit (£600 instead of £220 in the example) raises a more important problem. There does not seem to be any strong reason against treating it all as divisible; it is the measure of old realised trade profits in up-to-date terms (and, in the sense that it contains no element of time-lag error, is even conservative). If, however, this view is sound, the directors of innumerable companies can, by revaluing mixed totals of corrected profits, raise their dividend ceiling without impropriety. This opens up a perhaps unnerving prospect—if not of wholesale dividend increases, at least of doubt and upheaval in concepts and case law.

Equity capital

Our approach to revaluation has left equity capital in a rather passive role—as little more than a residual balance. Logic suggests that the normal (often mixed) historical figure should be stabilised with the general index, i.e. raised in the eyes of the owner to the current equivalent of his historical contributions. Company law presumably forbids similar change in ordinary accounts, but could hardly prevent the increase (e.g. the £2000 in Table 12.5) from being shown next to capital as a separate 'valuation adjustment' or 'capital reserve'. From time to time, the balance sheet might then be tidied up by using this surplus for the issue of bonus shares.

Some ingenious minds have suggested a far more radical attack: if each asset, loan, etc., ought to be restated at its market value, why should the company's own shares too not be restated in a way that reflects the *ex-ante* value of the going concern (most simply, at their market quotation, so that the total gives the company's 'market capitalisation')? Here we have returned to the issue raised at the start of this chapter, i.e. the distinction between the total of the separate (net) assets and the *ex-ante* value of the whole firm. If we accept that the most useful task of the balance sheet is to give information about the 'size of the tools', and not about the going-concern value of the whole firm, then the owner's balances must do no more than reflect the net assets. To mix the two types of value is to invite maximum confusion.

Conclusions on revaluation

Though we may hope that the balance sheet of the future will contain defensible values, we must recognise that the task of finding them will involve the accountant in many new troubles.

This chapter has explained some of the difficulties (notably ones that arise when the given asset is divorced from market dealings, or would be replaced by something very different). But there are still others. Two of these must be mentioned. They tend to become important where values are interdependent, i.e. where it is misleading to measure the given asset by itself.[25]

First, it sometimes happens that the loss of the one asset would cripple the firm. This is unlikely where the firm's cash benefits are high relative to the asset's replacement cost: given the 'normal circumstances' (plenty of time available, etc.) envisaged by p. 210, a deprived firm would here make itself whole by replacing the asset; and so replacement cost is a suitable measure of value. But if the benefits are low relative to the replacement cost, a deprived firm might decide to close down the whole rather than replace. An example is a costly bridge or tunnel on a moribund railway. Deprival may lead not to replacement but to the line's closure, and thus to loss of the net receipts from the whole; so this one asset's deprival value is the present value of the line's future net receipts. But the same may hold for other bridges and tunnels as well. To sum such deprival values is to reach an absurdly high total.

Second, the plant as a whole may be semi-obsolete, and yet its parts—viewed piecemeal—may still be worth replacing. If the chance arose (e.g. if a fire wiped out the plant), the whole would be replaced by an improved set of assets, working on a quite different system. But, in the absence of such a clean sweep, a machine of the improved kind may not fit in, and so the firm must keep up the old system; the loss of an existing machine would lead merely to its replacement by a more or less similar machine. Here each single asset can sensibly be valued at its replacement cost, and yet the sum of such values fails to allow for the general obsolescence.

It seems desirable, where the parts add up to an unwarrantably high total, to remove the excess from the balance sheet. But can one do so by writing down the individual values? There may be no logical way of apportioning the excess between them; we may question even the practice of writing it off from fixed assets, leaving the current assets unscathed. A more defensible plan may be to list the assets at their full values, and then to deduct some comprehensive provision for obsolescence, etc., from their sum.

The net total should be the price that the firm, if deprived of all the net assets, would be willing to pay for a similar set—a price low enough to enable it to compete with today's most efficient new plants.

The difficulties of finding balance sheet values mainly arise, as earlier pages have said, from the inherent crudeness of all value concepts that are not founded on an *ex-ante* treatment of composite cash flows. If this glum view is right, we must accept that all concepts for individual assets are beset by faults, and that the balance sheet must often be blinkered and ritualistic. The deprival concept shares the general weakness; but it seems at least to be sufficiently useful and reasonable to merit a trial.

Notes and References

1 Mr H.P. Barker, Parkinson Cowan, Ltd, Annual Report, 1964.

2 See, e.g. Turvey, R. (1971) 'Rates of return, pricing, and the public interest', *Economic Journal*, September, p. 489.

3 See MacNeal, K. (1962) 'What's wrong with accounting', in *Studies in Accounting*, 3rd edn, W.T. Baxter and S. Davidson, (eds) p. 168 ICAEW. This is outspoken on the ill-results of using historical cost (justified on the 'going concern principle of value') instead of current value: 'accepted accounting principles permit new types of exploitation on a scale that makes plain stealing look tame. This exploitation is not crude stealing; it is horse-trading on plush carpets with a background of authentic period furniture; it doesn't give the smartest Indian a chance, nor is it supposed to'.

4 Solomons, D. (1965) *Divisional Performance: Measurement and Control,* p. 123, Financial Executives Research Foundation.
5 See e.g. Stamp, E. (1981) 'Multi-column reporting', in Thomas A. Lee (ed.), *Developments in Financial Reporting*, Philip Allan.
6 Mr Justice Danckwerts in *Holt* vs. *Commissioners of Inland Revenue* [1953] 32 ATC 402.
7 These matters are set out more fully and skilfully by Professor J.C. Bonbright, of Columbia Business School, in his massive and incomparable *Valuation of Property*, Michie, 1965. Merrett, A.J. and Sykes, A. (1973) *The Finance and Analysis of Capital Projects*, Longman, provide a useful alternative treatment linked with long-term budgets.
8 The size of the brokers' charge or the 'inside dealers' margin' depends on 'the degree of perfection [in] the market in which they operate and on the amount of "processing" or "transformation" performed by them', e.g. transportation, packaging, physical transformation through manufacture, etc. It depends, too, on how far they act as shock-absorbers by varying their quantity of stocks held; thus they may buy when prices are sagging, and sell later when prices rise—'an intertemporal transfer of goods . . . fundamentally no different from any geographical transfer'—Kaldor, N. (1972) The irrelevance of equilibrium economics', *Economic Journal*, December p. 1248.
9 Chambers, R.J. (1966) *Accounting, Evaluation, and Economic Behaviour*, p. 92, Prentice-Hall.
10 'When I say, "My house is worth $10,000 to me", I mean (if I am precise in my use of language) that the retention of the house is worth to me as much as the acquisition of $10,000 in cash would be worth to me. But this is the same thing as saying that the anticipated loss of my ownership interest in the house has an adverse value to me of $10,000. Such negative terms as "anticipated loss", "damage", and "injury", when used as quantitative terms to which dollar signs may be attached, are simply the converse of such positive words as "value", "worth", and "importance"'—Bonbright, J.C. *op. cit.*, p. 72. Professor F.K. Wright seems to hit the nail on the head when he uses 'opportunity value' in this context (see 'Towards a general theory of depreciation', *Journal of Accounting Research,* Spring, 1964).
11 See Boersema, J.M.J. (1979) 'Does current cost accounting yield deprival value?', *The Accountants' Magazine*, July.
12 Knight, F.H. (1957) *Risk, Uncertainty and Profit*, p. 63, London School of Economics reprints.

A member of the ASC (we are told) enlivened the revaluation debates on 'modern equivalents' with verse:

Said the husband of Emily Crassett:
'She has many a praiseworthy facet.
But this is a case
Where I'd rather replace
With a modern equivalent asset.'

13 This 'revenue approach' is amplified and discussed in Baxter, W.T. (1971) pp. 43 and 101, *Depreciation,* Sweet & Maxwell.

14 When the facts warrant, a just compensation law will allow for dramatic circumstances, though perhaps by distinguishing more than one type of loss rather than valuing the asset at an unusually high figure. Professor Bonbright (*op. cit.*, pp. 75–6) takes as illustration an imaginary legal system in which a man deprived of his car sets the damage at $1500: if he should claim for 'a total loss of $1500 due (a) to the necessity of buying another car for $1000 and (b) to missing an important business engagement that would have yielded him a profit of $500, most courts would distinguish between the loss of a car "worth $1000" and the incidental loss of an opportunity to make a profit. They would not be likely to think of the car as having been temporarily worth $1500 to the owner because of its usefulness in preventing the owner from missing his engagement. But unless "value" is defined to mean market value, or else to mean the value that the automobile *would* have to the owner under *hypothetical* conditions, the distinction is invalid.'

15 These and similar views are discussed critically by (among others) Bromwich, M. (1975) 'Asset valuation with imperfect markets', *Accounting and Business Research*, Autumn, and 'The general validity of certain "current" value asset valuation bases', *ibid.*, Autumn (1977); Gee, K. P. and Peasnell, K. V. (1976) 'A pragmatic defence of replacement cost', *Accounting and Business Research*, Autumn; Gray, S.J. (1977) 'Accounting values and inflation: A review', *Abacus*, June; Ma, R. (1976) 'Value to the owner revisited', *ibid.* December; Parker, R. H. and Harcourt, G.C. (1969) Introduction to *Readings in the Concept and Measurement of Income,* Cambridge; Revsine, L. (1977) *Replacement Cost Accounting*, Prentice-Hall; Sterling, R.R. (1975) 'Relevant financial reporting in an age of price changes', *The Journal of Accountancy*, February; Solomons, D. (1966) 'Economic and accounting concepts of cost and value', in Morton Backer (ed.), *Modern Accounting Theory*, Prentice-Hall; Whittington, G. (1983) *Inflation accounting: An Introduction*, Cambridge.

16 Baxter, W. T. (1978) 'Deprival value of assets: What if the parts exceed the whole?' *The Accountants' Magazine*, July.

17 Sorter, G. H. and Horngren, C. T. (1962) 'Asset recognition and economic attributes: The relevant costing approach', *The Accounting Review*, July.

18 Bonbright, J. C. *op. cit.*, page 79.

19 The following story was told in *The Times*, 20 February 1973, to illustrate Indian business capacity:

> Police in a village saw an Indian had come into some money. He told them he had received it from importing shoes. But you need a licence to do that, the police reminded him; did he have one? No, he admitted. Then surely the shoes must have been seized by the state and sold at public auction? They were, the man said; but in that case, the puzzled policeman asked, how did he benefit?
>
> 'Ah', the Indian said, 'I imported 10000 left shoes into Calcutta, and they were sold at public auction, but no one wanted them, so I got them very cheaply. Then I imported the right shoes into Bombay, and they, too, were sold, but no one wanted them. So I got them cheaply, too. Then I matched the pairs and sold them all at a good profit'.

20 Carsberg, B. V. (1966) 'The contribution of P.D. Leake to the theory of goodwill valuation', *Journal of Accounting Research*, Spring; Edey, H.C. (1962) 'Business valuation, goodwill and the super-profit method', in W. T. Baxter and S. Davidson (eds), *Studies in Accounting Theory*, Sweet & Maxwell.

21 See Bromwich, M. (1969) 'Inflation and the capital budgeting process', *Journal of Business Finance*, Autumn.

22 For instance: Egginton, D. A. and Morris, R. C. (1976) 'Holding gains on long-term liabilities', *Accounting and Business Research*, Summer; Grinyer, J. R. (1975) 'Holding gains on long-term liabilities', *Accounting and Business Research*, Autumn; Kulkarni, D. (1980) 'The valuation of liabilities', *Accounting and Business Research*, Summer; Kerr, J. (1980) 'Liabilities in a current value accounting system', in D. M. Emanuel and I. C. Stewart (eds), *Essays in Honour of Trevor R. Johnston*, University of Auckland; Ma, R. and Miller, M. C. (1978) 'Conceptualising the liability', *Accounting and Business Research*, Autumn; Martin, C. A. (1983) 'The current cost of a quoted long-term liability', *Accounting and Business Research*, Summer.

23 Whittington, G. (1975) 'Baxter on inflation accounting', *Accounting and Business Research*, Autumn.

24 A possible book-keeping scheme for handling gain and loss on prior obligations is given in E. O. Edwards and P. W. Bell, (1960) *The Theory and Measurement of Business Income*, p. 204. University of California Press. This even shows the variance between actual interest charges and what would be paid on loans raised at current rates.

25 Edey, H. C. (1974) 'Deprival value and financial accounting', H. C. Edey and B.S. Yamey (eds), *Debits, Credits, Finance and Profits* p. 83, Sweet & Maxwell.

13

The Revaluation of Depreciating Assets

The main concern of this chapter is the revision of depreciation charges and asset values after price change. But it cannot deal with these matters without first discussing the traditional values, i.e. the starting point for revision.

The asset viewed as a store of inputs

Sometimes an asset is best viewed as a quantity of inputs bought ahead of needs. A tank of fuel-oil at a factory is a store of gallons awaiting use: likewise, a machine is a store of service-units (e.g. ton-miles) awaiting use. Such stores are bought in big purchase-lots, and not in driblets, for the sake of convenience, the economies of bulk-buying, etc. Thus a brand-new lorry may be preferred to a series of shortlived, secondhand ones because it is thought to cost less per ton-mile.

If a whole purchase-lot is used-up within an accounting period, no problem of balance sheet valuation arises. If some of the lot spills over into later periods, the units still on hand must be valued. The task seems easier where the number of units can be gauged with simple physical measures of weight, volume, and so on—e.g. as so many gallons of oil. It seems much less easy where the units cannot be so gauged. Usually 'depreciating asset' means an asset that is subject to this difficulty: we often find it hard to quantify the remaining physical services of a machine, and lack any obvious guide to their value per unit. For valuation theory, however, such assets do not appear to differ much from other stores of input, and the analogy with raw materials, etc., should serve as a useful starting-point.

The chapter will run most easily if it separates value movements due to aging (with depreciating assets such as machines, from a peak at acquisition to a low point at disposal) from those due to changing market forces. It starts with the former.

Reasons for calculating depreciation

Like other assets, a depreciating asset can be valued by several different concepts, e.g. at replacement cost or sale price; and, if we define annual depreciation cost as the change during a year in one of these values, the cost charge also has a corresponding range of possible sizes. It was suggested on p. 24 that rival income figures should be judged by their informativeness, and that sometimes one figure may be the most informative for purpose A and another for purpose B. In the same way, the rival figures for depreciation cost should be judged by their informativeness, and one may be the best for A and another for B.

Thus it is helpful to remind ourselves of the occasions when information about depreciation may be wanted:

In final accounts (a) The cost figures of the *income statement* are sometimes looked on as a test of efficiency. More important, they influence profit, i.e. guide the owners' consumption and investment (see p. 25); thus depreciation charges that err on the high side could result in unduly low dividends and failure to attract the capital needed to expand plant to its best size.

(b) The values for plant, etc., in the *balance sheet* are evidence of the 'size of the tools' and capital maintenance.

In decision budgets Here depreciation costs may help with, e.g. problems of pricing, and of deciding whether a given job will be worth doing. Depreciated asset values may help with decisions on when to sell and replace the asset.[1] They should therefore be linked in some logical way with replacement and secondhand prices—so that, if book value threatens to sink below sale price, this should be a reliable signal that the time for disposal is near.

In calculating tax Here the procedure depends on legal rules, not economic goals, and so lies beyond the reach of reason.

The traditional methods

Where asset values are linked with historical cost, accountants have dealt with depreciation by writing off the cost by one or other of their traditional 'depreciation methods'. The rationale of these methods ('matching cost and revenues') seems crude, and the grounds for choosing a particular method are seldom stated in a clear way. Moreover the methods produce a limited range of somewhat rigid value patterns. Even if the link with historical cost is retained, there seems no reason why the patterns should not be more flexible. And if assets are instead to be shown at current values, their valuation method must be agile enough to respond to all manner of ups and downs. It must be able to cope, for instance, with the pattern for a cow: this will vary not only with changes in market conditions, but also with age—upsurge in youth, a summit at maturity, and fall thereafter.

This chapter must try (with the help of deprival logic) to find if there is an ideal method; and, if there is, whether and when a traditional method can adequately deputise for it.

The well-known methods

The well-known bookkeeping methods are: (a) the straight-line method, (b) the fixed-percentage (more clearly, the 'fixed percentage of the diminishing balance') method, (c) (especially in North America) the sum-of-the-digits method, and (d) the double-declining balance method. Occasionally, other simple methods are employed, for instance, (e) a fixed annual charge to cover both depreciation and repairs, and (f) a charge varying with use—the 'service-unit' or 'production-unit' method. Even more rarely, the methods recognise the desirability of discounting, i.e. of allowing for 'interest' at some suitable rate. As we shall see, the case for doing so (in these as in other calculations that deal with cash flows of widely different dates) is strong. The methods that allow for 'interest' include, (g) the annuity method, and (h) the sinking-fund method.

The nature of the methods can best be shown with diagrams such as those in Figure 13.1.

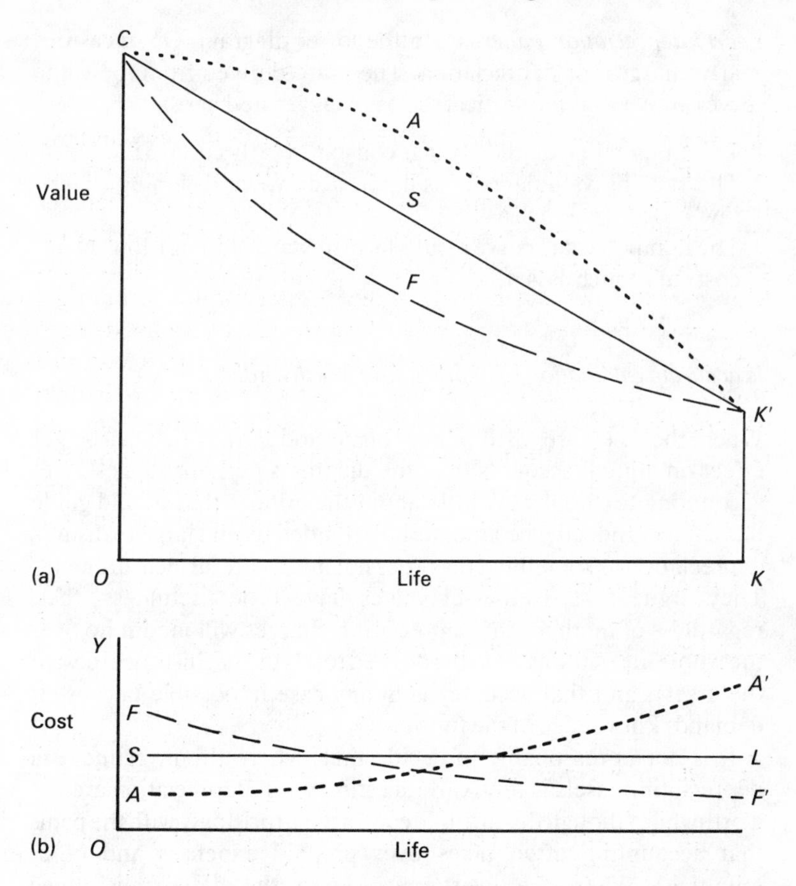

Figure 13.1 Patterns of value and depreciation costs. (a) Asset value patterns, (b) yearly depreciation costs

Asset value patterns *OK* is the asset's life. *OC* is its initial cost. *KK'* is its final sale price (i.e. scrap or 'salvage' value).

The methods result in yearly values traced by the lines between *C* and *K'*.

1 The straight line method produces *CSK'*.
2 Most of the other well-known methods (e.g. the fixed percentage) produce 'sagging' curves like *CFK'*.
3 When interest is allowed for, the curve tends to 'hump' like *CAK'*.

Yearly depreciation patterns In the lower diagram, OY measures yearly charges for depreciation. These are derived from the value curves above (but the vertical scale is exaggerated here).

1 The straight line method brings constant yearly costs, *SL*.
2 The sagging value curve results in a downward-sloping ('high–low') cost curve such as *FF'*.
3 The humped value curve results in an upward-sloping ('low–high') cost curve such as *AA'*.

Is accurate calculation of depreciation worthwhile

Where the assets are costly, choice of method can have a much bigger effect on annual accounts than the diagrams perhaps suggest. Yet accounting textbooks say little about the criteria that should guide this choice. Indeed, accountants have tended by and large to dismiss depreciation as something that does not merit careful measurement. They argue that fixed-asset values have little usefulness; that, regardless of method, the depreciation charges will mount up over the whole life of the asset to the desired total (the net historical cost of the asset); and that accuracy is in any case impossible because it demands knowledge of the future.

It is not unreasonable to decide that, where the investment in depreciating assets is tiny, careful estimates of depreciation are not worthwhile (though this attitude contrasts surprisingly with the pains that accounting often takes over prepaid expenses and other minutiae). Where the investment is large, the matter must hinge mainly on whether the figures have a useful part to play, and in particular on how far they help with decisions.

Definitions

Before one can come to grips with the main problem, certain preliminary points must be cleared up.

Use-assets and time-assets The lives of some assets end when the asset is worn out by use. The lives of others are ended by events that time must bring anyway, regardless of use, e.g. the expiry of a lease or the invention of a better asset. Thus it is convenient to talk of 'use-assets' and 'time-assets'. (It may be that some assets depreciate partly because of time and partly because of use—e.g. my car's life may end when a better model is put on the market, but its trade-in value then may be affected by its mileage.) Possibly time is the more usual cause of depreciation, and so the following pages tend to concentrate on time-assets.

If an asset's value depreciates during a year, this fall is normally a cost for purposes of income measurement, i.e. must be charged in the income statement. With use-assets, there is a cause-and-effect link between the use of the asset on a job, etc., and the fall; so the fall is an avoidable cost of the job, and should be shown as such in budgets for the job, as well as in the income statement (ideally with the direct costs). With time-assets, however, use does not cause the fall; time depreciation is therefore not an avoidable cost of the job, and should be left out of decision budgets, but included with other fixed costs in the income statement.

Depreciation and obsolescence If the word is used in a narrow sense, 'depreciation' is due to physical factors such as wearing-out and to the resulting rise in repair costs, fall in output, etc. Perhaps because our naïve minds often find it hard to accept economic loss that is divorced from physical decline (we shrink from throwing out white elephants if they look 'as good as new'), we tend to use a special word—'obsolescence' instead of 'depreciation'—when value sinks for non-physical reasons. Obsolescence may be due, for instance, to a fall in demand for the product (because, say, fashion changes or a better product is invented) or the arrival on the market of a better asset; it may be sudden or slow; and it may be unforeseen or predictable.

This distinction between depreciation and obsolescence can on occasion help understanding. But it does not usually seem to serve much purpose in accounts; and, as the two kinds of decline are often difficult if not impossible to unravel, this chapter treats them in principle as one.

Primary and secondary assets It was suggested on p. 151 that it is convenient to give the name 'primary asset' to the depreciating asset whose figures are being studied, and 'secondary assets' to the extra net assets that accumulate as a result of providing for depreciation (and restricting dividends to a matching extent). As the primary asset falls, the secondary assets rise: together they should maintain the owner's capital. This changeover can be envisaged in terms of Figure 13.2. Here *OC* represents the amount of capital invested in the primary asset at the start of its life. *OK* represents its life-span. Its value falls over the years along some such pattern as *CK*. But, if secondary assets accumulate in the quantities suggested by the area *CC′K*, the owner's capital is maintained.

Secondary assets may at first take the form of cash. But in time this cash will tend to enrich the whole net asset structure; for instance, it may be used to buy more stocks or even other depreciating assets, or to repay interest-bearing loans. In this way, the secondary growth normally becomes part and parcel of the general structure, and (though their total size is measured by the cumulative depreciation provision) the secondary assets can no longer be identified. But occasionally they are put aside as earmarked financial securities, with some such name as 'sinking-fund investments'.

The rising secondary assets will in time earn revenue or lessen

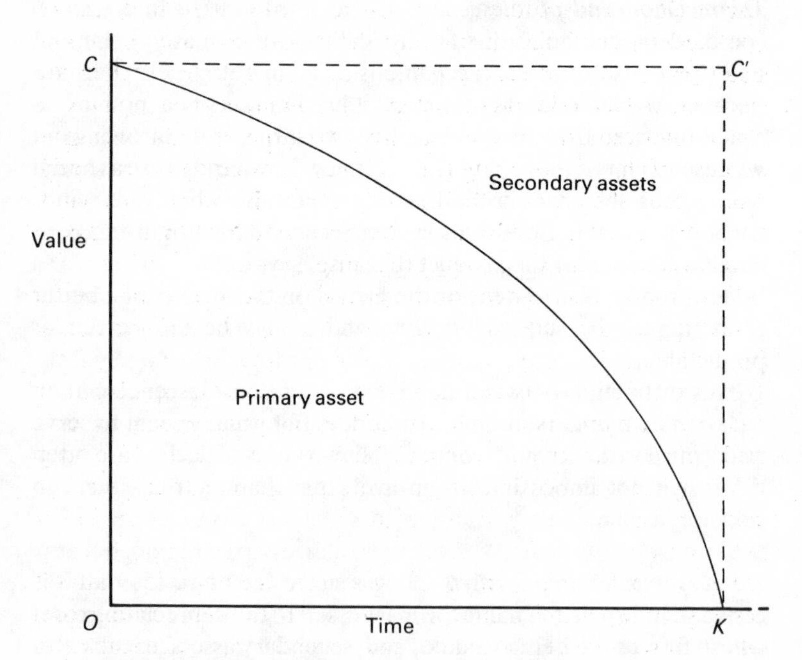

Figure 13.2 Depreciation and the firm's asset structure

costs. Thus they create 'secondary revenue'. A full discussion of depreciation must treat this revenue (= 'interest') as part of the relevant flows.

Deprival budgets for depreciating assets

Deprival value depends on the difference between two cash budgets—one for the figures if the owner is deprived, the other for the figures if he is left in possession. We shall continue to call the former the *Have not* budget, and the latter the *Have* budget. It will be convenient also to call the existing asset Old, and its potential replacement New.

Relevant cash flows for deprival budgets Which cash items should be put in the budgets for depreciating assets? We are concerned with the *contrast* between the two sets of figures; as usual, therefore, any figures that are common to both sets—*in date as well as size*, i.e. after discounting—are irrelevant and can be left out. The well-known bookkeeping methods put most of their stress on initial price and scrap proceeds; and certainly these in most instances affect the contrast, and then should be included. But many other items may be just as relevant. The obvious example is repair cost. If this increases because of the asset's aging (i.e. because of 'wearing out' through time or use), then it too will affect the contrast. If, on the other hand, it would not be changed by a switch from Old to New (because both have the same constant charges), it can be ignored.

Where there is a close link between the asset's age and the pattern of tax payments, tax becomes a relevant flow. This holds in particular for the leasing industry; here the lessor's profit comes mainly from Treasury largesse in the asset's first year. Lessors are perplexed by their accounting problem; they could solve it by basing depreciation on deprival values that allow for tax flows.[3]

Yearly receipts may in some cases be as relevant as outflows. For instance, they will vary where an old asset loses customer-appeal or works only by fits and starts; the rent of an apartment may fall as it grows old and dingy; and a plane or car may cease to attract passengers when it becomes comparatively slow and unreliable. Often, however, receipts do not affect the contrast, particularly if the asset does not earn them independently, but is only one link in the productive chain. Compare a taxi with a machine in a long assembly line; as the machine grows old, usually the owner suffers not because his receipts dwindle, but because he has to pay for higher repairs to that asset and finally for its replacement.

For many assets, then, the budgets can be confined to a few outflows.

'Interest' and deprival budgets In budgets that stretch over long tracts of time, discounting of the figures may greatly increase accuracy. The figures in the *Have not* and *Have* budgets for depreciating assets will often become more helpful if they are reduced to present values; and this discounting process is sometimes essential while we are exploring theory.

With depreciation problems, it is often sensible to start with figures that ignore interest; the results are easy to understand, and are all that traditional accounting demands. Then, to look at the problem in a more profound way, one should introduce interest. The results by the two attacks will differ a good deal if the interest rate is high and the life long.

Assumption of knowledge of future If value depends on budgets, i.e. is forward-looking, serious discussion of our subject is impossible unless we concede that some estimate, however rough, can be made of the cash flows for the asset's whole life, and sometimes indeed for longer periods. Even the usual rule-of-thumb methods use estimates of life-span and scrap proceeds; and they in fact rely on still other assumptions about the future—all the more dangerous because they are not spelled out.

Simple example

Suppose that a time-asset costs £100, has a scrap value of £20 at the end of a five-year life, and needs an overhaul costing £30 at the end of year 3.

The argument will be simpler if we assume use of the method that writes off a fixed annual charge to cover both 'capital' items and running costs. The £30 is thus added to the asset balance, and the annual charge is $1/5(100 + 30 - 20) = 22$.

The resulting patterns for the whole life can be arranged as in

Table 13.1 Simple Example of Asset Values and Depreciation Charges

Year end	*0*	*1*	*2*	*3*	*4*	*5*
	£	£	£	£	£	£
(i) Cost of asset	100			30		−20
(ii) *Less* Annual equivalent charge		22	22	22	22	22
(iii) Change in value		−22	−22	+8	−22	−42
(iv) Value at end of year	100	78	56	64	42	—

Table 13.1. Line (iii) shows each year's change in value, i.e. the depreciation charge. A year's end-value (see line (iv)) must be the sum of the charges still to be written off during the rest of life (see line (iii)).

Note that in year 3 the depreciation is outweighed by the costly overhaul: the value in line (iv) *rises* following the net improvement. This seems realistic and informative; second-hand market values would respond similarly to the improvement. I shall therefore assume that the desired method will reflect the asset's state of repair (shorthand for all the year's relevant flows) in a similarly sensitive way, i.e. will charge as yearly depreciation either (a) a constant sum as in line (ii) of the table (repairs being capitalised), or (b) a varying amount that complements the repair charges in the income statement, as in line (iii). Values and total yearly charges are of course the same whether form (a) or (b) is used.

The deprival approach supports this method. As accountants normally put repairs and other relevant flows into the income statement, form (b) is the more convenient.

Deprival budgets

Table 13.1 gives all the information needed in deprival budgets. Line (i) has the data for a *Have* column. Provided the owner would replace with a New whose flows are like Old's (and this is a sensible assumption with which to start the argument), line (ii) has the *Have not* data—in a handy annualised form that will be justified below. Line (iii) gives the yearly charges, and line (iv) the balance sheet values.

Suppose the owner wants to value Old at the end of year 2; and that he would, if deprived, buy an identical but new model. For clarity, we shall call the years 19x0 (when Old was bought), 19x1, and so on. Table 13.1 can be rearranged in our usual two-column form.

Have not: The owner, if deprived, will pay £100 at the end of 19x2, and £30 in 19x5; he will get £20 in 19x7.
Have: If left in possession, he will pay £30 in 19x3, and get £20 in 19x5.

But these time-spans overlap. Comparison demands that they must be restricted to the same period. Let us choose 19x2–5. We then must round off the *Have not* budget with a kind of 'closing stock'—an allowance for the future benefits of owning New during 19x5–7. These are worth (if we can trust Table 13.1) £64. The budgets run as in Table 13.2.

Table 13.2 Deprival Budgets of a Depreciating Asset

		Have not	*Have*
		£	£
19x2	New's price	−100	
19x3	Old's repairs		−30
19x5	Old's scrap receipts		20
	New's repairs	−30	
	New's value	64	
		−66	−10
Deprival value (costs obviated by ownership) at 19x2		56	

So this familiar form of budgets agrees with the figures of Table 13.1; the 19 x 2 value is £56.

Annual equivalent cost ('notional rent')

But Table 13.1 relies on the annual figure of £22 as a representation of New's flows. We must consider whether this is valid.

The market can and does on occasion reduce a series of varying yearly flows to a constant flow: instead of buying as asset, one can hire it at a fixed yearly rent. Contract hire firms provide and maintain cars, etc., on this basis. So £22 need not be dismissed as an artificial allocation. If helpful, we can envisage a firm as two departments, Owning and Operating: Owning buys and maintains assets, and hires them out to Operating at a rent that just covers costs; Operating charges its income statement with rent instead of normal depreciation and repairs.

The notion of a yearly equivalent cost (or notional rent) greatly simplifies depreciation theory. For instance, Table 13.2 can be shortened by putting only 'rents', for three years, in the *Have not* column:

Table 13.3 Simplified Budgets

		Have not	*Have*
		£	£
19x2–5	New's costs, three years' rent at £22	−66	
19x3	Old's repairs		−30
19x5	Old's scrap receipts		20
		−66	−10
Deprival value		56	

Cost and value diagrams[4]

The case can be strengthened with diagrams. Figure 13.3(a) shows cumulative cost curves.

1 Old's flows are represented by *OCRTJS* (in effect, the *Have* budget).

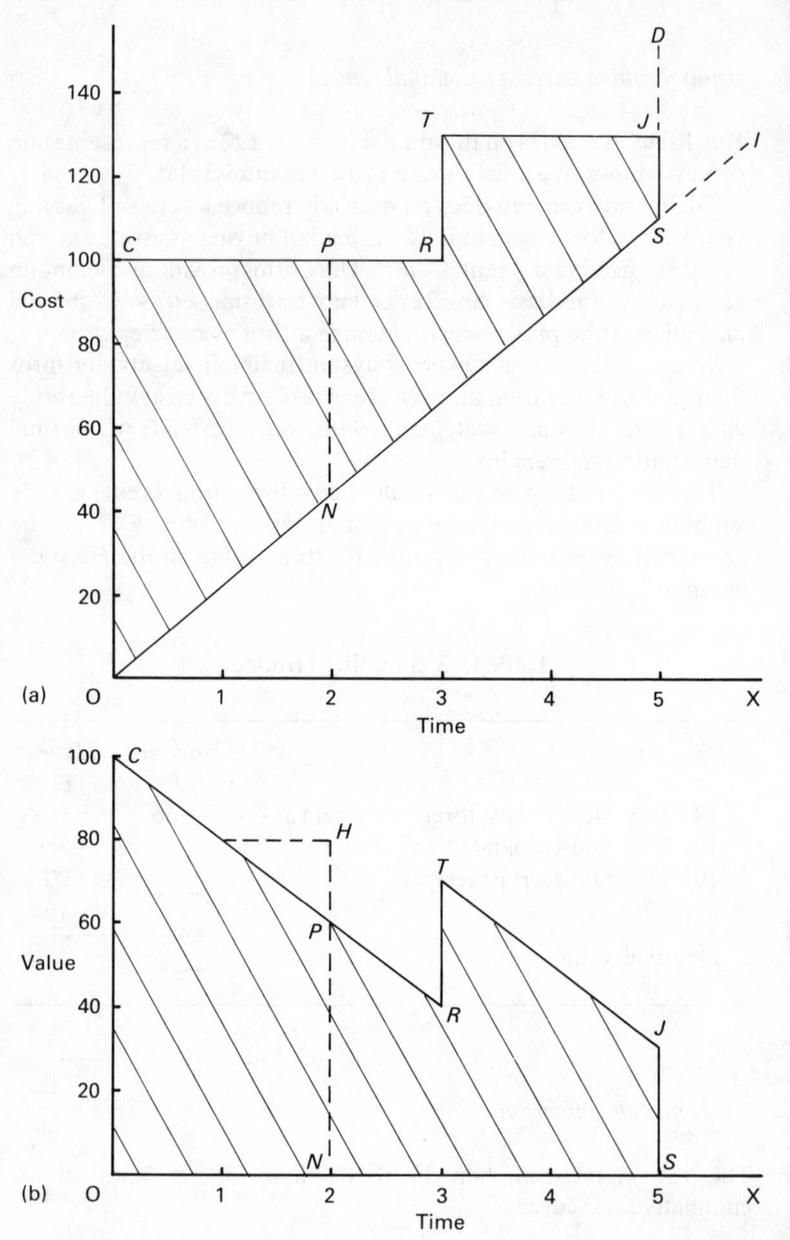

Figure 13.3 Cost and value curves. (a) Cumulative cost curves, (b) asset value curve

OC is purchase price, *RT* is repair cost, and *JS* is scrap receipt. (If Old were not scrapped at year 5, a prohibitively high repair cost such as *JD* would be incurred.)

2 New's flows, expressed as a constant yearly equivalent, are represented by *OSI* (in effect, the *Have not* budget).

At any date, the upper curve: shows Old's future flows, and the lower curve shows New's: the vertical difference between them thus shows cost obviated by ownership, i.e. deprival value. This starts as *OC*. It dwindles from year to year (e.g. to *NP* at year 2); but it gets a boost at year 3 (*RT*) because of the overhaul.

Figure 13.3(b) shows asset value curve. Old's life story can be more readily recognised if the shaded bit of the top diagram is twisted down to its position in the lower diagram. Again the year 2 value is *NP*; the year's depreciation (=drop in value) is *HP*. But this diagram is defensible only if one recalls that *OX* is a clumsy surrogate for New's cumulative 'rent'.

Testing the traditional patterns

Old's value pattern in Figure 13.3 is quite different from the patterns in Figure 13.1. These were produced by methods that clearly do not cater for one big repair cost (or, more precisely, for a small number of big relevant flows). The deprival budgets suggest that, when there are a few big flows, one should use a method that is specially tailored to the particular asset, e.g. the fixed annual charge to cover both depreciation and repairs.

Sagging value curves

Suppose now that there are many repairs, and that these tend to increase over the asset's life. The deprival arithmetic can be set out as in Table 13.4.

Old's flows are in section (i). They add up to a net total of £700 over a seven-year life. So the average (the notional yearly cost or 'rent' of an identical New) is £100, as in section (ii).

The lower sections give the usual details of deprival value. Section (iii), for the net benefit of owning, shows the extra cash outlay for

Table 13.4 Calculation of Deprival Value with Rising Yearly Costs

Year of life	*0*	*1*	*2*	*3*	*4*	*5*	*6*	*7*
	£	£	£	£	£	£	£	£
(i) *Have budget*								
Old's price	620							
Old's repairs		10	20	30	40	50	60	70
Old's scrap receipt								−200
	620	10	20	30	40	50	60	−130
(ii) *Have not budget*								
Less New's yearly 'rent'		100	100	100	100	100	100	100
(iii) *Net benefit of owning* for year (=write off at year-end)		90	80	70	60	50	40	230
(iv) *Deprival value* (= future years' benefits per *(iii)*)	620	530	450	380	320	270	230	—

each year that would face a deprived owner, and thus the advantage of ownership during a year. This benefit evaporates by the end of the year, and so must be written off. If the repair is (the common practice) debited in the income statement, (iii) gives the depreciation charges; if it is added to the asset's value, (ii) gives the depreciation charges. The cost of depreciation plus repairs is constant. At any year-end, the sum of the remaining years' benefits is *deprival value*, shown on (iv)—e.g. at the end of year 4, deprival value is the sum of the remaining benefits to the right in (iii) above: £50 + £40 + £230 = £320.

Diagrams With these data, the cumulative cost curve will look like the stepped line *OCJS* in Figure 13.4. It rises more steeply each year. Little harm will be done if we smooth it into the dotted curve *CJ*. Deprival reasoning converts these cumulative costs into a constant yearly equivalent for the *Have not* budget, represented by the straight line *OS*. Values of each year are shown by vertical distances between points on *CJ* and *OS*, e.g. *PN*.

As before, the shaded area *OCJS* can be twisted to produce the

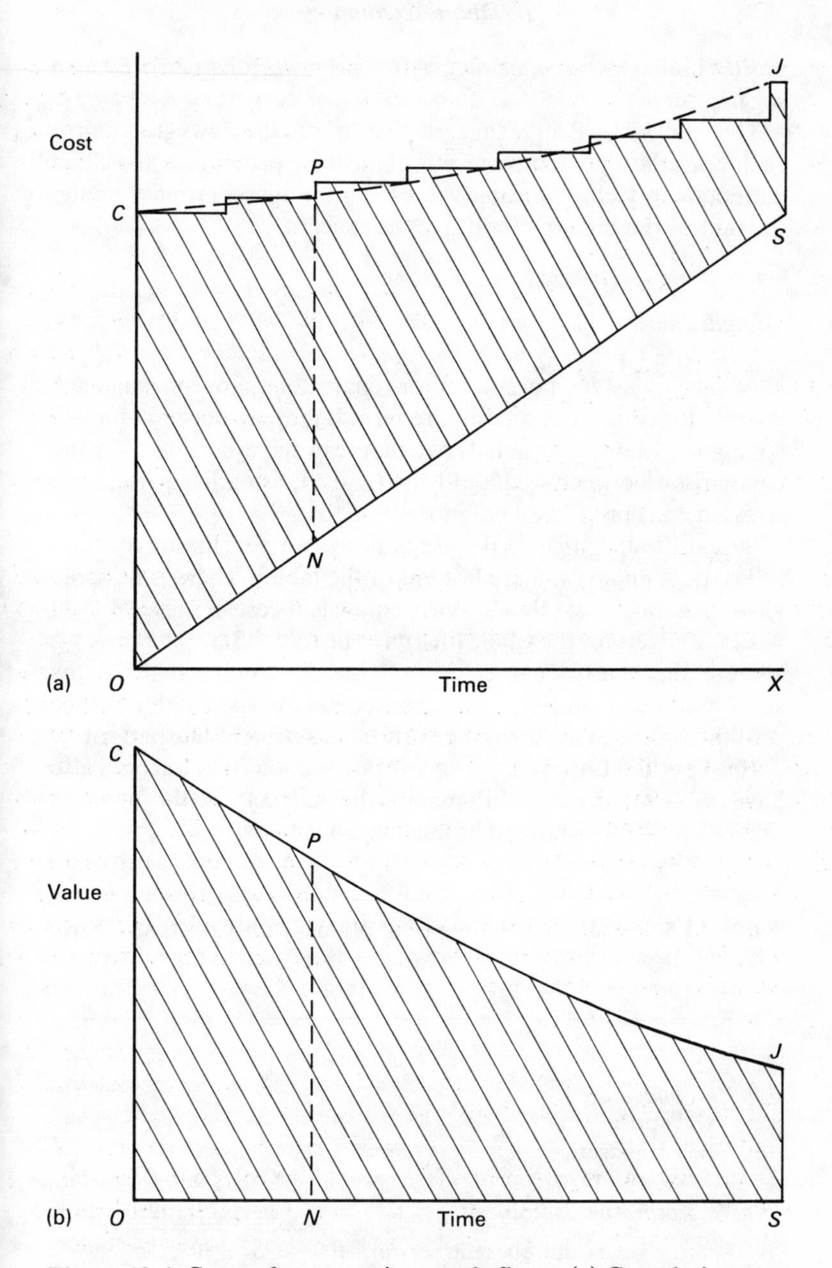

Figure 13.4 Curves for worsening yearly flows. (a) Cumulative cost curves, (b) asset value curves costs

more familiar asset value shape (in the lower diagram). *CJ* is a sagging curve.

Thus the deprival logic suggests that, where the flows grow worse each year, the high–low write-offs of the fixed percentage and allied methods may yield defensible values. For the figures in our example, the sum-of-the-digits method gives an exact fit.

Straight line

Next take an asset whose flows for repairs, etc., are constant each year. In the simplest case, they are zero. If they are not zero, but are common to both Old and New, they can have no effect on the comparison between Old and New (and so, as earlier pages have stressed, may just as well be ignored).

Suppose initial price is £100. Repairs over a 4-year life are constant at £20 per annum (and are left out of the table). There is no scrap value. Average cost (New's yearly equivalent cost) is thus $\frac{1}{4} \times$ £100 = £25. Budgets for the whole life run as in Table 13.5.

Here the yearly depreciation charge (i.e. the benefit of the services 'used up' during a year, per section (iii)) is always £25. The resulting values in section (iv) clearly have a straight-line pattern.

If we put the £20 a year of repairs into section (i), we should also have to put it into section (ii), making the 'rent' £45. So the figures in sections (iii) and (iv) would be unchanged.

Table 13.5 Calculation of Deprival Value with Constant Yearly Costs

	Year of life	*0*	*1*	*2*	*3*	*4*
		£	£	£	£	£
(i)	*Have budget*					
	Old's price	100				
(ii)	*Have not budget*					
	Less New's yearly 'rent'		25	25	25	25
(iii)	*Net benefit of owning* for year		25	25	25	25
(iv)	*Deprival value* (future benefits per *(iii)*)	100	75	50	25	—

Diagrams If the £20 repairs cost is ignored, the cumulative cost curves can be represented by *CJ* and *OJ* in the upper part of Figure 13.5. If the repairs are included, we must change to *CJ'* and *OJ'*. In either case, the resulting value pattern is traced by the straight line *CJ* in the lower part.

Thus the deprival logic confirms that, where flows are constant each year, the straight-line method suits the facts.

Humped value curves

From the above discussion, it is easy to perceive that the value curve will be humped if the yearly flows *improve* over the asset's life (e.g. if repairs have a high–low pattern).

Experience suggests that such improvement in the obvious flows is rare. Typically old age brings rising repairs (and, if it affects revenue at all, declining receipts).

But there is one flow, namely 'interest', that does improve. Consider the case in which (a) an asset is bought with the help of a loan, and (b) the depreciation quotas are used, not to pile up secondary assets, but to repay the loan. Plainly the loan interest will each year get less. So here we have a cost, certainly if not very obviously created by the asset, with high–low flows that may be substantial.

If instead the asset is bought with the firm's own funds, its purchase will deflect cash from other uses. Again there is a hidden 'interest' cost—the loss of potential benefits from the uses forgone. And again the cost will each year dwindle as the depreciation quotas produce secondary assets and then secondary flows of benefits.

One way or another, then, a firm with a big depreciating asset can expect the 'interest' flows to make predepreciation profits curve upwards throughout the asset' life. At the end, when funds are reduced by replacement, profits will tend to fall back abruptly. Such profit cycles give a poor picture of the firm's progress. Constant 'unit costs' would be more realistic, and again can be obtained by complementing the high–low cost of 'interest' with low–high depreciation charges.

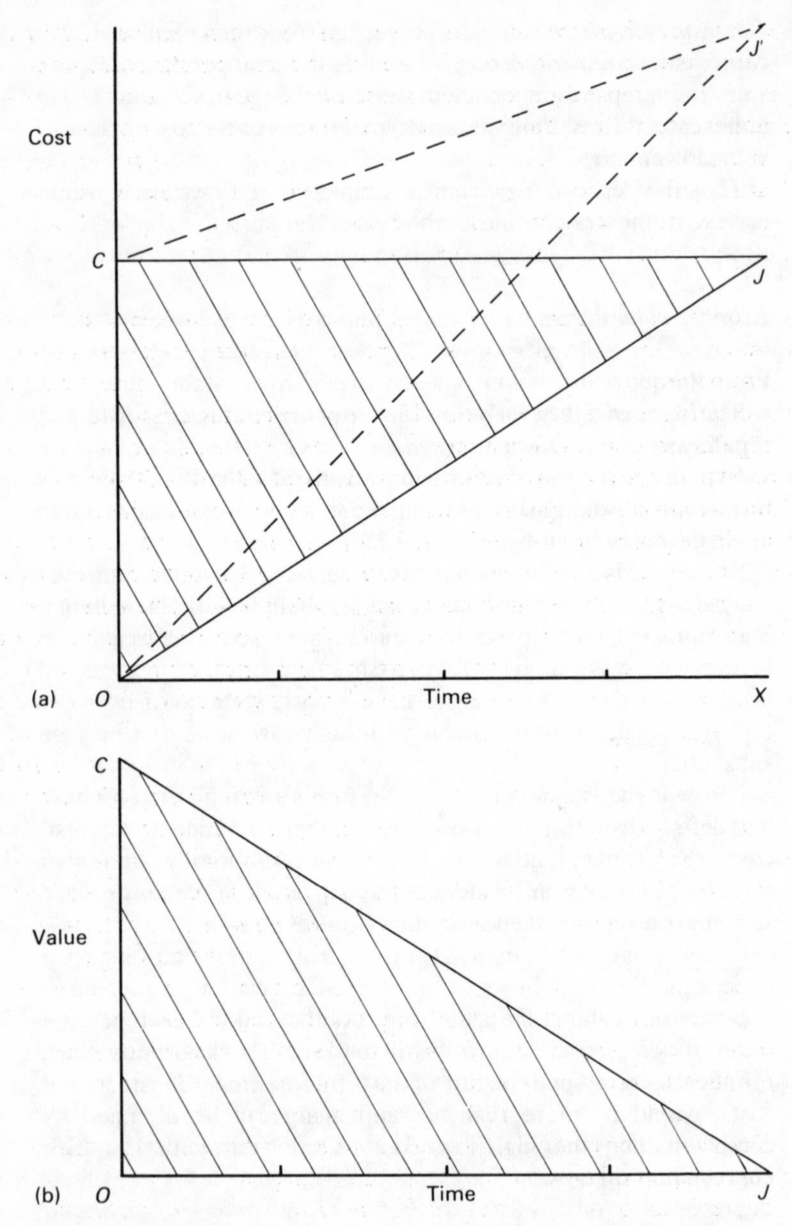

Figure 13.5 Curves for constant yearly flows. (a) Cumulative cost curves, (b) asset value curve

The deprival arithmetic with interest[5] To allow for 'interest', the usual table of *Have not* and *Have* budgets must be adapted in two ways. First, *Have's* section (i) must include the series of yearly interest costs (found as a percentage of asset value at the start of the year). Secondly, *Have not's* section (ii) must no longer use an arithmetical average (of the flows in section (i)) as yearly 'rent'; instead, it must use the yearly sum that the present value of those flows would yield if invested in an annuity.[6]

Example Let us again use the example of Table 13.5 (cost £100, four-year life) but superimpose interest at 30 per cent on the straight-line patterns.

Section (i) will now include a high–low series of interest charges, e.g. £30 in year 1 (30 per cent of the year's £100 opening balance shown on line (iv)). Annuity tables state that £100 will at 30 per cent buy a four-year annuity of £46.16 p.a.; so section (ii) uses this figure as New's yearly 'rent'—see Table 13.6.

Table 13.6 Deprival Value Calculation Allowing for Interest

Year of life	*0*	*1*	*2*	*3*	*4*
	£	£	£	£	£
(i) Have budget					
Old's price	100				
Old's interest cost		30	25.15	18.84	10.65
(ii) Have not budget					
Less New's yearly 'rent'		46.16	46.16	46.16	46.16
(iii) Net benefit of owning for year		16.16	21.01	27.32	35.51
(iv) Deprival value (future benefits per *(iii)*)	100	83.84	62.83	35.51	—

Section (iii) shows that the net benefits 'used up' each year (= depreciation charge) have now a markedly low–high slope. (Compare the figures with the £25 straight-line charge.)

Diagram The curves in Figure 13.6 reflect Table 13.6. The value curve in part (2) now humps perceptibly. For good measure, annual depreciation cost is shown also in Figure 13.6(c) (whose vertical scale for clarity exaggerates the changes in (b)); *DD'* traces the deprival charges, *SL* those of the straight-line method.

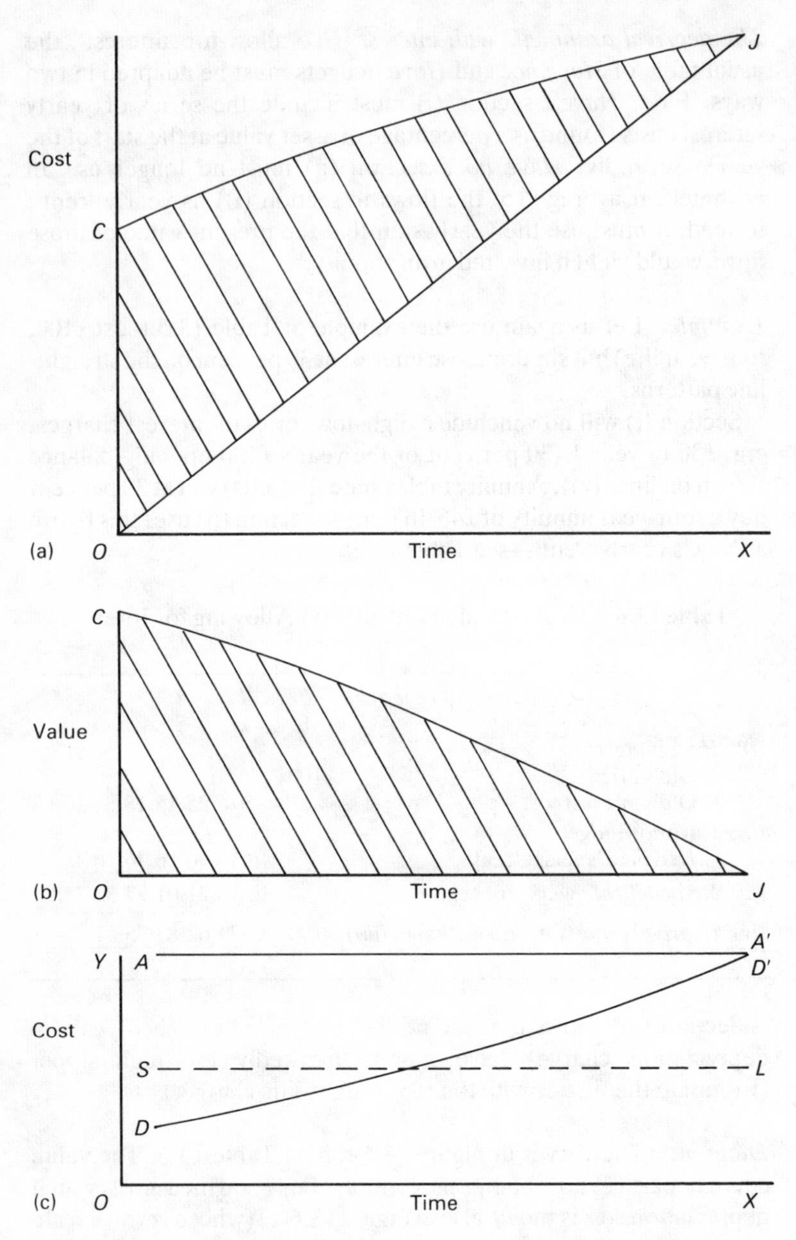

Figure 13.6 Curves showing effect of interest. (a) Cumulative cost curves, (b) asset value curves, (c) yearly depreciation cost

The annuity method *DD′* reflects the low–high charges of section (iii) in Table 13.6. Such charges might be called *net* depreciation. They are simple and satisfactory. But text books, when they illustrate the bookkeeping (under the heading 'annuity method'), prefer a grander approach. They first capitalise interest (i.e. raise the asset's value with the figures shown in section (i), and credit interest expense or some other suitable account); then they write off a constant *gross* depreciation charge—in our example, the £46.16 in section (ii) of Table 13.6, and AA′ in Figure 13.6(c).

This roundabout variant ends with the same value and income patterns as the net method. It has at least one advantage. If gross depreciation is charged to the annual accounts of a department, its manager gets a forceful reminder that ownership of costly assets means high yearly sacrifice by the firm. This is one of the reasons why the interest rate should reflect the firm's cost-of-capital rate, or (with capital rationing) the cut-off rate that is used for project assessment.

The perpetuity approach Our discussion on interest has so far tended to portray it as a past cost. Our specimen accounts were backward-looking, i.e. recorded former items such as price, repairs to date—and interest cost to date on loan, etc.

However, forward-looking concepts often yield more satisfying results. Past interest is here displaced by discount on future flows; deprival budgets use present values.

But how far forward must the owner look? When the existing asset's life is over, he will probably replace it with a second, bringing much the same set of flows. And so on. In the absence of special circumstances, ownership involves him in sets of flows that stretch to his time-horizon. He can estimate their size by treating them as a perpetuity, and finding its present value. On our assumption that the relevant flows are mainly costs, the present value is a *burden*—the bad side of the decision to own such an asset permanently.[7] Because discounting reduces the remote flows to negligible size, the figures are less intimidating than one might suppose.

The burden is greatest just before purchase of the asset; its size then is the right figure for any *Have not* budget. Just after a purchase, it is reduced (by the price) to its minimum size; during life, it gradually grows again as replacement cost looms nearer; at a valuation date, it is the right figure for the *Have* budget.

This arithmetic is no doubt too elaborate for ordinary use; and, when static conditions are predicted, it gives the same answers as the annuity method. But it seems essential for understanding changeable conditions. It thus brings realism when the valuer tries to cope with rising prices, improving technology, and the like.[8]

Market values and interest The main argument for depreciation methods that allow for interest is that they mirror the market. The latter's prices for limited-life assets tend (in the absence of other factors such as rising repairs) to follow a humped pattern like *CJ*. Thus the price of leasehold property usually sinks little in the early years of a long lease, but steeply in the final years. Again, one would expect a close match between the deprival and market values of financial assets such as annuities-certain. *CJ*'s shape reflects a powerful force.

Use-assets

So far, our discussion has centred on time-assets, and so has assumed that depreciation does not depend on extent of use during a year.

If the asset is instead a use-asset, deprival reasoning suggests that we must pay regard to extent of use (cf. the yearly consumption of stores and the depletion of minerals). The total net outlay must be divided over units of expected physical use, to find average cost per unit. Cost is then spread across section (ii) of the tables in proportion to yearly use. In other words, New's cost is expressed as a rent per ton-mile, etc., instead of per year.

Conclusion on choice of method

There seems no reason why the traditional methods should not be adapted. A mixed method may best reflect the facts. The deprival table can produce such a mix. Thus it can blend service units with rising repairs; and, with a little ingenuity, the valuer can superimpose interest on the other date.[6]

However, as many of the projected flows must be only rough guesses, there are some grounds for choosing the simple method that approximates to the findings of the deprival table. And we can perhaps permit ourselves another comforting thought. With most assets, repairs probably have a low–high pattern. But interest has a high–low pattern (and, whether or not the firm appreciates the fact, is a potent force). Common sense suggests that often the two forces may just about cancel one another, thus giving unexpected support to the simplest of the methods—the straight line.

Optimum life-span

The preceding pages assume that the owner has found out the optimum life, i.e. knows which life-span will best suit his pocket. How does he find the right number of years?'

Simple approach (interest ignored)

When a man decides to own a depreciating asset, he is involving himself in a new and lengthy series of future cash flows. For his value calculations, he should select the flows that affect deprival budgets—notably the flows that vary because of the asset's aging. They probably include a price paid at once, and varying repair charges, etc., paid at later dates; they may also include some varying receipts, such as final scrap proceeds.

Let us assume the relevant cash flows of this asset, and its replacements, to be dominated by the outlays (initial price, repairs, etc.), so that the net total can be pictured as a cost or burden. If initial prices were the main thing to consider, then the burden would be lightened by keeping each asset longer. But a longer life must at some point entail disadvantages such as higher repairs and lower resale value. These make for a heavier burden. Thus the owner must weigh two conflicting forces, and try to find the compromise that minimises his burden. By drafting alternative budgets for series of different life-spans—i.e. by comparing flows for, say, ten-year lives, eleven-year lives, twelve-year lives, and so on—he can discover which life gives the lowest burden.

The budgets' *totals* are of course no help, since they rise as life lengthens. Once again the notion of yearly equivalent comes to the rescue. The owner must turn each life-span's total into the arithmetical average per year of life. The life-span with the lowest average ('rent' or 'service charge') is the most economical: at least in a rough-and-ready way, it points to the policy that will minimise long-run cost for a series of successive future lives.

Arithmetic To illustrate, suppose the asset's price is £1000, and the owner expects that the repair costs and scrap values will be:

Year	*1*	*2*	*3*	*4*	*5*	*6*
	£	£	£	£	£	£
Repairs		100	100	150	300	450
Scrap receipts if asset is sold at end of year	690	540	420	350	300	270

The alternative budgets for the various possible life-spans run as in Table 13.7. So the minimum rate of yearly cost (£250) is achieved if this asset is kept for four years.

It may be helpful to check such findings with a marginal test. At some point near the end of Old's optimum life, the yearly rise in its flows must become greater than New's average. (In the table, 1350 – 1000 = 350 > 250.) The owner of an old television set uses this

Table 13.7 Alternative Budgets to Find Optimum Life

Life-span, years:	*1*	*2*	*3*	*4*	*5*	*6*
	£	£	£	£	£	£
Cash outflows						
Year 0	1000	1000	1000	1000	1000	1000
1	—	—	—	—	—	—
2		100	100	100	100	100
3			100	100	100	100
4				150	150	150
5					300	300
6						450
	1000	1100	1200	1350	1650	2100
Cash inflow (scrap)	690	540	420	350	300	270
Net outflow	310	560	780	1000	1350	1830
Average per year	310	280	260	250	270	305

approach if he works out that it will now come cheaper to hire a new set than to pay the rising repair bills on the old one.

'Life' should thus be looked on, not as a physical matter, but as a balance between the 'capital' flows (at the start and end) and the intermediate flows. If the balance is disturbed, the owner should adjust the life. In 1807, the British Navy curbed the slave trade from Africa; prices of slaves in America rose—and their lives grew longer.[9]

Interest

Long-run budgets that ignore interest are clearly imperfect. They improve if (a) the future flows are discounted, and (b) the total for each likely life-span is then expressed, not as an arithmetical average, but as the yearly sum that the total could buy as an annuity. The life-span with the lowest yearly sum (rent or 'full service charge') is the most economical. The first section of Appendix 3 shows this arithmetic.

It is possible to use perpetuity arithmetic. And this makes for realism where change in future prices, etc., is expected.[10]

Effect of allowing for interest When my cash position is so tight that I am desperately anxious to husband every penny, I try to put off big payments until later, even if this costs me extra small payments now. Recognition of interest likewise makes an owner tend to put off replacement and pay instead for more repairs, etc.

If Table 13.7 allowed for interest, the lowest yearly average (now modified to the full service charge) would tend to shift to the right. Thus it might shift to the foot of the five-year column, i.e. show the optimum life to be a year longer than the undiscounted figures suggest.

Revision of life estimates and values

Most kinds of asset would appear seldom to 'die' at the age foretold by early estimates. Yearly repairs may in the event prove unexpectedly light or heavy: a much improved New may arrive later or sooner than predicted. Such statistics as exist, as 'mortality tables' for large groups of like assets, suggest that at best only a third dutifully die at the average age. With more eccentric types, there is even less of a peak; if the average life is expressed as 10 periods, a few assets die in period 1, a few linger on after period 20, and less than 8 per cent die in period 10.[11]

Thus one would expect the values of depreciating assets to be revised frequently. They are not. And, where life estimates are revised, probably the most usual procedure is to leave the existing book-value unchanged, but to write it off over a future period that conforms with the new estimate. Current value accounts surely should be as responsive to life estimate change as to price change.

As a half-hearted form of inflation accounting, some companies have been writing off historical cost over unrealistically short lives. This leads to an awkward clash if the company later produces current value accounts.

Revaluation of depreciating assets

So far, our discussion of asset values has for the most part assumed that Old's cash flows will continue as first predicted, and that New will also have these same flows. But in fact changes in both prices and technology may affect the flows. One of the attractions of the deprival approach is that its tables can then be altered, without much trouble, to show current values and charges.

As earlier chapters explained, revaluation problems should be analysed in three steps, by considering (a) general price change alone; (b) price change of the given asset alone, i.e. specific change when general prices are stable; and (c) the combination of general and real changes.

General price change

If general and specific prices move to much the same extent, and are expected to go on doing so, the current value of assets can be found by adjusting historical cost with the general index. Adjustment with the index cures also the time-lag error on annual cost (see Chapter 10), and thus gives the most defensible net profit figure.

Budget revision after price change Suppose for simplicity that all prices suddenly go up by x per cent, and are expected to stay constant at the new level. In the *Have* budget, Old's post-change flows must be raised by x per cent. But New's flows too will jump by x per cent, and so average cost in the *Have not* budget must be raised by x per cent in the post-change columns. The post-change depreciation charges and values thus are shown to be x per cent higher. (Such arithmetic may seem otiose proof of the obvious; but it is an easy introduction to tables for specific change.)

The figures of Table 13.7 can be used to illustrate general change. They showed that, when the asset was first acquired, its optimum life was put at four years, and yearly cost (with constant prices) at £250; its expected value pattern is shown by the usual deprival table:

Year	*0*	*1*	*2*	*3*	*4* *(before scrapping)*	*4′* *(after scrapping)*
	£	£	£	£	£	£
(i) *Have* flows	1000	—	100	100	150	−350
(ii) *Have not* average flow	—	250	250	250	250	—
(iii) *Net benefit* for year	—	250	150	150	100	350
(iv) *Deprival value*	1000	750	600	450	350	—

If all prices rise (say) by 40 per cent at the end of year 2, a rift appears in the table. The amended figures are in Table 13.8.

Inflation has raised the *nominal* figures (the yearly charges of section (iii), and the values of section (iv)) by 40 per cent. The new figures should appear in curent value accounts. But, if these are stabilised in £s of date 0, they will of course revert to the original estimate; there has been no real change. Stabilised accounts will show too that here a backlog problem does not exist.

Inflation fails to affect not only real value patterns but also optimum life. On our assumption that all prices move to the same extent, the balance between the asset's price and repairs, etc., is not disturbed, so optimum life is unchanged.

Diagram Earlier diagrams can be readily adapted for change in nominal values. Figures 13.7 shows once-and-for-all change. The asset's value curve was first expected to be CFK'. At date E, prices jump sharply; nominal value rises from F to H, and thereafter

Table 13.8 Calculation of Deprival Values, with General Price Change

Budgets at end of year	*0*	*1*	*2a*	*2b*	*3*	*4*	*4′*
			Price change			*Scrapping*	
			Before	*After*		*Before*	*After*
(i) Have							
Old's flows	1000	—	100	—	140	210	−490
(ii) Have not							
Less New's average flow		250	250	—	350	350	—
(iii) Net benefit for year		250	150	—	210	140	490
(iv) Deprival value	1000	750	600	840	630	490	—
(v) Unforeseen write-up				240			

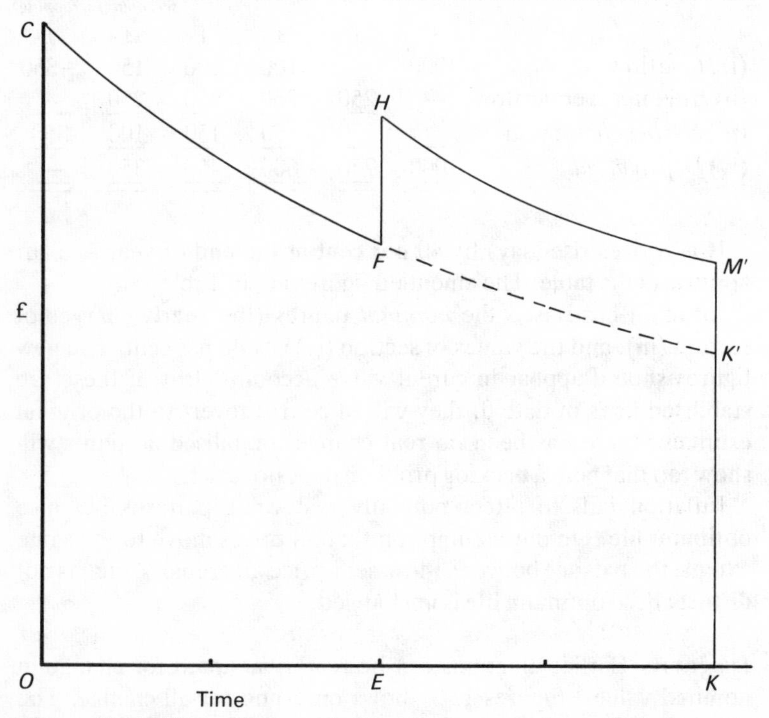

Figure 13.7 Effect of general price change on a depreciating asset's value

follows the pattern *HM'K*. The optimal life still ends at *K*.

Inflation is more likely to be gradual. Then there will be a series of small jumps. The value pattern may well form a fairly smooth curve between *C* and *M'*.

Specific price change when general prices are stable

The phrase 'specific price change' here means change per unit of input; it thus occurs when a better New is marketed at the same price, as well as where New's price moves in a more obvious way. After the change, the deprival budgets must be revised to match the new expectations.

Budget revision after price change In the *Have* budgets, the future cash flows for Old's repairs, etc., may be unchanged (but its resale price is likely to alter). Some of New's flows change, and so the yearly 'rent' (average cost or full service charge) must be revised in the *Have not* budget. As a result, Old's deprival values may go up or down, in both the current and later years.

The figures in Table 13.7 can again be used as illustration. Suppose that a better New is invented unexpectedly at the close of year 2. The improvements seem likely to reduce the price, the running costs, and scrap value of the replacement by 20 per cent. As the balance between 'capital' flows and 'repairs' is (in this example) unaltered, New's optimum life stays at four years. Its average cost per year falls to only £200.

The owner should now use the marginal test (page 260) to review Old's life, i.e. to find the date at which the yearly rise in its new flows exceeds £200. An important factor here is Old's revised pattern of resale values, which New's advent may depress. If they fall fast in years 3 and 4, life must tend to shorten; whereas a slow fall makes for longer life. Let us here assume a pattern such that life still ends at the close of year 4, when the sale receipts will be £280.

Table 13.9 gives the revised figures. At the end of year 2, but before New's advent is announced, Old is worth £600, and the year's write-down is £150. But when New's attractions become known, the gap between the *Have* and *Have not* budget shrinks, and Old's value drops sharply by a further £170 to £430. This windfall loss is a good example of how technical improvement brings obsolescence; owners

Table 13.9 Calculation of Deprival Values, with Specific Price Change

Budgets at end of year	*0*	*1*	*2a*	*2b*	*3*	*4*	*4'*
			Price change			*Scrapping*	
			Before	*After*		*Before*	*After*
	£	£	£	£	£	£	£
(i) *Have*							
Old's flows	1000	—	100	—	100	150	−280
(ii) *Have not*							
Less New's average flow		250	250	—	200	200	—
(iii) *Net benefit* for year		250	150	—	100	50	280
(iv) *Deprival value*	1000	750	600	430	330	280	—
(v) *Unforseen write-off* ('obsolescence')				170			

of assets may well look askance at the onward march of technology. Old's own prospects are almost unchanged, but if suffers in comparison with the 'modern equivalent asset' (New), and so the future benefits of ownership fall. Here again the figures stress the *relative* nature of value.

Diagram Specific price change can alter value patterns in various ways. Figure 13.8 shows some of the possibilities.

Let us start with downward movement in value. An old asset's curve was expected to be *CFK'K*. New, with lower price and upkeep costs, appears unexpectedly at date *E*. At once the relative advantage of possessing Old is lessened. Old's value curve falls vertically from *F*. If the comparison of Old with New gives New a moderate advantage only, the drop may be to a point such as *G*, and the revised curve may be *CFGL'L*, i.e. the optimum life is here shortened to L. But many other effects are possible. As we have seen, Old's value and life depend on the gap between Old's future annual outlays and New's full service charge. If at *E* the former already exceed the latter, Old will be scrapped at once (i.e. *L* coincides with *E*) as its value is less than its scrap price. If they remain

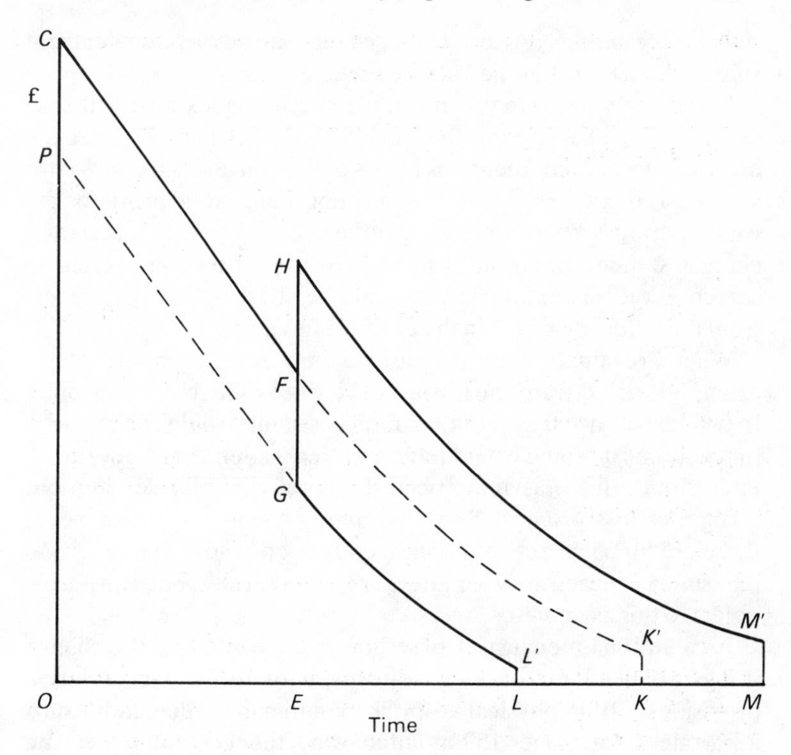

Figure 13.8 Some possible effects of specific price change on a depreciating asset's value

lower until K, Old's earlier life estimate still holds (i.e. L coincides with K) though its value curve GL' is beneath FK'.

If New's price, etc., are above Old's, the book-value should be raised, and Old's life tends to be extended. Its revised value pattern may for instance be $CFHM'M$.

Gradual value change This will result in a series of small movements instead of steep jumps such as FG and FH. And, when changes in a future year are foreseen, the revised *Have not* budgets must at once tend to affect deprival value, i.e. to spread the value changes back towards early life. Realistic value patterns should probably follow gentle curves from C to L' or M'. This is one of the situations in which depreciation and obsolescence are almost indistinguishable.

Accounting entries After specific change, all advocates of current value will wish to alter the balance sheet figures.

In the years following revision, the specific-index man will base depreciation charges on the revised value. Chapter 8 argued however that, where there is real loss or gain on assets that are later used up as input, such loss or gain cannot change total profit for the whole period. Where for instance there is real gain, depreciation charges should remain at historical cost; or, if they are raised to current level, the extra charge should be offset by yearly transfers from the holding gain (as in the example in Table 10.3).

Where revaluation results instead in a fall (as in the above example), strong tradition favours its charge against current income. In defence of such treatment, many accountants would cite the need for caution. But some would rely on the realisation test. As normally understood, this is asymmetrical; it ignores gain till sale, etc., but recognises loss promptly; an 'accounting event' occurs whenever there are 'impairments of nonmonetary economic resources'.[12] As realisation is necessarily a matter for arbitrary rules, one can hardly object to this asymmetry.

If capital maintenance is based on real wealth, specific change brings no need for backlog adjustment of former depreciation provisions. But physical capital maintenance demands such adjustment; as page 159 pointed out, the cost may become exorbitant.

Use value and sale value In our example, the revised values of years 3 and 4 can still be defined as replacement cost of future input (though the potential replacement is a changed model). But consider the more extreme situation where New is so superior that it should be bought at once. Old's year 2 value there falls below replacement cost. If the best plan is to get rid of Old, deprival value is sale price. If the best plan is to keep Old (say, as a standby in case New breaks down or is overstretched), deprival value is value in use. Perhaps it is best thought of as what the firm would be willing to pay as a kind of once-and-for-all insurance premium to keep the reserve capacity available. This premium might be assessed by considering the cost of buying or hiring a suitable alternative asset, and then reducing this cost by a probability factor to allow for the chance that it will never be incurred.

Mixture of differing specific and general price changes

If real change is superimposed on money change, the approach of Table 13.9 again yields current deprival values. Often the real change will be downwards (because of technological improvement) and the money change will be upwards (because of inflation).

Reformed accounts should show the asset at current value. And they should try to unravel the real from the illusory movements. Thus the balance sheet should show the real appreciation, as revaluation surplus with some such label as 'real holding gain (unrealised)', in the way illustrated on p. 53.

The specific-index man would have us gear the depreciation charge and income measurement to the asset's current value. The general-index man is satisfied with net charges that maintain real capital—a goal at once more practicable and defensible. The accounts in Table 10.4 and Table 10.5 both illustrate these matters in the year of change; Appendix 2 of this chapter has a more ambitious study of an asset's whole life.

A table of stabilised figures for a long period will show that, when there is a mixture of real and nominal changes, the former affects real value and optimum life, but the latter does not.

Gross and net value

A normal balance sheet gives three figures for most depreciating assets: (a) the original gross cost, (b) cumulative depreciation, and (c) a net value. These figures are useful, in that they enable readers to form some picture of the age of the plant. Consistency demands that a revalued asset also should be provided with (a) and (b) as well as (c). But how does one now define and measure (a) (i.e. what is a suitable substitute for Old's original cost in a revalued balance sheet)? In the example, three figures suggest themselves for the balance sheet of year 2:

1 The current price of another asset (at the start of its life) of the Old type.
2 The current price of whatever other asset (new) would in fact be the replacement.

3 A notional price. Suppose that another asset of the Old type was bought (new) at the end of year 2, just before New appeared; and that its £1000 price was at once written down after New's appearance. Arithmetic like that in Table 13.9 shows that the written-down value (i.e. deprival value of a brand-new asset) would be £730. This seems a suitable notional price (and is represented by OP in Fig. 13.8).

These three possible sets of figures could read:

	(1) £	(2) £	(3) £
Depreciating asset's value:			
(a) Gross			
Price, Old	1000		
Price, New		800	
Notional price, Old			730
(b) Cumulative depreciation	570	370	300
(c) Net value	430	430	430

Method 3 (above), putting gross value at £730, seems least unsatisfactory.

Interest and revaluation

Our discussion has suggested that, in any sophisticated treatment of depreciation, interest must play a part. This holds for revaluation; interest can have a big effect where the rate is high and the life is long. Appendix 3 illustrates the arithmetic.

As usual, the perpetuity variant makes for greater realism if future change is expected.

Conclusions

This chapter helps to clarify the earlier tentative definitions of deprival value—on p. 204 (stocks) and p. 221 (assets that yield interest, etc.). The cash flows of a depreciating asset tend to be more complex than those of other assets; but they give excellent support to the notions behind alternative budgets and deprival value.

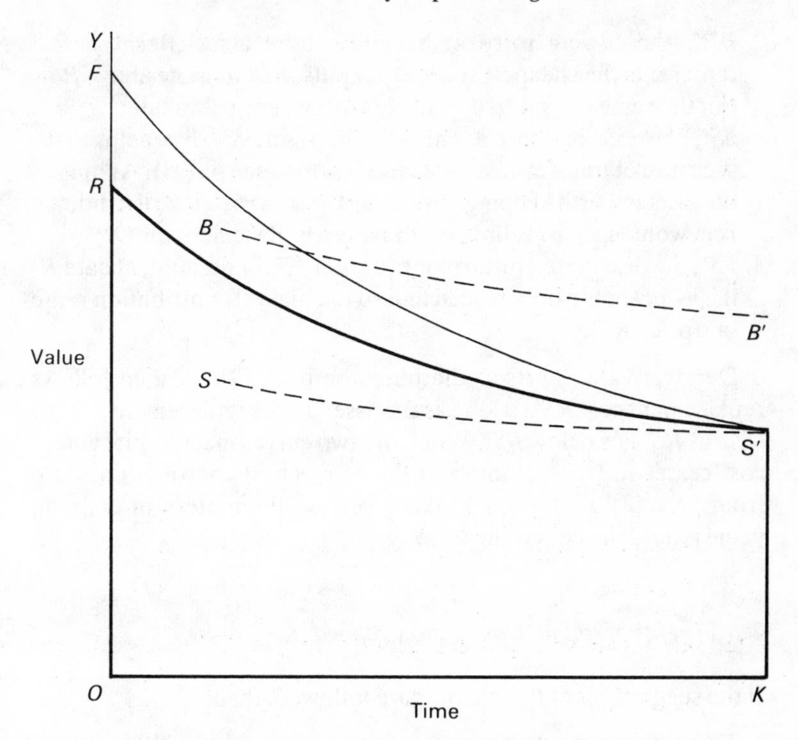

Figure 13.9 Various values of a depreciating asset

Deprival and other values over the whole life

It may be helpful to add a diagram that shows, over the asset's whole life, the patterns of the four main kinds of value.

The curves in Figure 13.9 assume that the cheapest input units come from an asset (new or secondhand) whose future life at purchase date *O* is *OK*; its price is *OR*. Preliminary capital budgets show such an asset to be worth buying because its contribution *OF* (the present value of its net cost savings or revenues, and of its final sale proceeds) exceeds *OR*; so the asset is duly bought.

The four patterns are as follows. (We here assume that they sag and are smooth.)

1 *RS'*, the net *replacement* outlay avoided thanks to owning the remaining stock of input units.

2 BB', the *buying* price of a similar used asset. Because RS' represents the cheapest source of inputs, BB' must lie above RS'. For the same reason, BB' is irrelevant to deprival value.
3 SS', the *sale* price of a similar used asset. SS' lies below BB' (because of transfer costs, specificity, etc.—see p. 195). As long as the asset is worth keeping, SS' does not rise above RS'; if it did, the firm would gain by selling and buying a replacement for OR.
4 FS', the discounted future contribution. This falls until, at date K, the asset should be replaced and so the highest contribution is the sale price KS'.

Deprival value starts as the purchase price OR. It then follows replacement cost RS' so long as the asset merits replacement, i.e. so long as RS' lies below FS'. When the two curves meet, replacement cost ceases to be relevant, and the asset's best contribution (here from prompt sale for KS') takes over. So the pattern of deprival value is here the heavy line $ORS'K$.

The benefits of sound depreciation values

If the suggestions of this chapter are followed, then:

1 The balance sheet value of a depreciating asset will be closely linked with current prices. It will also reflect managers' views of the benefits that the asset still can yield as input; the same value will tie in with many kinds of decision calculation on the best use of the asset.
2 The stabilised balance sheet will (by showing real holding gain on the asset) give some idea of management's skill in buying assets when they are cheap.
3 The income in corrected accounts will be free from the distortion of the time-lag error.
4 If cost-of-capital is recognised, the firm's operating divisions, etc., will be charged with an expense that may be important yet is normally neglected.
5 In successive income statements, the total net charges for the asset—depreciation, varying repairs, etc., and cost-of-capital, less real gain realised—will work out as a constant real amount per unit of time or use. This will smooth out some spurious fluctuations in the income pattern—and thereby give better information for

decisions on, e.g. dividends, further investment in fixed assets, and (at least with use-assets) pricing of the product. It will also give an improved check on the worthwhileness of past decisions to buy assets.

As an example of the harm done by inept methods, consider the firm that charges its branches with straight-line depreciation on delivery vans (with a low–high repair pattern). As a van ages, a branch manger will see his combined depreciation and repair charges rising, and will start to press for the renewal of the van—before its optimum life has run out; should his argument be accepted, the firm as a whole suffers. If depreciation cost is instead tapered in a high–low pattern, the branch's total charges tend to be constant throughout the optimum life, and the branch manager is not tempted to press for premature replacement. Consider too the firm that expands its plant for some years, and then stops expanding. If the plant has a low–high repair pattern, and cost-of-capital is unimportant, a high–low depreciation pattern is desirable. Otherwise, the total of these charges will be too small in the early years and too high in the late years, and the income figures will at first be too cheerful (thereby encouraging excessive dividends and investment) and then too gloomy (again prompting bad decisions).

Appendix 1: The well-known accounting methods for depreciating assets

The methods can be illustrated with the following figures. An asset's cost is C, expected resale value S, and life-span n years.

Straight-line Here the depreciation charge is $(1/n)(C - S)$ in all years. For example, if the asset costs £1250 and will fetch £50 after a three-year life, the charge is £400 p.a.; the book-values for successive year-ends run £1250, £850, £450, and £50.

Fixed percentage The diminishing balances are written down by a rate r (a fraction of 1) found from

$$r = 1 - \sqrt[n]{\frac{S}{C}}$$

or

$$n \log (1 - r) = \log S - \log C.$$

In the example, the rate is 0.658; the charges run £822, £282, and £96; the book-values £1250, £428, £146, and £50.

Sum-of-the-digits The years are represented by the digits 1, 2, 3, . . ., n. The fractions of $(C - S)$ charged in years 1, 2, 3, . . ., n are the digits in reverse order, divided by their sum. In the example, the fractions are

$$\frac{3}{1+2+3} \text{ in the year 1}$$

$$\frac{2}{1+2+3} \text{ in the year 2}$$

and

$$\frac{1}{1+2+3} \text{ in the year 3}$$

the charges run £600, £400, and £200; the book-values £1250, £650, £250 and £50.

Double rate, declining balance This is a handsome gift to US business by the tax authorites. The rate is twice that for the straight-line method. It is applied to the whole of the declining balance (i.e. ignores S). In the example, the rate is 0.6; the charges run £833, £278, and £93; the book-values £1250, £417, £139, and £46.

Fixed annual charge to cover depreciation and repairs Let R = total expected repairs during life. The charge is $(1/n)(C - S + R)$ in all years, and repair outlays are added to the value of the asset. In the example, suppose R consists of a £300 overhaul in year 2. The charge is £500 p.a.; the book-values £1,250, £750, £550, and £50.

Service-unit $(C - S)$ is divided by the expected total of units during the life; the unit-cost is multiplied by the number of units 'consumed' in a year, to give that year's depreciation charge. In the example, suppose the asset is a car, expected to run 100000 miles; unit-cost is thus £0.012 per mile. Yearly mileage is 25000 in year 1, 60000 in year 2, 15000 in year 3. The charges are £300, £720, and £180; the book-values £1250, £950, £230, and £50.

Annuity Convert S into its present value, S'. Find the annual sum that $(C - S')$ buys for n years. Use this sum as yearly depreciation. Each year, debit the asset account with interest on its opening balance, and credit interest expense.

In the example, suppose primary revenue is £738 p.a. and secondary assets earn 10 per cent. The whole firm's accounts for the three years run:

Year	*1*	*2*	*3*
	£	£	£
Balance sheet			
Primary asset			
Balance brought forward	1250	887	488
Add 10% cost-of-capital	125	89	49
	1375	976	537
Less Depreciation	488	488	487
Net value	887	488	50
Secondary assets	363	762	1200
Total (= capital)	1250	1250	1250
Income statement			
Operations			
Revenue	738	738	737
Less Depreciation	488	488	487
	250	250	250
General			
Secondary earnings		36	76
Cost-of-capital added to primary asset	125	89	49
Total	125	125	125
Total profit (= dividend)	375	375	375
Rate of return on £1250 investment	30%	30%	30%

A whole life table for the firm is a check against weak reasoning. Note that, with constant primary revenue, profit and composite rate of return are also constant.

Appendix 2: Price change throughout the depreciating asset's life

It is not easy to squeeze a complete example into a small table. The figures should cover many kinds of events, and illustrate many alternative modes of treatment. But the following example shows at least the mixture of general and real change. It assumes a short life (only three years), and its solution in Table 13.10 gives three versions of each year's accounts:

1 Ordinary accounts
2 Stabilised accounts, in £s of 31 December of each year. The assets are revalued at their current prices. The depreciation charge is based on the resulting end-of-year value; but the real holding gain in this charge is brought in as extra income, so the net profit is the figure that would be found by general-index adjustment.
3 As 2 but the depreciation charge is based on *mid-year* specific values (adjusted between July and December with the general index). It was argued on p. 172 that this is the best measure of a year's current input cost. As the fall in the charge (compared with 2) is matched by a fall in the credit for real holding gain, profit stays the same as in 2.

Data of example

The firm has a capital of £3000, with which it buys the primary asset on 1 January, year 1. The asset has no scrap value at the end of its three-year life. The primary revenue is £1540 in year 1, and rises with the general index. Secondary assets appreciate with the general index (which implies that net money-assets are *nil*), but otherwise have no earnings. The straight-line method is appropriate. Profit (as measured over-generously in the ordinary accounts) is all paid out as dividends at mid-year. The general index rises over the three years from 100 to 160, and the specific index from 100 to 200; each year's average and end-figures are shown near the top of Table 13.10.

Solution

The ordinary accounts of columns (1a), (2a), and (3a) in Table 13.10 tell the usual story of rising profits. Because these uncorrected sums are paid out as dividends, real wealth is eroded: the secondary assets at the end of year 3, shown at their cost of £3000 though worth £3813 if revalued,[13] are less than the real opening wealth (£3000 at the start of the three years = £4800 at the end), let alone the replacement price of £6000.

The stabilised income statements reveal the rising yearly deficits. The stabilised balance sheets value all the assets at current prices, and show the real holding gain on the primary asset—written off as the asset is consumed. The depreciation charges of version (b) tie in with the December values, but not with the replacement costs of the dates when inputs are consumed; the versions in (c) are geared to those dates, and so give a better view of the year's costs.[14] Where the main aim is comparison over the years, the stabilised accounts should be restated in a common £, say that of 1 January, year 1.

If the owners had instead restricted dividends to the profit figures of (b) and (c) (i.e. if they had used the general-index concept of capital maintenance), there would be no deficits, and the value of the secondary assets would in the end have risen to £3813 plus £987, i.e. to £4800. This sum falls short of replacement cost (£6000), but maintains real capital.

If the owners had preferred the specific-index view of capital maintenance, they would have reduced profits and dividends further, by not crediting real holding gain realised to the income statement. Their resulting savings would in the end have raised the secondary assets[15] to £5390. So, even if they follow the precepts of the specific-index man faithfully, their funds still fall short of replacement price. To reach the latter, they would in years 2 and 3 need to top up the accumulated provision.

Table 13.10 Life History of a Depreciating Asset Subject to Price Change

		Year 1			*Year 2*			*Year 3*	
General index: Average		110			126			147	
End		120			140			160	
Specific index: Average		115			136			160	
End		130			145			200	
	(a)	(b)	(c)	(a)	(b)	(c)	(a)	(b)	(c)
	Ordinary accounts £	*Stabilised accounts*	*As (b), but input at mid-year price*	*Ordinary accounts* £	*Stabilised accounts*	*As (b), but input at mid-year price*	*Ordinary accounts* £	*Stabilised accounts*	*As (b), but input at mid-year price*
		£ of 31 December			*£ of 31 December*			*£ of 31 December*	
Income Statement									
Sales, *less* Current costs	1540	*1680*	*1680*	1764	*1960*	*1960*	2058	*2240*	*2240*
Depreciation									
Historical cost	1000			1000			1000		
Replacement cost									
End of year		*1300*			*1450*			*2000*	
Mid-year			*1255*			*1511*			*1742*
Current operating profit		*380*	*425*		*510*	*449*		*240*	*498*
Real holding gain realised		*100*	*55*		*50*	*111*		*400*	*142*
Net profit	540	*480*	*480*	764	*560*	*560*	1058	*640*	*640*
Less Dividend	540	*589*	*589*	764	*849*	*849*	1058	*1152*	*1152*
Deficit: for year	—	*(109)*	*(109)*	—	*(289)*	*(289)*	—	*(512)*	*(512)*
brought forward	—	—	—	—	*(127)*	*(127)*	—	*(475)*	*(475)*
total	—	*(109)*	*(109)*	—	*(416)*	*(416)*	—	*(987)*	*(987)*

Balance Sheet								
Primary asset (cost, new)	3000	*3900*		3000	*4350*		3000	*6000*	
Less Depreciation	1000	*1300*	as (b)	2000	*2900*	as (b)	3000	*6000*	as (b)
	2000	*2600*		1000	*1450*		—	—	
Secondary assets									
Of year 1	1000	*1091*		1000	*1273*		1000	*1455*	
2				1000	*1111*		1000	*1270*	
3							1000	*1088*	
				2000	*2384*		3000	*3813*	
	3000	*3691*		3000	*3834*		3000	*3813*	
Capital	3000	*3600*		3000	*4200*		3000	*4800*	
Real holding gain (unrealised) on primary asset	—	*200*		—	*50*		—	—	
Profit deficit	—	*(109)*		—	*(416)*		—	*(987)*	
	3000	*3691*		3000	*3834*		3000	*3813*	

Appendix 3: Interest and revaluation

Example

Facts

Old's cash flows are:

		£
Annual cost savings		900
Initial price		1000
Repairs:	year 3	100
	year 4	—
	year 5	500
	year 6	800
Scrap value, all years		Nil

The firm's interest rate is 20 per cent p.a.

At the end of year 2, the initial price unexpectedly rises to £1500 (but other flows stay unaltered).

Required

Value pattern over the whole life.

Solution

1 Find optimum life		*3 years*	*4 years*	*5 years*	*6 years*
Old					
Outlays: Of year 0	Price	1000	1000	1000	1000
3	Repairs £100 discounted to 0	58	58	58	58
5	Repairs £500 discounted to 0			201	201
6	Repairs £800 discounted to 0				268
		1058	1058	1259	1527
Yearly equivalent: Full Service Charge (FSC)		502		421	459
Optimum (4 year life)			409		
New					
Outlays: As Old, plus £500 extra price			1558	1759	2027
Yearly equivalent (FSC)			602		610
Optimum (5 year life)				588	

2 Find Old's revised life estimate at end of year 2.

Its life will be extended till its repairs equal New's FSC, just after year 5.

3 Find Old's deprival value at end of year:

	0	*1*	*2*	*3*	*4*	*5*
Comparative budgets:						
(i) Before New's advent						
Have Future flows, till 4:						
£100 discounted from 3	58	68	83	–		
Have not Future FSCs						
at 0 $a_1 \times 409$	1058					
1 $a_3 \times 409$		860				
2 $a_2 \times 409$			624			
3 $a_1 \times 409$				341		
Deprival value	1000	791	541	341		
Depreciation charge		209	250	200	341	
(ii) After New's advent						
Have Future flows, till 5:						
£100 discounted from 3			83	–		
£500 discounted from 5			289	347	417	–
			372	347	417	
Have not Future FSCs						
at 2 $a_3 \times 588$			1239			
3 $a_2 \times 588$				898		
4 $a_1 \times 588$					490	
Deprival value			867	551	73	
Depreciation charge				316	478	73

4 Enter holding gain

		2	*3*	*4*	*5*
Unrealised gain	cr.	326			
	dr.		116	137	73

As gain is realised in years 3 to 5, it is transferred to the income statement (to meet the rules of real capital maintenance), as excess of revised over original depreciation charge.

References

1 Lewis, W. A. (1977) 'Depreciation and Obsolescence as Factors in Costing', in W. T. Baxter and S. Davidson (eds), *Studies in Accounting*, ICAEW, is helpful on these matters.
2 These are briefly described in Appendix 1 of this chapter (p. 273).

3 See my 'Lessors' depreciation and profit', *Journal of Business Finance and Accounting*, Spring, 1982.
4 Based on Solomons, D. (1962) 'The determination of asset values', *Journal of Business of the University of Chicago*, January.
5 My *Depreciation*, Sweet & Maxwell, 1978, Chapter 8 of this volume has further examples.
6 Let
V_0 = initial price:
i = relevant cost-of-capital rate;
v = present value factor—that is $1/(1+i)$;
k = number of years in the whole life;
$0(k)$ = sum of the present values of the relevant cash flows, e.g. variable repair outlays, during the life;
Sv^k = present value of the scrap proceeds.

Then A, the present value of all these flows, is found from:

$$A = V_0 + 0(k) - Sv^k$$

For fuller treatment, see Merrett, A. J. and Sykes A., (1973) *The Finance and Analysis of Capital Projects,* Chapters, 1, 18 and 19, Longman.

The yearly charge or rental U is found from:

$$U = A \times \frac{i}{1 - v^k}$$

A good rule-of-thumb for finding the approximate charge is to add together (a) the straight-line depreciation charge, (b) interest for a year on two-thirds of the asset's price, and (c) yearly average of any relevant repairs.
7 P, the perpetuity, is found from:

$$P = \frac{A}{1 - v^k}$$

or from:

$$P = \frac{U}{i}$$

8 For formulae, see Baxter, W. T. and Carrier, N. H. (1971) 'Depreciation, replacement price, and cost of capital', *Journal of Accounting Research,* Chicago, Autumn.
9 Hicks, J. R. (1969) *A Theory of Economic History*, Oxford University Press.
10 Bhaskar, K. N. (1973) 'Optimal asset lives', *Accounting and Business Research,* Autumn.

11 Watson, P, and Baxter W. T. (1984) 'Depreciation and probability', in B. Carsberg and S. Dev (eds), *External Financial Reporting*, Prentice Hall.

12 Monroe Ingberman and George H. Sorter, 'Accounting Rules of Recognition, Quantification and Reporting', a paper read at New York University, 1982.

13 Provision of mid-year 1 = 1000 × (160/110) = 1454.5
Provision of mid-year 2 = 1000 × (160/126) = 1269.8
Provision of mid-year 3 = 1000 × (160/147) = 1088.4
3812.7

14 For instance, during year 1 the average current cost of input is only £1000 × 115 = £1150. For stabilisation in end-£s, this is raised with the general-index factor 120/110 to £1255 (column (1c)).

15 Extra provision, version (b), by end of life:

Year 1	£100 × (160/120) =	133
2	£ 50 × (160/140) =	57
3	£400 × (160/160) =	400
		590
General-index provision		4800
		5390

14

Conclusions

Earlier chapters have covered many topics—some concerning principles, others techniques. This final chapter must try to put the topics into perspective and to sum up.

Because ordinary accounting is in the main a historical record, it is an imperfect means for giving current information. Even when general prices remain tolerably steady, its defects evoke proposals for improvement. With inflation, the defects become much worse, and the proposals more radical.

The defects can be summarised under two heads—asset values and income measurement.

Asset values

Chapter 12 set out the main arguments for revaluation. If balance sheets are to be of maximum service to their readers, they should be revised from time to time.

The most important kind of reader is usually the investor, actual or potential; the balance sheet is the firm's 'invitation to the financial market to participate in the profit'. To be sure, investors would prefer an invitation in the form of a forward-looking valuation of the firm as a whole. But, unless and until directors become more reliable prophets, investors must be content with the balance sheet, and use it to form their own judgments. The better the balance sheet, the better the judgments.

Investors can be misled by historical values in several ways. Such values paint a spurious picture of a firm or industry with old assets. They give little notion of the assets' earning potential or sale value. They yield unduly high income:asset ratios (especially when reinforced by the time-lag error). And they fail to warn investors of possible takeovers.

Other important groups of readers are creditors and managers. The former would plainly prefer current to out-dated values. If managers lack current values, they are likely to be misled in several ways—for instance when they study the rates of return on the assets of different departments, or make decisions that lead to the using-up of existing stocks and machines.

The fact that the owners' balances (retained earnings, etc.) are 'mixed' historical totals means that they too give muddled information. They fail for instance to show whether the owners' real capital has been maintained after price change. Still less do they analyse the various forms of realised and unrealised appreciation over the years.

Income measurement

Income statements are apt to deduct costs of one date from revenues of another. The curing of this time-lag error seems to be the most urgent need in the field of income measurement.

Consequences of the time-lag error

If the error has a marked effect on income figures (as it assuredly has in certain kinds of firm, especially when the rate of inflation is high), then they fail in their functions as guides to consumption, investment, and efficiency.

Thus an owner may, during inflation, suppose that his capital is intact, whereas in reality it is diminished (particularly where his dividends have been based on uncorrected profit). Again, investors may be misled about the relative profits of firms A and B, or industries C and D, so new resources may be misdirected. Manager E can be made to seem more efficient than manager F, and method G than method H. Thus decisions of efficiency may be warped. 'Make or buy' budgets, for instance, will tend to compare 'make' figures that are historical costs with 'buy' figures that are current prices. Decisions on sale price may be made wrongly if cost figures are historical; and, even if the firm's own accountant is enlightened on this point, the accountants of competing firms may not be.

Conceivably a gifted manager or analyst knows intuitively of the existence of the error and tries to allow for it in his calculations. We can only guess how far he succeeds. In view of the many difficulties, complete success seems unlikely.

The gravity of the error is shown by the composite figures for British companies. The Bank of England has published tables that compare the real rate of return (corrected profit to revalued assets) with the nominal rate (uncorrected profit to historical cost assets). Even before the inflation grew severe, the gap was considerable, e.g. in 1964 the two rates were 11.5 per cent and 16.5 per cent. When inflation reached its worst (1974), the rates were 4 per cent and 16.8 per cent.[2]

Social consequences

It is reasonable to think that an error of such size, repeated in many lands, must have bad side-effects.

Thus it may aggravate the trade cycle. As page 165 explained, it makes for high profit figures in times of general price increase, which (in the past at least) have tended to coincide with the upswing of a trade cycle; it may then raise the expectations of businessmen and inject undue optimism into their investment budgets, and so add fuel to the boom. Conversely, when prices are falling on the down-swing, it depresses the profit figures, and so may have bred extra pessimism and checked investment. If this view is right, accounting malpractice has aggravated the ills of boom and slump: reform is an urgent social duty.

Again, the miscalculation of profit leads to miscalculation of tax. The British Government saw its error in 1974; many other governments still have not reformed their rules adequately. In the absence of reform, the time-lag error gives rise to an extra tax—never envisaged by the legislature—on those who hold stocks or depreciating assets, or make capital gains. Particularly if dividends as well as tax are linked with uncorrected profit, seemingly prosperous firms may fail (in real terms) to expand or even maintain their wealth, and may suddenly face cash shortages when assets have to be renewed. And the extra tax must presumably act as a disincentive to the holding of stocks and depreciating assets. To quote President Eisenhower, illiberal treatment of depreciation 'discourages long-range investment on which the risks cannot be clearly foreseen. It discourages the early replacement of old equipment with new and improved equipment, and it makes it more difficult to secure financing for capital investment, particularly for small business organisations.'[3] It does not seem too fanciful to suppose the tax was one of the forces that held back investment in recent years, and so contributed to the world depression.

Real and nominal gain

Traditional accounts can be faulted moreover for their inability to test value change with the general index, i.e. to analyse the nominal change into real and fictional parts. They thus give poor information about fixed asset appreciation, realised or unrealised. And—a major defect—they cannot record gain from owing money and loss from owning it.

Ailments and cures

Earlier chapters have also suggested how each fault in traditional accounting might be remedied. So perhaps we can best summarise their content by drawing up a table of ailments and cures. There are only two of the latter, namely the general index (CPP) and specific revaluation (CCA):

Section 3 of Table 14.1 (income measurement) might be set out in more colourful language, as, (a) sins of commission (the time-lag error), and (b) sins of omission (failure to show real gain and loss).

The hybrid system

The 'cure' column of the table does not, alas, show that reform can be ultra-simple. Some ailments will respond to CPP, others to CCA; 3(b) needs both, since real gain and loss are found by comparing CPP and CCA values.

Thus full-blooded reform demands a hybrid system (illustrated for instance in Table 9.7).

Table 14.1 Ailments Induced by Inflation, and Suggested Cures

	Ailment	*Cure*	
1	Figures of different dates are not comparable	CPP	(Chapter 4)
2	Values are out-of-date and mixed:		
	(a) Balance sheet		
	Assets (non-monetary)	CCA	(Chapter 12)
	Equity	CPP	(Chapter 12)
	(b) Input costs in decision budgets	CCA	(Chapter 12)
3	Income measurement is defective:		
	(a) Illusory gain is shown (the time-lag error on stocks, depreciation, and asset sales)	CPP*	(Chapters 7–10)
	(b) Some real gain/loss is not shown:		
	On monetary items	CPP	(Chapter 6)
	On non-monetary items	CPP and CCA	(Chapter 8)

* Or CCA, provided real gain is credited.

Degree of reform

However, anaemic reform may be much better than no reform; it can at least serve as an educational stepping-stone. A single cure—either CPP or CCA—may in favourable circumstances bring substantial improvement.

Once the cure has been selected, a further choice must be made—of extent of application. The possibilities range from 'first-aid' adjustments (of, say, the costs in the income statement) to some full stabilisation package of both income statement and balance sheet.

The first-aid is by no means to be despised. It demands a minimum of change in the normal figures and methods. It seems specially appropriate where the time-lag error is confined to a few items. And most readers of accounts are likely to feel more at home with figures that are still mainly of the familiar kind—though admittedly the new-fangled charges may at first need a lot of explaining.

But full hybrid reform seems preferable, at least for the large and sophisticated firm. Besides curing the time-lag, it brings improvement in other areas, and leaves fewer inconsistencies; for instance, its income statement dovetails neatly with its balance sheet. It can deal with the various forms of real gain and loss, notably those on holding money. And, as stabilised accounts can be readily updated, comparison between the results of different periods is easy.

The future

As I write, inflation Standards have for several years been in force, both in Britain and North America. They are now being reviewed, and possibly will be revised (or even abandoned). This prospect has touched off a vigorous debate on their merits and faults.

Thanks to the Standards, most big companies have been constrained to issue reformed accounts. Preparers and users have thus had a chance to grow familiar with the new ideas. Familiarity has not bred universal affection. Attitudes are very divided: some are cordial, others lukewarm, and many seem increasingly hostile.[4]

Reasons for approval

A good deal of research is being done on these conflicting attitudes. The companies that like reform cite its familiar merits. In particular, they stress its usefulness as a guide to dividend policy. They say they are helped by its 'rate of return' statistics, and other tests of operating efficiency. They are helped too by asset revaluation, as this improves their debt cover and chances of getting fresh funds from banks and long-term lenders. In internal management, current costs are specially useful for testing whether some given activity should be retained or given up; thus current depreciation may warn that costs would become prohibitive if old plant is renewed.

Reasons for hostility

The reasons given for hostility are mainly the obvious ones. The corrected figures are hard to understand. They are subjective. They are costly to prepare. They are ignored by the accounts' users. They are not accepted by the tax authorities. Initially they cannot be compared with previous figures. They lead to the publication of two conflicting sets of 'true and fair' results, which is absurd. And so on.

Is it being unduly cynical to wonder whether there is not a deeper reason for hostility (and one that the most conscientious of researchers cannot lay bare)? Accounting is not an easy subject, and most of us have invested much time and effort in acquiring some knowledge of it. So we cannot take kindly to the idea that its principles and methods are faulty, and that we must now start afresh on an arduous relearning task. This view gets support from the attitudes in companies that adopted reform many years ago (e.g. Philips Lamps); staff who have grown up with the new methods find them simple and eminently effective.

Faced with so much hostility, leaders of the accounting profession have shown courage and persistence in their campaign for reform. Unfortunately these virtues have not been matched by wisdom in choice of methods. One reason for the hostility must surely be the inflation Standards' complexities and stress on physical capital.

Enthusiasm and type of firm

Not unexpectedly, a firm's attitude to reform would seem often to depend on the attitude of its leaders. Their enthusiasm or otherwise infects the whole.

The size and type of firm may also have an effect. There is some evidence that big firms are more likely than small ones to take kindly to reform; perhaps they are better able to re-educate staff, or have greater need for sound statistics. Again, a mature firm, with old assets and strong competitors, tends to find reform helpful; whereas the managers of a thrusting new firm may be more concerned with the technological race than with improvement of accounts.

The uncertain outlook

Inflation accounting has many merits. Yet the outlook for reform still seems highly uncertain.

To judge from the important (and neglected) experiment of Brazil, inflation accounting is most likely to prosper if four conditions obtain, (a) the chosen cure is simple, (b) all users adjust with the same few indices, (c) these indices, being common to many firms, tend to maintain real capital rather than individual assets, and (d) the tax authorities accept corrected profit.

It lies within accountants' power to meet the first three conditions; a wise Standard could pave the way. And, if these three conditions were met, tax authorities would have fewer sound reasons for hostility.

Continuance of inflation would greatly strengthen the arguments for reform. But even if (as one hopes) inflation dwindles, a serious depreciation error will linger on until all plant bought in the inflation era has disappeared. And, since many specific prices are always in lively motion, the case for asset revaluation would persist even with stable general prices.

To my mind, a main cause for concern is the seductive appeal of physical capital. This has led reformers badly astray. Chapter 8 tried to explain its practical difficulties, complexities, and faults of principle. We smile when we hear of simple tribes that assess a man's wealth by the number of his cattle, regardless of whether the beasts are sleek and well, or decrepit and diseased; yet this is precisely how accountants behave when they take physical size as guide.

But we need not end on a note of gloom. Though inflation has brought many ills, it has at least made accountants look afresh at doctrines long taken for granted. In particular, it has forced us to question the sanctity of historical cost. The search for better theories and methods now seems too vigorous to subside. Improvement, perhaps in directions still unsuspected, must surely follow.

References

1 Lehtovuori, J. (1972) *The Foundations of Accounting*, Helsinki School of Economics.

2 Bank of England, *Quarterly Review*, March 1976, p. 37.
3 *New York Times*, 22 January 1954.
4 Archer, S. and Steele, A. (1983) 'The Implementation of SSAP 13—A research report', University of Lancaster.

Index